T0305153

EUROPEAN UNION AT THE CROSSROADS

STUDIES IN ECONOMIC TRANSFORMATION AND PUBLIC POLICY

General Editor: Christos C. Paraskevopoulos, *Professor of Economics and Chair, Department of Economics, York University, Canada and President, the Athenian Policy Forum Inc.*

The major objective of the Athenian Policy Forum (a non-profit research organization) is to promote independent objective analysis and stimulate public discussion on issues and problems relating to economic adjustment. This series contributes to this goal by disseminating the results of innovative research on the economic implications of the changing forces of demography, the environment, social and political transformation, technology and trade.

Recent titles in the series include:

Global Trading Arrangements in Transition
Edited by Christos C. Paraskevopoulos

European Union at the Crossroads
A Critical Analysis of Monetary Union and Enlargement
Edited by Christos C. Paraskevopoulos

European Union at the Crossroads

A Critical Analysis of Monetary Union and Enlargement

Edited by

Christos C. Paraskevopoulos

York University, Canada and the Athenian Policy Forum

STUDIES IN ECONOMIC TRANSFORMATION AND PUBLIC POLICY
IN ASSOCIATION WITH THE ATHENIAN POLICY FORUM INC.

Edward Elgar

Cheltenham, UK · Northampton, MA, USA

© Christos C. Paraskevopoulos 1998

All rights reserved. No part of this publication may be reproduced, stored in a retrieval system or transmitted in any form or by any means, electronic, mechanical or photocopying, recording, or otherwise without the prior permission of the publisher.

Published by
Edward Elgar Publishing Limited
8 Lansdown Place
Cheltenham
Glos GL50 2HU
UK

Edward Elgar Publishing, Inc.
6 Market Street
Northampton
Massachusetts 01060
USA

A catalogue record for this book
is available from the British Library

Library of Congress Cataloguing in Publication Data

European Union at the crossroads : a critical analysis of monetary
    union and enlargement / edited by Christos C. Paraskevopoulos.
        — (Studies in economic transformation and public policy)
        1. Monetary unions—European Union countries. 2. Monetary policy—
    European Union countries. 3. Europe—Economic integration.
    I. Paraskevopoulos. Christos C. II. Series.
    HG925.E97   1998
    333.7'142—dc21   97–47509
                                                                       CIP

ISBN 1 85898 762 8

Printed and bound in Great Britain by Bookcraft (Bath) Ltd.

To my children
Dean, Dennis, and Christina

THE ATHENIAN Policy Forum Inc.

We Athenians, in our own persons, take our decisions on policy or submit them to proper discussions: for we do not think that there is an incompatibility between words and deeds; the worst thing is to rush into action before the consequences have been properly debated

Thucydides (460–400 BC)
Pericles' Funeral Oration

Contents

Figures

Tables

xi

Contributors

Angelos A. Antzoulatos, Federal Reserve Bank of New York, USA, and Research Fellow Athenian Policy Forum

Nicholas C. Baltas, Athens University of Economics and Business, Greece

Bala Batavia. DePaul University, USA, and Research Fellow Athenian Policy Forum

Jiten Borkakoti, Middlesex University, UK, and Research Fellow Athenian Policy Forum

Patrick M. Crowley, Saint Mary's University, Canada, and Research Fellow Athenian Policy Forum

George D. Demopoulos, Athens University of Economics and Business, Greece, and Research Fellow Athenian Policy Forum

Theodore A. Georgakopoulos, Athens University of Economics and Business, Greece, and the Athenian Policy Forum

Christis Hassapis, University of Cyprus, Cyprus

Bernd Kempa, University of Essen, Germany, and Research Fellow Athenian Policy Forum

Alexander J. Kondonassis, University of Oklahoma, USA, and the Athenian Policy Forum

A.G. Malliaris, Loyola University of Chicago, USA, and the Athenian Policy Forum

Leo Michelis, Ryerson Polytechnic University, Canada, and Research Fellow Athenian Policy Forum

P. Nandakumar, Delhi School of Economics, India

Eleni Paligninis, Middlesex University, UK, and Research Fellow Athenian Policy Forum

Christos C. Paraskevopoulos, York University, Canada, and the Athenian Policy Forum

Nikitas Pittis, University of Cyprus, Cyprus and Union Bank of Switzerland, Switzerland

Kyprianos Prodromidis, Athens University of Economics and Business, Greece

Robin Rowley, McGill University, Canada

Nicholas A. Yannacopoulos, University of Piraeus, Greece, and Research Fellow Athenian Policy Forum

Acknowledgements

Most of the contributions to this volume were originally presented at an international conference held in Athens, Greece, in August 1996, organized by York University and the Athens University of Economics and Business, in co-sponsorship with the Athenian Policy Forum. The Athens conference was the third major joint activity of the two universities, under an exchange agreement signed in 1991. The Athenian Policy Forum serves as the research and publications arm of the Exchange Agreement. I would like to thank the two organizing universities, the Athenian Policy Forum, and all participants for their contribution to its success. The Athens University of Economics and Business, as host, should in particular be cited for outstanding organization and publicity.

Special thanks go to Rector Andreas Kintis for embracing the idea of establishing the exchange (an idea conceived on the island of Spetses), and Theodore Georgakopoulos (conference chair) for his involvement and support in making this idea a reality. Livy Visano, Dean, Atkinson College, has provided generous support and encouragement throughout.

In addition, as editor and conference co-chair, I would like to thank the following colleagues who served on the organizing committee or helped in other ways: D. Bourantonis, N. Christodoulakis, G. Eaton, M. Evriviades, G. Karydes, F. Lazar, and T. Moutos. Special thanks are due to W. Northover and J. Smithin for editorial advice, and R. Cook for research assistance.

We appreciate the financial support provided by the following non-academic sponsors: Aspis Bank; Commercial Bank of Greece SA; Eurobank; European Commission; General Bank; General Secretariat for Research and Technology; Hellenic Industrial Development Bank SA; Ministry of Culture; and National Bank of Greece.

We received excellent secretarial support from Eleftheria Apostolidou of the Athens University of Economics and Business who did a superb job, as Conference Secretary, in handling the local logistical arrangements and publicity, and Agnes Fraser (York University) who was equally superb in coordinating the Toronto arrangements.

As General Editor of the series I would like to thank the members of the editorial board for their help in reviewing and approving the manuscripts accepted for publication in this volume. In addition, thanks are due to the anonymous reader (referee) at EE Publishing for comments and

suggestions which have improved the contributions. Above all I would like
to thank the publisher, Edward Elgar, for his support and encouragement.

Finally thanks are due to Jane Croft, Dymphna Evans, Ian Garbutt,
Julie Leppard, Francine O'Sullivan and other members of the staff of
Edward Elgar Publishing Limited, both at Aldershot and Cheltenham, for
their customary high quality work on this volume.

Introduction
Christos C. Paraskevopoulos

This volume is one of the first two under the imprint of the newly established series – 'Studies in Economic Transformation and Public Policy' – published by the Athenian Policy Forum Inc. collaboration with Edward Elgar Publishing Limited, A companion volume, *Global Trading Arrangements in Transition*, is also forthcoming in the same series.

Most of the contributions in this volume were originally presented at an international conference, held in Athens, Greece, in August 1996, organized by York University and the Athens University of Economics and Business in co-sponsorship with the Athenian Policy Forum (APF). Many of the contributors are either Associates or Research Fellows of the APF.

The Athens (1996) conference on the theme 'Economic Integration in Transition' was the third in a series on the broad theme of economic integration – the largest ever conference on economic integration – and was a follow-up to the earlier conferences held in Athens (1992) and Toronto (1994), respectively.

The aim of the conference – with specialists in attendance from several different countries and four continents – was to evaluate the deepening and widening of the integration process both between the existing trading blocs such as the North American Free Trade Agreement (NAFTA) and the European Union (EU) and elsewhere. The present volume includes a selection of papers that focus on the European experience.

The chapters in this volume provide a state-of-the-art analysis of key issues facing the European Union on the road (albeit rocky) towards monetary union and enlargement. A wide range of topics is covered from a diverse and largely critical perspective. The diverse methodologies and perspectives tackled make for an unusually broad presentation that will engage the economic theorist, the empirical social scientist, the policy-maker, and also the informed general reader who wants to understand the challenges and dilemmas facing the EU. The significant number of Greek economists participating in both the conference and this volume provide a unique perspective. Greek accession to the EU is an important case study dealt with in several of the chapters.

This book concentrates on the effects on member nations of inclusion in the European Monetary Union (EMU). Part I focuses on the implementation of the EMU and its feasibility. In Chapter 1, Alex Kondonassis and

Tassos Malliaris examine the EMU and prospects for further integration. The benefits and costs of monetary integration are discussed as well as some lessons learned from the international monetary system. In Chapter 2, Patrick Crowley and Robin Rowley discuss the evolution of the European Union and EMU. They note that the development of the EMU will be highly dependent on internal political developments and inter-member bargaining. In Chapter 3, Christos Hassapis, Nikitas Pittis and Kyprianos Prodromidis consider the question of the German Dominance Hypothesis with regard to the EMU. An empirical analysis of the question finds that there is symmetry between members of the EMU and dominance on the part of the United States in monetary policy. In Chapter 4, Leo Michelis and Chris Paraskovopoulos extend work done by Rose and Svensson on devaluation expectations, increasing the number of explanatory variables used. Italy and France are presented as case studies. The extended model is found to be superior in that it offers a better explanation of devaluation expectations than does the standard model. In Chapter 5, George Demopoulos and Nicholas Yannacopoulos present a game-theoretic analysis of a monetary union. Using a cooperative framework, the feasibility of a monetary union is analysed and it is concluded that such a union is feasible when there exist increasing returns to scale in the union.

Part II of this book deals with some policy aspects of the integration taking place in the EU. Theodore Georgakopoulos, in Chapter 6, compares current and future VAT arrangements within the EU. It is concluded that the argument that the current VAT system places a financial burden on domestic supplies, and that the proposed VAT is neutral in its treatment of sources of supply, is not correct. It is suggested that there is room for further analysis of this problem. In Chapter 7, Nicholas Baltas looks at the effects of the Common Agricultural Policy (CAP) on Greek agriculture. It is found that the CAP significantly affected agricultural trade flows and the agricultural trade balance of Greece. Furthermore, the structure of agricultural output was also changed. Eleni Paliginis, in Chapter 8, looks at the effect of economic integration on Greece, Portugal, Ireland and Spain. The effects of EU membership on this group of countries are mixed. While Spain and Portugal have experienced some degree of convergence, it is found that Greece has actually experienced divergence. It is suggested that the EU could do more to assist these countries during the integration process. In Chapter 9, Jiten Borkakoti looks at the criteria set by the Maastricht Treaty for monetary union. In particular, he is concerned with whether or not the necessary convergence between members is taking place. It is argued that the emphasis being placed on nominal criteria is inappropriate and real variables such as capital per head are better indicators of whether convergence is, in fact, taking place. Finally it is suggested that primary divergence is actually taking place. Angelos Antzoulatos in Chapter 10 examines the different responses of Latin American and Asian countries to inflows of capital, using a dynamic model of a borrowing constrained individual. The model's results are tested empirically and are found to be supported by the data.

Part III looks at the experience of the Nordic and southern members of the EU with respect to their transition to an integrated market. In Chapter 11, P. Nandakumar and Bala Batavia look at the effects on Sweden of integration into the EU. It was found that trade increased and, at the same time, the structure of Sweden's trade with EU countries changed. In addition, the effects of economic integration on direct investment were examined and the results were found to be disappointing. In Chapter 12, Bernd Kempa looks at the effect on Greece, Italy, Portugal and Spain of participation in the Exchange Rate Mechanism (ERM). It is asked whether or not membership in the ERM reduced volatility in the real exchange rates of these countries. It is pointed out that these countries make an ideal target for study since they all had varying degrees of involvement in the EMU. The results of a statistical analysis could not conclude that ERM membership helped to stabilize the countries' real exchange rates.

While the arguments presented in this book cannot be considered the last word on European economic and monetary integration, it is hoped that the discussion here – with particular emphasis on the contentious issues which arise in a process of integrating unequal partners – will help to clarify some of the issues faced when economic partners move towards a closer relationship. The scope and perspectives, however, of the set of studies in this volume are unusual and worthy of a broader audience, and it is hoped that the reader will feel that, collectively, they do represent a valuable further step in the ongoing study of these complex phenomena.

PART I

IS EUROPE READY FOR EMU?

1 The European Monetary Union in transition

Alexander J. Kondonassis and A.G. Malliaris

1 Introduction

The Treaty of Rome of 1957, which established the European Economic Community, did not address the important issue of monetary integration. One significant reason for this omission was the fact that the Bretton Woods international monetary system of fixed exchange rates was still functioning well at that time. The early difficulties of the Bretton Woods system during the 1960s and its eventual collapse in 1971 forced the European Union to face the challenges of the monetary dimension.

The purpose of this chapter is to review critically the evolution of European monetary integration by contrasting it to the remarkable changes of the world monetary system during the past twenty-five years. For example, it is worth noting that while the world monetary system has evolved from strictly fixed exchange rates under the Bretton Woods regime to flexible exchange rates, with some degree of intervention by the central banks of the G7, the European monetary system has been driven largely by fixed rates.

The chapter also focuses on the recent developments initiated by the Maastricht Summit and argues that achieving fixed exchange rates among all EU members simply by adhering to inflation, interest rates and public debt requirements is highly unlikely. Thus, only three practical alternatives seem to exist: (i) to maintain the present system with its imperfections as the world itself maintains the managed float; (ii) to achieve monetary union among a small subset of EU members; or (iii) to essentially force monetary integration politically much like that between East and West Germany.

2 The evolution of the European Monetary Union

The origins of the current efforts to move the European Union (EU) beyond the single market to a single currency go back to the Hague Summit in 1969. At this summit, European governments appointed a committee chaired by Pierre Werner, then Prime Minister of Luxembourg, to study the prospects for European monetary union. The Werner report, published in 1970, recommended the development of the European Currency Unit (ECU), a centralized European credit policy, a unified capital market policy, a common policy on government budgeting finance and the gradual narrowing of exchange rate fluctuations.

The monetary crisis of the early 1970s, which led to the rescinding of the gold convertibility of the dollar on 15 August 1971 and the floating of the guilder and mark, created great pressures for finding an alternative solution to the abandoned Bretton Woods system of fixed exchange rates. The major economic powers, known as G7, in their Smithsonian Accord agreed to allow their participating currencies to fluctuate within a 4.5 per cent band *vis-à-vis* the US dollar and EU currencies to vary as much as 9 per cent against each other. It was agreed that if a participating country's currency moved outside a band, this country's central bank would be responsible for sufficient intervention to reestablish the acceptable range.

EU countries concerned about the difficulties that such a wide variation in their exchange rates would cause to their Common Agricultural Policy, proposed a more limited exchange rate mechanism, which was called the *snake*. Such a snake allowed a maximum total band of 2.25 per cent against the EU currencies. However, because some EU countries were unable to maintain such a narrow band, Denmark, France, Ireland, Italy and the United Kingdom left the arrangement at various times during 1973 and 1974.

In October 1977, Roy Jenkins, President of the Commission, reactivated EU efforts at establishing a European monetary union. His efforts led to the birth of the European Monetary System (EMS) which became operational in March 1979. At the time, all EU members joined in the EMS with the exception of Italy and the United Kingdom. The Italian lira was allowed a wider margin of fluctuation and the United Kingdom did not become an active participant because of concerns about national sovereignty. Actually the EMS was basically a super-snake that imposed less strict exchange rate conditions on the participating currencies because it was founded on the ECU. As such the EMS did not attempt to maintain direct parity with currencies outside the EU, specifically the US dollar or the Japanese yen. The details of the EMS and a brief evaluation of its performance may be found in Giavazzi and Giovannini (1989) and Kondonassis and Maillaris (1994).

3   The Delors Report

At the Hanover Summit of June 1988, the Council agreed that in adopting the Single European Act, an implicit objective was monetary integration. The task for making such a goal explicit was assigned to the Jacques Delors Committee and the analysis, findings and recommendations of this committee are known as the Delors Report. This report contains three major stages. Stage one was unanimously adopted by the EU members at the June 1989 Madrid Summit.

The first stage of the Delors Report addresses the issue of the non-participating member states in the Exchange Rate Mechanism (ERM) of the EMS and the expansion of the role of the Committee of Central Bank of Governors in coordinating monetary policy. The second stage would create a European System of Central Banks (ESCB) much in the spirit of the US Federal Reserve System. The Euro-Fed would be responsible for price stability, exchange rate and reserve management, banking and monetary policies and general support of macroeconomic policies agreed upon at the EU level. Finally, the third stage of the Euro-Fed would be to transfer the authority of monetary policies to the EU and to establish such a narrow band for the existing exchange rate fluctuations of all the currencies involved that effectively a convergence would occur to one ECU.

Although the Delors Report outlined the process towards monetary integration, it was in the December 1991 Maastricht Summit that EU addressed a little more specifically the timetable of the various stages. In the detailed 90-page treaty on European monetary union produced at the Maastricht meeting, the EU heads of state reached an agreement, the Maastricht Treaty, which is aimed at fixed exchange rates and a single currency by 1 January 1999. More specifically, EU members must abolish all restrictions on the movement of capital and adopt, if necessary, multi-annual plans to ensure the lasting convergence necessary for monetary union.

Between January 1994 and January 1996, each member of the EU has started a process leading to the interdependence of its central bank. To facilitate this process a European Monetary Institute (EMI) has been established to strengthen the coordination of monetary policies between central banks, to monitor the functioning of the EMS and to facilitate the use of the ECU. At this summit, it was agreed that the ECU would eventually replace the D-Mark. This ECU will not be the current composite basket of the EU Currencies. The EMI, as a precursor of the Euro-Fed, will oversee and promote the development of the ECU, which has recently been named.

According to the agreement, if a majority of members states meets the strict economic criteria necessary for the European Monetary Union (EMU) (that is, an inflation rate not more than 1.5 per cent higher than the three lowest rates among the members; a budget deficit not higher than 3 per cent of GDP, a long-term interest rate no more than 2 per cent higher than the EU's three lowest; no devaluation of a currency against any other currency with the ERM of the EMS for at least two years), then stage three of the EMU would be implemented. These issues are discussed further in Kondonassis and Malliaris (1995).

If the criteria established are not met as outlined above, the EU leaders would decide in 1998 which countries are ready for EMU and without the requirement of a majority of the members, those countries meeting the criteria would proceed with a currency union on 1 January 1999.

European monetary union received another boost at a European Union finance ministers' and central bankers' meeting in Verona, Italy in April 1996. They agreed to set up a new ERM to link the planned single currency, the euro, to currencies of countries that do not join. The future European Central Bank, which will police monetary union. will also be empowered to demand alignments of currencies in the new ERM rather than waiting for countries to ask for a devaluation. The decisions in Verona were seen as significant as they will meet German demand for a strong monetary union and euro.

4   The post-Maastricht crisis

The three years, 1992–94, after the Maastricht Summit have been turbulent, both politically and financially. Politically, the rejection of the Maastricht Treaty by the Danes on 2 June 1992 and the approval of the treaty by the Irish on 18 June 1992 caused a number of concerns to resurface. The Danish rejection underscored fear of centralization and dominance of Denmark by the Brussels bureaucracy. The approval of Ireland raised major concerns among the less-developed areas of the EU about their economic survival under the Maastricht Treaty.

The marginally favourable French referendum on 20 September 1992 offered renewed optimism and at the 12 December 1992 meeting of the EU leaders there was a new commitment for the Maastricht Treaty. Following the second favourable vote by Denmark in June 1993, all EU members had ratified the treaty and the former name of European Economic Community was changed to European Union.

Ironically, although the EMU has been repeatedly reaffirmed and politically ratified the ERM, as a forerunner of such a monetary union, has experienced major difficulties during 1992–94. Much of the pressure on the ERM stemmed from Germany's high interest rates necessitated by the cost of East German unification. As is well known, Germany funded such costs through borrowing, avoiding the politically unpopular alternative of taxation.

With German interest rates rising during the first half of 1992, the pressure increased enormously for the weaker currencies of the ERM. Speculative attacks against the Italian and British, Spanish and Portuguese currencies took place. After an increase of British interest rates from 10 to

15 per cent failed to stabilize the pound, on 16 September 1992, both the British and the Italian currencies withdrew from the ERM and allowed their currencies to float. Spain devalued by 5 per cent and reintroduced capital controls, and Portugal also reimposed capital controls. The reluctance by the German Bundesbank to bring down its short-term rate substantially, fuelled periodic speculative attacks on the remaining currencies of the ERM until the August 1993 decision by the EU to widen the margins of currency fluctuations to ±15 per cent on each side. Thus, the progress made by the EU since 1990 towards removal of controls and stabilization of exchange rates was negated. Within a day of the Brussels decision to widen the bands for most currencies in the ERM to 15 per cent on each side, German, French and Belgian officials were insisting that EMU was not an extinct idea and that the EU would try to meet the second stage of the Maastricht Treaty by establishing the EMI during 1994, which actually did take place.

During the spring of 1996, the governments of both Germany and France announced several measures to prepare their nations for EMU. These measures include tax cuts, privatization, deregulation and better access to venture capital. It is as yet difficult to evaluate the impact of these policies to the Maastricht criteria.

It appears that both France and Germany are faced with most difficult challenges as a result of Germany's economic slowdown and France's social unrest from the planned French government spending cuts. Moreover, the December 1996 Dublin conference has underscored continuing differences between Germany and France as the time for the establishment of the European Union and the adoption of a single currency, the euro, is approaching. While the Germans place primary emphasis on a strong euro and support an anti-inflationary policy, the French are looking for more flexibility in goal setting, including concern with economic growth and employment. These differences have once again surfaced in connection with the German proposal to adopt after 1999 a currency stability pact under which countries with budget deficits in excess of 3 per cent of gross domestic product would be penalized by fines of as much as 0.5 per cent of GDP. On the other hand, the French have counterproposed that circumstances of 'severe recession' would warrant running higher budget deficits. The compromise reached seems to suggest that any punishment would be subject to political debate rather than bureaucratic decisionmaking.

Another event of some importance is that on 29 March 1996 the heads of state of the EU's members met in Turin, Italy. This intergovernmental conference was designed to open negotiations on revamping the EU and its institutions. In anticipation of substantial growth in the number of members of the EU it was agreed that the decisionmaking procedures and bodies of the EU would have to be overhauled. This package of reforms of the Maastricht Treaty, which has been labelled Maastricht II, will be presented in late 1997. The prospective new members will not be in a position to join the monetary union soon. However, negotiations are scheduled to commence late in 1997.

5   The rationale for EMU

The brief presentation of the central developments of the EMU movement during the past 25 years, naturally raises the question: why is the EU interested in monetary integration? Economists have reformulated this simple question by asking: what are the potential benefits and possible costs of monetary integration? The central argument in favour of a monetary union among several sovereign countries usually involves both a macroeconomic and a microeconomic dimension. It is argued that a single currency eliminates macroeconomic uncertainty and also reduces microeconomic currency transactions costs.

Both benefits can be illustrated with a representative example. Suppose that trade growth encourages one European firm to consider building a factory in another country which is a member of the Union. The transfer and convertibility of the currency involves transaction costs. More importantly, future fluctuations in exchange rates, possibly due to dissimilar shocks and/or macroeconomic policies, may increase economic uncertainty and reduce the investment profitability.

The existence of transaction costs and economic uncertainty because of multiple currencies does not necessarily justify one currency. One must also consider potential costs of a monetary integration rather than highlighting only potential benefits. The most significant cost of any monetary integration scheme is the loss of a national autonomous macroeconomic policy. Such an autonomous policy is immediately eliminated with the abolition of separate national currencies.

Thus, monetary unification offers both benefits and costs. One cannot on theoretical grounds claim that benefits are more significant than costs, nor does economic reality offer an opportunity to conduct laboratory experiments to compute benefits and to count costs. This may partially explain why EMU has been neither implemented nor abandoned as a goal by the EU. In other words, it may be argued that the possibility of potential benefits has kept the goal of EMU alive, while the reality of costs has prevented its accomplishment.

This may also support the speculation about a monetary union among a small number of EU members including Germany, Belgium, Luxembourg, France, the Netherlands and Denmark. Note that such a union will not offer significant benefits nor will it impose any important costs. These countries have experienced fairly stable exchange rates and thus macro-economic uncertainty has been rather minimal. The elimination of transaction costs will offer some small benefits. Also, the costs will be small because these countries have not followed independent monetary policies; rather they have coordinated their policies with those of Germany.

Suppose that one accepts the general idea that EMU will offer certain benefits but will also impose costs on its members. Suppose, further, that it is neither clear theoretically nor possible empirically to assess the net outcome from such benefits and costs. Can we judge from the current EMU policy debates the most likely evolution of European monetary integration?

The Maastricht Treaty and the recent developments of the period 1992–96 offer mixed signals. Observe that the key intentions of the Maastricht Treaty were to coordinate fiscal and monetary policies to achieve certain targeted macroeconomic goals about inflation, interest rates, ratio of public debt to GDP, and so on. One way of interpreting these goals is to say that the Maastricht Treaty attempted to reduce the degree of autonomy for the macroeconomic policies of its members. On the other hand, the collapse of the European ERM on 2 August 1993 and the currency crisis show that not all members of the EU were willing to forgo their autonomous macroeconomic policies in favour of EMU. Thus the Maastricht Treaty with its firm goal of EMU and the collapse of the ERM since 1992 as the centrepiece of European monetary integration offer mixed signals about the future of EMU. Put differently, the pendulum of economic reality has not unambiguously confirmed the goal of macroeconomic policy coordination among all EU members as a prerequisite for EMU.

6   Lessons from the current international monetary system

As one reflects about the future of the EMU, what lessons have been learned from the current international monetary system? There are several detailed accounts, such as McKinnon (1993), which offer a detailed historical perspective. We are not interested in offering such a detailed review. Instead we wish to highlight some important lessons since the collapse of the Bretton Woods system in 1971.

First, the G7 (the US, Japan, Germany, France, the United Kingdom, Italy and Canada) have learned that totally flexible exchange rates create macroeconomic uncertainty which discourages trade and investments. During the past twenty-five years, these G7 countries have met regularly to establish target zones for the world's key currencies and have committed their monetary authorities to maintain these currency ranges. Of course, numerous shocks have always prevented currency fluctuations within the targeted ranges and new zones were often selected to acknowledge the underlying macroeconomic realities of the G7. The lesson, however, appears clear: both the international monetary system and the EMU have practised target zones with frequent reviews to make allowances for structural changes. The EU has been less willing to make changes in target zones than the G7. Actually, the resistance of the EU in making gradual changes in its currency zones has forced it to experience speculative attacks simply because of the willingness of the G7 to accept the economic realities more readily.

Second, an important corollary to the first lesson of target zones is the imperative of policy coordination. Beyond the establishment of currency zones, the G7 have made serious efforts to coordinate their monetary and fiscal policies because both economic reasoning and political realities make it clear that coordination is more beneficial than autonomy in economic policy. The EU has actually gone beyond the policy coordination reality of the international monetary system by advocating the specific Maastricht criteria that actually necessitate a high degree of cooperation among the EU members.

Third, the international monetary system has learned the discipline imposed by world financial markets. Countries that have not followed appropriate macroeconomic policies to support their currency within a desired zone have experienced speculative attacks. The recent history of Mexico offers a typical example. This lesson was also learned by the EU with speculative attacks against the British pound and other currencies discussed earlier. Both for the international monetary system and for the ERM these speculative attacks may be viewed as valuable experiences that impose market discipline.

Finally, the international monetary system has taught us that, independent of the imperfections of target zones and their periodic adjustments, the world's major economic powers have coordinated their macroeconomic policies sufficiently to avoid continuous difficulties. Actually, one may view the very small number of crises as evidence that the system has performed reasonably well. Independent of the discipline imposed by financial markets, the emergence of derivative markets to manage interest rate and currency risks has contributed to the stable performance of the world system.

7 Conclusions

Since the collapse of the Bretton Woods international monetary system in August 1971, both the EU and the G7 have put forth enormous effort to developing and maintaining the managed float as a world monetary system and the ERM as an EU monetary system.

This chapter traces the history of monetary developments in the EU but also briefly presents several lessons learned from the international monetary system. One natural conclusion seems to be the reality that both systems are evolving and although we may be a little far from the ideal of a total EMU with one currency for the one market of the EU, the managed float has taught us that world trade can continue to grow despite the current imperfections of the international monetary system.

References

Eichengreen, B. (1993), 'European Monetary Unification', *Journal of Economic Literature*, **31**, 1321–57.

Giavazzi, F. and A. Giovannini (1989), *Limiting Exchange Rate Flexibility: The European Monetary System*, Cambridge, MA: MIT Press.

Kondonassis, A.J. and A.G. Malliaris (1994), 'Toward Monetary Union of the European Community: History and Experiences of the European Monetary System', *American Journal of Economics and Sociology*, **53**, 291–301.

Kondonassis, A.J. and Malliaris A.G. (1996), 'European Monetary Integration: Lessons for other Trading Agreements' in C. Paraskevopoulos *et al* (eds) *Economic Integration in the Americas*, Cheltenham, UK: Edward Elgar Publishing Limited, pp 129–36.

McKinnon, R. (1993), 'The Rules of the Game: International Money in Historical Perspective', *Journal of Economic Literature*, **XXXI** (1), 1–44.

2 Configurations and prospects for European integration and monetary unification

Patrick M. Crowley and Robin Rowley

1 Introduction

Only recently have the economists dealing with European integration focused attention on political frameworks within which macroeconomic decisions are taken, due in part to developments in related fields of economics dealing with central bank independence, fiscal federalism and the devolution of government responsibilities, GATT transformation and the evolution of trade patterns, and voter models. A new interest in political context and feasibility has also been influenced by the debate among political scientists over appropriate conceptions for the European Union (EU). But there are few illustrations of an integrated theory in the professional literature of economists, with efforts by Eichengreen and Frieden (1994) and Winkler (1995) being notable exceptions. Economic research continues to evolve independently of the research agenda of political science, which has gradually assimilated economic issues – Dyson (1994) and Sandholtz (1993) illustrate the inclusion of additional economic material. Our chapter melds notions and facts from the contemporary literature of economics and political science on the European Monetary Union (EMU) into a unified package.

The nature of institutionalized, cooperative policymaking in the EU has changed in scope and depth during recent years. Intergovernmental bargaining has been a creative force behind the drive to more cooperative policymaking, and important areas of decisionmaking have shifted from their national bases to the European arena. The Council is a major forum for expressions of national interests, with a small group of 'European' civil servants, but commissioners are appointed by the national governments. The Commission also uses epistemic communities of experts, whose advice supposedly abstracts from political and ideological influences.

The structural evolution of the EU occurs at discrete intervals through deliberations at irregular intergovernmental conferences (IGCs), where major decisions affecting the Union are formulated and agreed upon – as with completion of the Single European Act (1986), qualified majority voting in the Council of Ministers, and the Maastricht Treaty (1991). The next reconsiderations will emerge from the deals struck at the 1996–97 IGC. A widespread perception is that a strong reliance on IGCs and the transfer of important competencies to the EU institutions have eroded the power of individual member states, thus diluting sovereignty and weakening the influence of interest groups in member states. This perception is overly strained, however, for the IGCs are merely cooperative (sometimes non-cooperative) bargaining sessions and qualified majority voting is invalid. Only unanimity ensures that policy initiatives and institution-building are accepted by the participants. Thus, to an important extent, major decisions regarding the building of European institutions and transfers of competency remain in the hands of governments and other agencies in member states.

Some past decisions are now being implemented. Thus (i) creation of an EMU is under way, with a European Monetary Institute (EMI) in operation as a precursor for the European Central Bank (ECB), which is expected to assume responsibilities by 1999 at the latest, (ii) the Schengen club of states, which promotes borderless travel and labour mobility within part of the EU, is seeking to extend its membership to include Sweden, Norway and Finland (and cooperative agreements with Norway and Iceland, which have a passport union with these Nordic countries), and (iii) most directives of the Single European Act have been enacted by all member states. We take these changes for granted and explore the future shape of economic policymaking in Europe, given the political competencies assigned to supranational institutions and the perceived development of integrationist tendencies (expressed in new institution-building or referential principles, such as subsidiarity). Our discussion begins with an account of the evolving EMU and the principal circumstances within which EMU agreement came to fruition. We evaluate potential configurations of member states during the third stage of an emergence of the EMU, before assessing aspects of relevance to the final stage of this process, and give special attention to the development of future monetary and fiscal policies. The anticipated development of the EU is considered and some concluding remarks are offered.

2 The EMU process

The Maastricht Treaty (1991) specifies an evolutionary multi-stage process by which member states would adopt a single currency. Stage one of this process has now been completed, while the second stage is expected to end by 1999. During this second stage, (i) the new EMI has been established, (ii) member states must encourage a greater degree of central bank independence for monetary policy, (iii) ERM realignments are to be vigorously resisted, and (iv) the EMI and European Commission must decide if the economic performances of member states satisfy 'convergence criteria' (specified in the Treaty itself) or approach satisfactory levels at a sufficient rate. During the final stage, exchange rates are to be 'irrevocably' fixed among the domestic currencies of member states who fulfil the criteria, the ECB is to start operations, and the 'euro' will become an international currency, alongside national currencies and superior to them in various respects.

Fulfilment of this process is an ambitious objective. The main features were not fixed by any procrustean edict, and the need for the current IGC was clearly envisaged at Maastricht. Economic commentaries on the process are provided by Buiter *et al.* (1993), Kenen (1995), and Crowley and Rowley (1996). Plans for the introduction of the single currency have been tabled and tentatively agreed upon, as clarified by the EMI (1995) and Commission of the European Communities (1995a, b, 1996). Portes (1996) and Crowley (1996b) explore implementation of the final stage for establishment of the EMU. From a political standpoint, the Maastricht compromise was surprising, given the initial positions held by member states. The nature of this compromise has been actively debated, as reflected in the favourable opinions of Sandholtz (1993), Eichengreen (1993) and Crowley (1996a), and the dissent expressed by Connolly (1995) and Minford (1992).

Much of the justification for a monetary union was originally provided by the Commission of the European Communities (1990). It was suggested that gains in efficiency from removing currency uncertainty and exchange costs might be worth as much as 10 per cent of gross national product for the EU. No explicit evaluation of the overall costs of monetary union was made, but estimates were made of the costs for a transfer of seigniorage from individual governments to a single supranational institution (ECB). Such estimated transfer costs were negligible in most cases, while the offsetting benefits from enhanced credibility and macroeconomic stability were presumed to come from the establishment of a new structure. It is now widely acknowledged that a purely economic or quantitative rationale is an incomplete basis for supporting the forceful advocacy of a monetary union. Indeed a wide bloc of significant concerns are relevant here and a suitable integration theory must draw on material from economic, political and legal spheres, as well as on realistic treatments of social regulation. Within economics, observers such as Eichengreen (1990) and De Grauwe and Vanhaverbeke (1991) have moved beyond the empirical focus on optimal currency areas, while Winkler (1995) offers a critical summary of the conventional approach. Within political science, rival views are split between 'intergovernmental' and 'institutionalist' perspectives, as illustrated by Moravcsik (1993), Keohane and Hoffmann (1991), Sbragia

(1992), Garrett and Weingast (1993) and Taylor (1991). Intergovernmentalists suggest that member states dominate EU politics, so any major outcome of the evolving bargaining among them reflects the individual interests and relative powers of the states, while the institutionalists insist that supranational institutions exercise an independent effect within the union and thus also affect outcomes.

Within the legal sphere, the drafting of a constitution for the EU, as reflected in the Resolution given in the European Parliament (1994), prompted a strong interest in establishing suitable legal forms for this new type of international organization. Legal uncertainties arise in many substantial areas (extending from new provisions for corporate structures, workplace and business contracts through the rules for harmonization and standards to issues governing the supervision and requirements of international and domestic payment systems). Relevant comments on legal issues are illustrated by Thurer (1995), Ladeur (1995) and various discussion papers from the European University Institute in Florence and elsewhere. Specific interest in a social chapter of the Maastricht Treaty has also stimulated development of a pan-EU social policy and wider appreciation of the growing significance of rulings from the European Court of Justice which have social aspects.

The signing of the Maastricht Treaty need not reflect a clear unanimity among its signatories as to the desirability of its primary clauses or the inviolability of its provisions and timetable for structural adjustments. Rather it can be viewed as stemming from the opportunistic and pragmatic nature of interstate bargaining within the EU, the domestic political interests of key member states (notably Germany) and the independent effects of supranational EU institutions in convincing the national governments, central bankers and other significant 'players' of risks from compromising the basic principles subsequently embedded in the Treaty. Derogations secured by the United Kingdom and Denmark on EMU indicate that pragmatic exclusions to a homogeneous package were necessary to reduce some particular obstacles to the pace of unification and to facilitate timely progress at IGCs. Without visible compromises, it seems the Maastricht Treaty would probably not have included EMU and the social chapter, and its determination may have been substantially delayed. Schneider and Cederman (1994) suggest that the Treaty can be viewed as a reaction to systemic constraints and point to the loss of sovereignty following globalization of capital markets. We should also note the spatial relocation of economic activity and employment, rapid political disintegration in Eastern Europe, creation of other trading blocs, changes in past trade flows and leadership patterns as disturbing influences for the political climate during the bargaining process.

In the aftermath of the Maastricht Treaty, it became clear that sections of the Treaty, apart from the explicit derogations, will indirectly affect sovereignty for particular areas of policy for the member state (Commission of the European Communities 1995b) in the post-Maastricht era. It is to these indirect obligations and constraints that we now turn.

3   Insiders and outsiders: possible post-Maastricht configurations

It has been suggested that the vagueness, ambiguity and rival interpretations of some sections of the Maastricht Treaty were anticipated and implicit reservations were left to be resolved during the subsequent process of implementation. Such legislated incompleteness is a common phenomenon in contract bargaining, as future situations cannot be fully specified in advance, and the use of 'soft' provisions permits sufficient flexibility for a subsequent dialogue among constituent parties to resolve specific problems or imprecisions when they occur or seem imminent. The EMU was perceived as a desirable objective by the Commission and as central to EU development. However, a consensus among member states for the detailed structure, entrance requirements, the longer-term obligations of membership of the EMU, and rules and institutions for treating interactions with non-members has not yet emerged, and conflicts have appeared in regard to the responsibilities to be honoured during the period after completion of the third stage of the Maastricht process. These conflicts often turn on rival interpretations of the convergence criteria, but not always.

Some general factors are likely to affect future configurations of the EU. These factors involve several areas of current imprecision, including changing perceptions for the desirability of the project as a whole, flexible interpretations of convergence criteria used to monitor members before and after admission, the scope and conduct of monetary policy by the ECB (and its relations and status relative to existing central banks), and new arrangements for the interfaces with non-participating member states and other national governments, involving discriminatory or discretionary access to the 'euro' payments systems, spillovers to futures contracts in alternative denominations, and short-term interest rates. An analysis of factors that may promote greater stability for the post-Maastricht environment is given by Eichengreen and Ghironi (1995). We offer a few terse observations.

For the interpretation of convergence criteria, it is clear that their initial specification was supplemented to allay the concerns of member states with large debt–GDP ratios. New dynamic criteria now focus attention on the pace with which states can approach 'satisfactory' performance according to the initial criteria. With a sufficient dynamic tendency, the Commission can request the Council to allow a state to proceed as if criteria were satisfied. Such a weakened qualification has already been exercised for Ireland, and it seems likely to be adopted if Italy and Belgium are to participate in the first wave to enter the third stage. The initial criteria collectively represent a hurdle that few states can leap without major changes in their economic performance. Consider, for example, the criterion whereby membership in the ERM of the EMS is required for at least two years without realignment, and with an exchange rate persistently within 'normal' ERM bands. Ambiguous 'normality' leaves considerable scope for ranges beyond a conventional ± 15 per cent band – the Nether-lands has retained a 2.25 per cent band, while states have either left the ERM or used the ± 15 per cent band in recent years.

In another area of imprecision, we have the ECB with its mandate for pursuing price stability, which was probably adopted to reduce German fears that a supranational central bank would have a lower commitment to price stability than is traditionally associated with the Bundesbank. Any policy to fulfil the mandate requires a clear definition in operational terms, in part to reduce over-reactions to the inevitable deviations from a very strict interpretation of the mandate. Also it has to be clarified whether stability means zero inflation over some determinate period or the use of a referential target range for acceptable inflation (Goodhart 1993). In Canada and New Zealand, the target option has been adopted with markedly different operating rules, enabling legislation and monitoring provisions. Perhaps Europeans will find it difficult to fully accept the independence of an active ECB in a 'federal' system if a monetary policy seeking price stability has deleterious impacts on social and economic concerns (a worsening of regional disparities, difficult credit conditions and financial complications). The hypothetical commitment to central bank independence and price stability must be subject to political erosion in difficult times.

In implementing the operational objective of price stability, other difficult choices have to be made for the ECB (Von Hagen and Fratianni 1994), notably with respect to measurement. Existing systems using consumer price indices already remove certain troublesome elements, such as those identified with changing energy costs, and they ignore the potential presence of technical biases (due to a failure to capture substitu-tion effects or recognize different reference populations, for example) except in so far as these biases affect the width of target bands, and they typically resist indices that are subject to major historical revisions (implicit deflators of national accounts). Further, in a union of member states, the ECB must determine how to produce an aggregate measure of price changes that is acceptable to its audience. A successful assault on inflation depends on the confidence generated by the central bank, and its credibility in this respect will be markedly affected by the choice of referential index for the targeted band.

The ECB can opt for an EU-wide price aggregate, or it can set individual target ranges for prices in each state and develop some aggregate measure to represent an average for the EU. Both options have awkward aspects. The second option, for example, permits inflation differentials within the EU and the excesses in one country must be countered by deflation elsewhere if price stability is to be achieved. Resistance to deflationary policies may mean that a decentralized approach yields a higher rate of inflation than the alternative approach using an EU-wide price aggregate. Politically too, the location of the EMI in Frankfurt and its high proportion of German staff might encourage the monitoring of reputations of central bankers themselves during the initial setting of EU monetary policy. A debate on reputations, beginning in the EMI Council but then pushed into governmental positions of individual states as the third stage starts, may encourage the EU council to tacitly accept the notion of a two-track EMU on credibility grounds (Alesina and Grilli 1993).

Turning to the complex set of arrangements that must be established to deal with interactions between members of the EMU and non-members, the Commission believes that all currencies for non-participating member states should eventually be compelled to join a revised ERM (Commission of the European Communities 1995b) on legal (Articles 109m and 109j:1 of the Maastricht Treaty) and economic grounds. The Commission holds that the convergence process should continue for non-participatory member states, relevant expectations should be stabilized as far as possible, and exchange rate fluctuations moderated as they may disrupt trade flows. The EMI also accepts this notion of a continuing process of convergence. It argues that those member states initially unable to meet convergence criteria or possessing a derogation from the EMU should tie their currencies to the euro in a revised ERM with a narrow band (an ERMII). Both the Commission and the EMI have sought to maintain the convergence criteria as a prerequisite for proceeding to the third stage of EMU. Agreement has recently been reached on a blueprint for a new ERM, centred on the euro, with ± 15 per cent bands, but membership will be voluntary.

What will the EU configuration look like after the third stage is completed? The 'Lamers Report' (1994) from the German CDU/CSU coalition proposed a 'hard core' of member states who would be committed to a 'fast-track' of more integration within the EU. Revising the framework used by Eichengreen and Frieden (1994), we can envisage various configurations, including: (i) an EMU of the 15 member states, with Denmark and the UK abrogating their derogations, (ii) a smaller

EMU of 13 member states, with the two countries keeping their derogations, (iii) a soft-edged core EMU involving Germany, Austria, France,
Belgium, Luxembourg, Ireland, the Netherlands, Italy, Sweden and Finland, (iv) a harder-edged core EMU involving Germany, Austria, France,
Belgium, Luxembourg, Ireland and the Netherlands, (v) the EMU abandoned as unworkable, and (vi) a mini-EMU with a revised treaty after
member states request a voluntary implementation of the mini-EMU.

Economically, configuration (i) may not be the best solution unless the
EU is a homogeneous optimal currency area, which has been questioned in
recent explorations of correlations for demand and supply disturbances
across member states by Bayoumi and Eichengreen (1994) – who found a
non-homogeneity or partial separability, consistent only with incomplete
blocs of member states and more favourable to configuration (iv). Erkel-
Rousse and Melitz (1995) indicate a potential lack of robustness of these
findings. They argue that sovereignty over monetary policy may be of little
value outside a strict monetary union, with the possible exception of the
UK, and that independent fiscal policies can mitigate costs of adjustment
at a later date, after monetary union is established. This view is overly
optimistic in the light of the creative fiscal accounting that pervades most
discussion of economic policies in Europe, and it ignores the constraints
likely to be exerted on any 'independent' fiscal policies by other member
states and the EU-imposed penalties introduced in the 'stability pact'.
Politically, it also seems likely that the collective interest of the EU is not
well served by the radical configuration (v), given the prior investment
made in the project and anticipations generated by it. Only if there is a
critical stalemate (with Germany unwilling to loosen the convergence
criteria and a large number of states unable to satisfy them), will this
configuration emerge as a viable alternative. The stability pact might
encourage states to tighten their fiscal policies, at least temporarily, to
satisfy most of the criteria. Configuration (vi) represents a scenario for
Germany going ahead with EMU but maintaining its support for the
criteria, even though their enforcement leaves only a minority of states
eligible to proceed. Again the configuration seems unlikely to occur.

We are left with the first four configurations as possibilities. The
Commission may prefer (i) but recent positions expressed by member
states have tended to undermine it and we are reduced to choosing among
configurations (ii), (iii) and (iv), all of which are 'intergovernmentalist'
solutions. The three options are differentiated, in practice, by the manner
in which the convergence criteria are to be applied. Choice is then to be
dominated by the prevailing political circumstances as much as by
economic factors. Whatever bargain is struck on convergence criteria,
another important issue still has to be resolved. Given a path dependency

of the Maastricht process, can the configurations (ii), (iii) and (iv) lead to a monetary union of at least 13 member states or will some states be isolated on an economic periphery? Alesina and Grilli (1993) argue that once a core group adopts the euro, there will be little incentive to ask high-inflation countries to join them – a misdirected argument since member states do not have to be invited to join. They have a right to proceed if and when the convergence criteria are satisfied. Persistent exclusion from EMU on other grounds would violate the founding principles of the European Union.

A different view of potential EMU configurations is given by Martin and Ottaviano (1995), who appraise a two-stage EMU and identify a perverse scenario in which countries initially excluded from a core are unable to join an integrated bloc, because of labour migration away from the periphery towards the initial core or agglomeration economies within that core. The longer a country remains on the periphery, the larger the barrier to subsequent entry as both agglomeration economies and migration gather pace over time. For peripheral states (Spain, Portugal, Greece and Italy, perhaps) and any new member states from Eastern Europe, the interpretation of convergence criteria is again crucial for it will affect how long these countries must wait before joining the favoured core. Clearly, there is an overwhelming need to clarify the dynamic consequences of irreversible path dependency and the processes which affect them.

4   Designing fiscal and monetary institutions for EMU

The design of effective fiscal and monetary institutions for the EU is not straightforward. Although the ECB is to be the central bank for the monetary union, the European Parliament (EP) does not fulfil a parallel function to that of a national parliament. The EP is mainly responsible for a secondary check on policies and has few powers with which to alter them. Its role is advisory and revisionary. This 'democratic deficit' (Verdun 1996) means that current disparities in degrees of centralization for monetary and fiscal policy provide no determinate European political authority to be held responsible for such policies. The ECB is designed as if it were a federal institution but yet it is firmly fixed within an intergovernmental or confederative structure as far as most areas of policy are concerned.

The role of Germany in influencing the design of the ECB and imposition of *ex ante* fiscal criteria for participation in EMU is well known. As De Grauwe (1995) notes, Germany committed to the Maastricht process only because the convergence criteria guaranteed subsequent domination by those states with records of low inflation, and because some aspects (independence, a commitment to price stability) of the ECB repeated similar ones attributed to the Bundesbank. But why did the Bundesbank promote a new arrangement which does not improve on its current situation relative to the German federal government? Determining the motives of major institutions is always hazardous but it is reasonable to infer that tacit agreement of the Bundesbank was attracted by a foreseeable accumulation of additional power and influence within Europe and Germany itself. The relationship between the Bundesbank and the Ministry of Finance in Germany has not always been cordial so there was scope for the Bundesbank to consolidate more power (Henning 1994). A lack of progress on European political union may have inspired fiscal convergence criteria to reduce the incidence of political disagreements similar to those experienced by the Bundesbank in Germany, producing a forum for deliberations and dispensing with democratic accountability, at least in the short term.

Another future problem affects the coordination of monetary and fiscal policies when monetary policy is made at a supranational level and implemented at a national level, while fiscal policy is to be made and implemented by member states. How will the ECB coordinate pan-EU monetary actions with 15 different sources for fiscal activities? Should the ECB be concerned only with those states that satisfy the fiscal convergence criteria or should it be more widely concerned with the overall stance for fiscal policy within the EU? Indeed, how should an overall stance be determined for fiscal policy? These are significant areas of uncertainty to be addressed by intergovernmental bargaining and settled by firm agreements – much beyond the bargaining already under way, and beyond the few arrangements accepted by member states. The penalties indicated in the 'Excessive Deficit Protocol' of the Maastricht Treaty for running excessive deficits are insipid and unenforceable, so as to render the established criteria as pointless and arbitrary guidelines. If a pan-EU fiscal policy is decided by member states and monetary policy is determined at the supranational level, the only way to effectively penalize a member state may be to limit its role in ECB policymaking, perhaps by a suspension of voting rights for a time (Gros 1995).

With respect to existing provisions for monetary policy, the Maastricht Treaty requires that the implementation of the common monetary policy must take place in accordance with the principle of subsidiarity, with the national central banks taking as full a role as possible (Committee on Economic and Monetary Affairs and Industrial Policy of the European Parliament 1994). Both the EMU and subsidiarity are enshrined into European law by the treaty, but it remains unclear how the principle of subsidiarity will be interpreted in the context of the ESCB. The historical experience of the Federal Reserve System in the US saw state representation evolving into regional representation through an emergence of the Reserve Banks (Giovannetti and Marimon 1995), but this regional dimension should not be exaggerated and its direct impact has diminished in recent years. The implications for a European system are also obscure since the American federal structure is far removed from the confederation being contemplated for Europe.

Even if we ignore subsidiarity and the implementation of monetary policy, we may still ask whether current arrangements in the Maastricht protocol for the ECB will offer the best means of ensuring credibility in the presence of opportunistic political cycles. Von Hagen and Suppel (1994) and Von Hagen (1995) suggest that the council representatives for a central bank, appointed supranationally, might deliver more efficient policy for stabilization than do state representatives, and the latter might deliver lower long-run rates of inflation. In the ECB context, supranationally appointed representatives will initially outnumber their state-appointed counterparts but this situation will be reversed as additional member states enter the third stage of the EMU. Since the state-appointed representatives to the ECB Council may be more attracted to reciprocal deals in strategic voting (Calvert 1989), establishing credibility in the initial phases of EMU is critical to the evolution of EU monetary policy. Further, a conservative 'culture' fostered by the initial appointees may be protected if the inclusion of new states in the EMU occurs incrementally rather than in groups.

Clearly, there may be significant problems in the coordination of fiscal and monetary policies in the EU and the ECB's monetary policy may be affected by the manner in which peripheral states enter the third stage of the EMU. Constitutional objectives of the ECB are inadequately specified, but retention of fiscal convergence criteria may ensure a modest continuity in monetary policy, with only incremental changes in monetary interventions. With the multilevel governance of economic policy, monitoring of any policy shifts may still be limited and the lack of democratic accountability for decisionmakers at the ECB could endanger the bank's credibility rather than enhance it.

5   The future of the EU

The EU faces unprecedented challenges to its future prosperity and stability. The participants in current deliberations seek to deepen existing levels of integration linking member states, and they are contemplating the potential expansion of the EU over the next decade. It is implicit in recent decisions at the 1996–97 IGC that deepening takes precedence over expansion but there are signs of dynamic pressures and structural differences that could produce permanent 'fault lines' separating some member states from others, perhaps through the emergence of a 'hard core' of countries at the expense of a weakened overall solidarity. Research into expansion, regional integration, and multi-tiered relationships is still in its infancy. There is scant evidence (economic or otherwise) to offer any substantial support to alternative structural strategies.

The EMU is laudable in many respects but there remain considerable doubts as to the viability and wisdom of the undertaking, particularly as we have no precedent for similar monetary unions and it requires a persistent coincidence of European political interests. The EU operates as an intergovernmental organization, which adversely affects the feasibility of its developing into a self-interested body politic. It lacks the institutional infrastructure of a federation and is dependent on the goodwill that makes a principle of collective consent operational. The lack of fiscal sovereignty and a unified social policy in the EU, for example, may significantly hamper pan-EU policymaking. Indeed we may have an organisation with different degrees of competency in various areas, subject to the principle of subsidiarity, but lacking coherence. Thus unified strategies for policy areas are difficult to implement and can create perverse incentives for the conduct of individual governments. The long resistance of the UK's government to a common social policy is symptomatic of a potential malaise, revealed too by differences among social policies of member states and by the UK incentive to leave the ERM so that a sterling devaluation would enhance the competitiveness of its traded products.

The erratic nature of integration is also worrisome. Difficulties in obtaining a sufficient degree of unanimity in decisionmaking have stalled projects at the EU Council level. If future compromises on new initiatives are dependent on the acquiescence or appeasement of domestic political factors, then any further institutional development is likely to be uneven at best, and unduly selective at worst. Nor is more progress towards an integrated future encouraged by the recent attacks on decisions of the European Court by national governments, especially those from the UK. Finally, in this legacy of flaws, current voting procedures are clearly in need of imminent reform, certainly before an expansion to include countries from Eastern Europe is contemplated.

6   Concluding remarks

It is difficult to summarize contentious issues and their imprecisions in a few bold statements, but these issues are too important to be left without some conclusions as reflected in the following list.

1. The evolution of the EMU will be path dependent, with the principal outcomes affected by historical compromises, deals struck by participants during the process, and special circumstances that arise, perhaps unexpectedly.
2. Treaty obligations, rulings, formal commitments and basic principles

are rarely inviolable. They can always be affected by an ongoing political dialogue, the ambiguities of diplomatic and legal language, incompleteness of contractual provisions, and pragmatic or strategic reinterpretations.

3. The rapid assimilation of a common currency is inevitable, as are some profound changes in financial markets and international business (affecting third-party countries and non-participating member states, too). From its modest accounting role, the euro will receive a substantial impetus – changing accounting rules, stimulating a spatial relocation of financial sector interests to Frankfurt or Luxembourg, and inducing new arrangements to facilitate restricted access to Target, the euro payments and settlements system.

4. The spillover of monetary union to other regulated activities will occur at a slower rate and will be fraught with difficulties. Concomitant adjustments are necessary for legal systems, labour and workplace regulations, commercial standards and aspects of spatial mobility.

5. The hegemonic and technical relationships between the future ECB and national central banks (and between the ECB and other financial players, such as large commercial banks) need careful definition as quickly as possible. Clarification of primary and secondary responsibilities and the means of resolving interjurisdictional disputes must be given high priority. The credibility of central banks is susceptible to the destructive impacts of uncertainty and ambiguity which will be enlarged by delays in establishing clear, fixed and realistic operational guidelines for the ECB. Such guidelines must be in place before any major shift in monetary responsibilities occurs.

6. The core–periphery distinction is unavoidable. States will inevitably be separated into groups according to visible differences of their economic performance and political priorities. Separation has significant consequences for economic prosperity, with heightened disparities stimulated by cumulative forces unless resisted by political pressures through new regional incentive programmes and other devices. It seems likely that these consequences will affect strategic voting and political deal-making in other non-economic areas.

7. A persistent fiscal obfuscation dims any sharp perception of the European future. Recent reinterpretations of convergence criteria and the severe restrictions on individual or collective fiscal activity have increased uncertainty in regard to the feasibility of effective economic management, given the 'voluntary' replacement of national monetary policies by a central supranational focus at the ECB.

8. Meaningful appraisals of actual and potential European developments must contain two primary features. They must be 'structural' in the

sense of recognizing the institutional character of economic evolution in Europe, and they must be multifaceted in drawing on contributions from economics, political science and both legal- and social-policy studies. Only an integrated theory has much chance of illuminating the complex developments that are under way.

References

Alesina, A. and V. Grilli (1993), 'On the Feasibility of a One or Multi-speed European Monetary Union', CEPR Discussion Paper, No. 792.

Bayoumi, T. and B. Eichengreen (1994), 'One Money or Many?: Analyzing the Prospects for Monetary Unification in Various Parts of the World', Princeton Studies in International Finance, No. 76.

Buiter, W., G. Corsetti and N. Roubini (1993), 'Excessive Deficits: Sense and Nonsense in the Treaty of Maastricht', *Economic Policy*, **16**, 58–90.

Calvert, R. (1989), 'Reciprocity Among Self-interested Actors: Uncertainty, Asymmetry and Distribution', in P. Ordeshook (ed.), *Models of Strategic Choice in Politics*, Ann Arbor, MI: University of Michigan Press.

(CDU/CSU) (1994), *Reflections on European Policy*, Bonn: Fraktion des Deutschen Bundestages. Commission of the European Communities (1988), *The Economics of 1992*, Luxembourg: Office of Official Publications of the European Communities.

Commission of the European Communities (1990), *One Market, One Money*, European Economy 44, Luxembourg: Office for Official Publications of the European Communities.

Commission of the European Communities (1995a), *On the Practical Arrangements for the Introduction of the Single Currency*, Green Paper.

Commission of the European Communities (1995b), *Relations Between the Single Currency and Currencies of Countries Which Do Not Participate From the Start*, Interim Report.

Commission of the European Communities (1996), *Scenario for Changeover to the Single Currency*, Press Release, 10 January.

Committee on Economic and Monetary Affairs and Industrial Policy of the European Parliament (1994), *Report on the Objectives and Instruments of a Monetary Policy*.

Connolly, B. (1995), *The Rotten Heart of Europe: The Dirty War for Europe's Money*, London: Faber & Faber.

Council of the European Communities, Commission of the European Communities (1992), *Treaty on European Union*, Luxembourg: Office for the Official Publications of the European Communities.

Crowley, P. (1996a), 'EMU, Maastricht, and the 1996 Intergovernmental Conference', *Contemporary Economic Policy*, **14** (2), 41–55.

Crowley, P. (1996b), 'The Final Stage of European Monetary Union: Economic Issues and Political Controversies', Presentation, European Communities Studies Association–Canada Meetings.

Crowley, P. and R. Rowley (1996), 'Flaws and Omissions in the Maastricht Process for European Integration', in C.C. Paraskevopoulos *et al.*, *Economic Integration and Public Policy in the European Union*, Kluwer, pp. 21–32.

De Grauwe, P. (1995), 'The Economics of Convergence Towards Monetary Union in Europe', CEPR Discussion Paper, No. 1213.

De Grauwe, P. and W. Vanhaverbeke (1991), 'Is Europe an Optimal Currency Area? Evidence from Regional Data', CEPR Discussion Paper, No. 555.

Dyson, K. (1994), *Elusive Union: The Process of Economic and Monetary Union in Europe*, London: Longmans.

Eichengreen, B. (1990), 'Is Europe an Optimum Currency Area?', CEPR Discussion Paper, No. 478.

Eichengreen, B. (1993), 'European Monetary Unification', *Journal of Economic Literature*, **31**, 1321–57.

Eichengreen, B. and J. Frieden (1994), 'The Political Economy of European Monetary Unification: An Analytical Introduction', *The Political Economy of European Monetary Unification*, Boulder, CO: Westview Press, pp. 1–23.

Eichengreen, B. and F. Ghironi (1994), 'European Monetary Unification: The Challenges Ahead', CEPR Discussion Paper, No. 1217.

Erkel-Rousse, H. and J. Melitz (1995), 'New Empirical Evidence on the Costs of European Monetary Union', CEPR Discussion Paper, No. 1169.

European Monetary Institute (EMI) (1995), *The Changeover to the Single Currency*, Frankfurt: EMI.

European Parliament (1994), *Resolution on the Constitution of the European Union*. Luxembourg: Office for the Official Publications of the European Communities.

Garrett, G. and B. Weingast (1993), 'Ideas, Interests and Institutions: Constructing the European Community's Internal Market', in J. Goldstein and R. Keohane (eds), *Ideas and Foreign Policy, Beliefs, Institutions and Political Change*, Ithaca, NY: Cornell University Press, pp. 173–208.

Giovannetti, G. and R. Marimon (1995), 'A Monetary Union for a Heterogeneous Europe', EUI RSC, Working Paper, No. 95/17.

Goodhart, C. (1993), 'The European System of Central Banks After Maastricht', in P. Masson and M. Taylor (eds), *Policy Issues in the Operation of Currency Unions*, Cambridge: Cambridge University Press.

Gros, D. (1995), 'Towards a Credible Excessive Deficits Procedure', Centre for European Policy Studies Discussion Paper, Brussels.

Henning, C. (1994), *Currencies and Politics in the United States, Germany, and Japan*, Washington, DC: Institute for International Economics.

Kenen, P. (1995), *Economic and Monetary Union in Europe: Moving Beyond Maastricht*, Cambridge: Cambridge University Press.

Keohane, R. and S. Hoffmann (1991), 'Institutional Change in Europe in the 1980s', in R. Keohane and S. Hoffmann (eds), *The European Community, Decision-making and Institutional Change*, Boulder, CO; Westview Press, pp. 1–39.

Ladeur, K.-H. (1995), 'Post-Modern Constitutional Theory: A Prospect for the Self-Organizing Society', EUI Law Working Paper, No. 95/6.

Martin, P. and G. Ottaviano (1995), 'The Geography of Multi-Speed Europe', CEPR Discussion Paper, No. 1292.

Minford, P. (1992), 'The Price of Monetary Unification', in P. Minford (ed.), *The Cost of Europe*, Manchester: Manchester University Press, pp. 125–41.

Moravcsik, A. (1993), 'Preferences and Power in the European Community: A Liberal Intergovernmentalist Approach', *Journal of Common Market Studies*, **31**, 473–524.

Portes, R. (1996), 'Implementing EMU', *American Economic Review*, **86** (2), 139–43.

Sandholtz, W. (1993), 'Choosing Union: Monetary Politics and Maastricht', *International Organization*, 47 (1), 1–39.

Sbragia, A. (1992), 'Thinking about the European Future: The Uses of Comparison', in A. Sbragia (ed.), *Euro-politics, Institutions and Policymaking in the 'New' European Community*, Washington, DC: Brookings Institution, pp. 257–91.

Schneider, G. and L.-E. Cederman (1994), 'The Change of Tide in Political Cooperation: A Limited Information Model of European Integration', *International Organization*, **48** (4), 633–62.

Taylor, P. (1991), 'The European Community and the State: Assumptions, Theories and Propositions', *Review of International Studies*, 109–25.

Thurer, D. (1995), 'Do We Need a Constitution for Europe', in *A Constitution for the European Union?*, EUI RSC Working Paper, No. 95/9, 13–22.

Verdun, A. (1996), 'The Democratic Deficit of the EMU: Who Governs the Domestic Economy', Presentation, European Community Studies Association–Canada Meetings.

Von Hagen, J. (1995), 'Reciprocity and Inflation in Federal Monetary Unions', CEPR Discussion Paper, No. 1297.

Von Hagen, J. and M. Fratianni (1994), 'The Transition to European Monetary Union and the European Monetary Institute', in B. Eichengreen and J. Frieden (eds), *The Political Economy of European Monetary Unification*, Boulder, CO: Westview Press, pp. 129–48.

Von Hagen, J. and R. Suppel (1994), 'Central Bank Constitutions for Federal Monetary Unions, *European Economic Review*, **36**, 774–82.

Winkler, B. (1995), 'Towards a Strategic View on EMU: A Critical Survey', EUI SRC Working Paper, No. 95/18.

3 The EMS interest rates: German dominance or else?

*Christis Hassapis, Nikitas Pittis and Kyprianos Prodromidis**

1 Introduction

Since the establishment of the European Monetary System, (EMS) (March 1979), the prevailing view has been that the national central banks of the EMS member countries have surrendered their monetary policy autonomy to the hegemony of the German central bank (Artis and Nachane 1990; Biltoft and Boersch 1992; Caporale and Pittis 1993; Fischer 1987; Giavazzi and Giovannini 1987; Karfakis and Moschos 1990; Wyplosz 1989). This implies that the Bundesbank independently fixes the reference level of interest rates and controls the exchange rate of the ECU *vis-à-vis* the US dollar, while the other EMS national central banks stabilize the parity of their currency *vis-à-vis* the Deutsche Mark (DM). This strong view has come to be known as the strict German Dominance Hypothesis (GDH).

The GDH has been challenged on several grounds, notably: (i) Germany is not the dominant, but still is a relatively strong player. This view is termed as the weak version of GDH (Von Hagen and Fratianni 1990; Smeets 1990); (ii) the monetary policies within the EMS are more symmetric (De Grauwe 1989; Katsimbris 1993; Katsimbris and Miller 1993); and (iii) the German monetary policy is not independent from the US monetary policy (Artus et al. 1991; Katsimbris and Miller 1993; Kirchgaessner and Wolters 1993).

Concerning the empirical work, a number of studies have focused exclusively on interest rate linkages within the EMS and aimed at revealing potential directions of causation between them (Karfakis and Moschos 1990; Katsimbris 1993; Katsimbris and Miller 1993). These studies have concentrated upon cointegration testing in the context of bivariate vector auto regression (VAR) systems, consisting of the German interest rate and the respective rate of each of the other EMS member countries. The null hypothesis of 'no long-run German dominance' is translated into 'non-cointegration' in the system. These authors are aware that, in general, non-

* Hassapis and Pittis gratefully acknowledge financial support from the Planning Office, the Rebuplic of Cyprus; Prodromidis acknowledges financial support from the Ministry of Development, General Secretariat for Research and Development, and the AUEB's Research Centre, Contract E368.

cointegration does not necessarily imply non-causality; therefore, they perform standard causality tests in the first-differenced VAR. However, they fail to acknowledge that lack of cointegration may simply be the result of a monotonic convergence of the member states' rates towards the German rate, which simply results in trending interest rate differentials. (For details, see Caporale and Pittis 1993.)

The methodologies of the preceding papers in elucidating the evolution of the EMS are varying. However, they have not dealt thoroughly with the possibility that the true dominant player may be outside the EMS. Specifically, the effects of the US monetary policy on each individual EMS country have not been compared with the corresponding effects from German monetary policy in a unified framework, allowing for monetary policy interactions between the US and Germany.

The chapter is organized as follows: In Section 2, we examine: (i) alternative versions of the GDH in the context of bivariate VAR systems; and (ii) augmented versions of the GDH, incorporating the impact of US monetary policies, in the context of trivariate VARs. In Section 3, we present the empirical results. In the context of bivariate first-order VAR systems, the empirical findings indicate that the German short-term interest rate is not cointegrated with the respective rate of each individual EMS country. These suggest that the (sufficient) condition for causality in at least one direction is not fulfilled. None the less, in the context of first-order trivariate VARs, the analysis reveals cointegration in all systems. This result implies causality between at least two variables in at least one direction; it implies interactions of monetary policies of the countries participating in the VARs. Hence, non-cointegrability in bivariate VARs may stem from the omission of an important 'causing' variable, which in our case is the US interest rate. The upshot of these considerations is the emergence of the US Dominance Hypothesis, over and above a variety of alternative versions of GDH. Section 4 summarizes the main findings and conclusions.

2   Methodology

Consider a trivariate VAR(1) system consisting of the processes y_t, x_t and w_t:

$$
\begin{bmatrix} y_t \\ x_t \\ w_t \end{bmatrix} = \begin{bmatrix} \gamma_0 \\ \gamma_1 \\ \gamma_2 \end{bmatrix} + \begin{bmatrix} \alpha_{11} & \alpha_{12} & \alpha_{13} \\ \alpha_{21} & \alpha_{22} & \alpha_{23} \\ \alpha_{31} & \alpha_{32} & \alpha_{33} \end{bmatrix} \begin{bmatrix} y_{t-1} \\ x_{t-1} \\ w_{t-1} \end{bmatrix} + \begin{bmatrix} e_{1t} \\ e_{2t} \\ e_{3t} \end{bmatrix} \tag{3.1}
$$

The series y_t, x_t and w_t stand for the short-term interest rates of an EMS member country (excluding Germany, see Section 3), Germany, and the US, respectively.

The dynamic behaviour of system (3.1) depends on the moduli of the three eigenvalues, λ_1 λ_2 and λ_3 of matrix $\mathbf{A} = [\alpha_{ij}]$, $i, j = 1, 2, 3$. Its dynamic stability is satisfied if $[\lambda_1]$, $[\lambda_2]$ and $[\lambda_3] < 1$. More specifically, to obtain three unit roots in the trivariate VAR(1), that is, $\lambda_1 = \lambda_2 = \lambda_3 = 1$ requires[1]

$$(\alpha_{11} + \alpha_{22} + \alpha_{33}) + (\alpha_{31}\alpha_{13} + \alpha_{21}\alpha_{12} + \alpha_{32}\alpha_{23} - \alpha_{11}\alpha_{22} - \alpha_{33}\alpha_{11} -$$
$$\alpha_{33}\alpha_{22}) + (\alpha_{11}\alpha_{22}\alpha_{33} + \alpha_{12}\alpha_{23}\alpha_{31} + \alpha_{21}\alpha_{32}\alpha_{13} - \alpha_{31}\alpha_{13}\alpha_{22} -$$
$$\alpha_{21}\alpha_{12}\alpha_{33} - \alpha_{32}\alpha_{23}\alpha_{11}) = 1. \tag{3.2}$$

That is, a sufficient condition for all three eigenvalues to be equal to one (non-cointegration) is that $\alpha_{11} + \alpha_{22} + \alpha_{33} = 1$, and $(\alpha_{12} = \alpha_{13} = \alpha_{21} = \alpha_{23} = \alpha_{31} = \alpha_{32} = 0$.

If w_t is independent of y_t and x_t, it can be dropped from the system, thus resulting in a bivariate VAR(1) system. In this case, condition (3.2) reduces to

$$(\alpha_{11} + \alpha_{22}) - (\alpha_{11}\alpha_{22} - \alpha_{12}\alpha_{21}) = 1 \tag{3.2a}$$

and the sufficient condition for both eigenvalues to be equal to one becomes $\alpha_{11} = \alpha_{22} = 1$, and $\alpha_{12} = \alpha_{21} = 0$.

The causality and cointegration properties of the bivariate and trivariate VAR(1) systems are analysed in our 1996 paper (Hassapis et al. 1996). The relevant statistical results obtained from that study are: first, regarding bivariate VARs: (i) sufficient conditions for unit roots to persist in VAR systems amount to Granger non-causality in any direction between the variables involved; (ii) a necessary condition for the disappearance of one unit root in the VAR involves Granger causality in at least one way; and (iii) in first-order models and for non-explosive time series, causality is also sufficient for cointegration. Second, in the context of trivariate VARs, the implications from the omission of an important 'causing' variable on causality and cointegration inference are discussed.

Our research strategy consists of the following steps. First, we estimate a bivariate VAR(1) in levels and test whether the Markoveness assumption holds for the data set available. This can be done by testing this model for its statistical adequacy and by comparing it with higher-order, competitive, in terms of information criteria, models (Akaike 1973; Schwarz 1978). If the estimates of α_{11} and α_{22} are close to one, we should expect no evidence in favour of Granger causality in any direction ($\alpha_{12} = \alpha_{21} = 0$); this is a sufficient condition for no cointegration between y_t and x_t. If, on the other hand, either one of these estimates is much lower than one, then Granger causality in at least one direction should be present. This implies that the necessary (but not, in general, the sufficient) condition for cointegration is fulfilled. Given the nature of the time series employed in this chapter, it is reasonable to argue that causality will almost surely lead to cointegration, since explosive situations such as $\alpha_{11}, \alpha_{22} > 1$ are highly unlikely to occur.

Second, we perform a formal cointegration test between y_t and x_t. Here, we distinguish between two cases: cointegration and non-cointegration. The former case formally establishes the presence of Granger causality in at least one direction; as such, it should coincide with an estimate of α_{11} or $\alpha_{22} < 1$. The direction of causality should be decided upon testing whether $\alpha_{12} = 0$ or $\alpha_{21} = 0$ by means of Johansen's likelihood ratio tests. In general, the case for non-cointegration coincides with either no causality (the estimates of $\alpha_{11}, \alpha_{22} \cong 1$) or with causality (at least one of the estimates of α_{11} or $\alpha_{22} > 1$) since both situations satisfy equation (3.2a). However, evidence of non-cointegration, in such a context, must imply the absence of causality in any direction, since European interest rates have not exhibited an explosive behaviour during the period under examination.

Third, in case the bivariate analysis provides evidence against cointegration, we follow the procedure discussed below. Recent developments in testing for unit roots in a univariate or a multivariate framework have shown that a once-off exogenous shock to the deterministic component (mean or trend) of a particular series can bias the standard unit root tests towards non-rejection of the null, with the degree of the bias rising with the magnitude of the shock (Perron 1989; Banerjee and Urga 1995). Therefore, before looking for other reasons that might have led to non-cointegration in a bivariate system, we should examine whether such deterministic breaks are responsible for the non-rejection of the null. Potential break dates that are also economically interpretable include the realignment dates of each individual EMS currency and the August 1993 episode, during which the EMS fluctuation bands were widened. Sequential tests for identifying these potential break dates are also available. The recursive sum of squared residuals is very useful in revealing such dates. A more formal testing procedure is suggested (Banerjee and Urga 1995) *inter alia* in the form of the sequence of one-step ahead Chow tests at each period i for the hypothesis that no structural break has occurred within the sample of size i. If the economically interpretable break dates coincide with those suggested by the tests, then the use of dummy variables is well justified. Hence, cointegration is reexamined by estimating the bivariate system with dummy variables, taking the value of one at the break dates and zero elsewhere. If the bivariate system is still non-cointegrated then we proceed to the next step.

Finally, the analysis on causality in incomplete systems (Hassapis et al. 1996) has shown that the omission of a 'causing' variable can affect the causality (and, hence, cointegration) inference between variables y_t and x_t of a bivariate system. Therefore, before concluding on possible linkages between y_t and x_t, the causality and cointegration analysis already described should be repeated in a trivariate context.

Applying the above theoretical findings in the empirical analysis reveals how erroneous could be a conclusion based on bivariate rather than on trivariate VARs. In particular, we examine the causality and cointegration properties of bivariate first-order VAR systems, consisting of the German short-term interest rate and the respective rate of each individual EMS country. A major finding of no cointegration emerges here. This implies that the sufficient condition for causality in at least one direction is not fulfilled. None the less, such a non-cointegrability in bivariate VARs may stem from the omission of an important 'causing' variable, notably the US interest rate. The respective analysis of first-order trivariate VARs reveals cointegration in all systems. This result implies causality between at least two variables in at least one direction. Thus, testing for the direction of causality is associated with interactions of monetary policies of the countries participating in the VAR. Our analysis brings to light an additional hypothesis, the US Dominance Hypothesis, over and above a variety of alternative versions of the GDH.

3 Empirical analysis

The data used in the empirical analysis are quarterly short-term (onshore) market interest rates covering the period 1979.3 to 1994.4. They concern Belgium (BE), France (FR), Germany (GE), Ireland (IR), Italy (IT), the Netherlands (NE) and the United States (US), and are obtained from OECD's *Main Economic Indicators*. In connection with the variables of Section 2, y_t, x_t and w_t correspond to the short-term interest rates of: the EMS member countries BE, FR, IR, IT and NE, taken separately, Germany, and the US. Similarly, the indices 1, 2 and 3 of matrix **A** represent the EMS country i, i = BE, ..., NE; Germany, and the US.

Hypotheses testing, both in a bivariate and a trivariate context, in relation to an asymmetric functioning of the EMS are given below:

I Bivariate context

- German Dominance Hypothesis (GDH) $\quad \alpha_{12} \neq 0$ and $\alpha_{12} = 0$
- symmetry $\quad \alpha_{12} \neq 0$ and $\alpha_{21} \neq 0$
- monetary autonomy in both countries $\quad \alpha_{12} \neq 0$ and $\alpha_{21} = 0$

II Trivariate context

- strong GDH (no direct or indirect
  causality from US) $\qquad \alpha_{12} \neq 0, \alpha_{13} = 0, \alpha_{23} = 0$
- weak GDH of type 1 (direct causality
  from US) $\qquad \alpha_{12} \neq 0, \alpha_{13} \neq 0, \alpha_{23} = 0$
- weak GDH of type 2 (direct and
  indirect causality from US) $\qquad \alpha_{12} \neq 0, \alpha_{13} \neq 0, \alpha_{23} \neq 0$
- semi-strong GDH (no direct causality
  from US, only indirect causality
  through Germany) $\qquad \alpha_{12} \neq 0, \alpha_{13} = 0, \alpha_{23} \neq 0$
- US Dominance Hypothesis (direct
  causality from the US with no direct
  causality from Germany) $\qquad \alpha_{12} = 0, \alpha_{13} \neq 0, \alpha_{23} \neq 0$

The empirical analysis is carried through as follows. First, estimates from bivariate VAR(1) models in levels, consisting of the interest rate of each individual EMS country and that of Germany, along with suitable misspecification tests are reported in Table 3.1. The choice of first-order models is well supported both by the misspecification tests, which reveal no departure from the model assumptions, and by the Schwarz information criterion (Akaike 1973; Schwarz 1978). The latter achieves its lowest value for a lag length equal to one. The α_{11} and α_{22} estimates are close to one for all countries except for the Netherlands. That is, in all bivariate systems at issue, but that for the Netherlands, Granger causality in any direction is absent. This implies that these systems are not cointegrated. The case of the Netherlands is different. The respective estimates are $\alpha_{11} = 0.59$ and $\alpha_{22} = 0.90$. Therefore, we should expect causality to run from Germany to the Netherlands ($\alpha_{12} \neq 0$). This is a necessary condition for cointegration. Furthermore, for non-explosive series, in the context of bivariate VAR(1) models, Granger causality in one direction is also sufficient for cointegration. In view of these findings, we proceed to conduct formal cointegration tests.

Second, Johansen's cointegration tests (Table 3.2) confirm the preceding finding that the Netherlands is the only EMS country cointegrated with Germany, and are in agreement with the findings of earlier studies (Karfakis and Moschos 1990; Katsimbris and Miller 1993). These studies utilize monthly data (1979.4–1988.11). Concerning the Netherlands, cointegration implies the existence of Granger causality in at least one direction. The direction of causality is identified via likelihood ratio tests. The hypothesis that the German interest rate does not Granger cause the Dutch rate is soundly rejected ($\chi^2 1 = 11.69$), whereas the hypothesis that no

Table 3.1 Bivariate analysis: VAR(1) in levels

Statistic	BE	GE	FR	GE	IR	GE	IT	GE	NL	GE
α_{11}	0.921		0.835		0.773		0.96		0.598	
	(0.061)		(0.051)		(0.071)		(0.032)		(0.112)	
α_{12}	0.052		0.061		0.229		0.068		0.327	
	(0.061)		(0.060)		(0.091)		(0.051)		(0.102)	
α_{21}		-0.028		-0.112		-0.101		-0.065		0.042
		(0.052)		(0.052)		(0.042)		(0.032)		(0.113)
α_{22}		0.931		0.978		1.000		0.958		0.901
		(0.057)		(0.056)		(0.053)		(0.054)		(0.102)
					P-values for misspecification tests					
AR(4)	0.615	0.912	0.051	0.104	0.285	0.011*	0.225	0.085	0.345	0.092
N	0.587	0.059	0.01*	0.102	0.033*	0.312	0.01*	0.074	0.063	0.135
ARCH	0.923	0.726	0.897	0.099	0.021*	0.182	0.313	0.688	0.452	0.087
LIN	0.165	0.558	0.396	0.978	0.405	0.489	0.186	0.783	0.128	0.567
SIC (4)	-0.73		-0.70		0.80		0.26		-1.60	
SIC (3)	-0.77		-0.93		0.57		0.05		-1.77	
SIC (2)	-0.93		-1.16		0.31		-0.14		-1.79	
SIC (1)	-0.92		-1.33		0.11		-0.21		-2.01	

Notes
1. A description of the misspecification tests is given in an appendix, available upon request.
2. An asterisk * denotes rejection of the null at the 5 per cent significance level.
3. SIC(i) stands for the Schwarz Information Criterion for lag i.

Table 3.2 Bivariate cointegration tests between the German and EMS interest rates

Country	Max eigenvalue		λ-max		Trace	
	D	ND	D	ND	D	ND
BE	0.08	0.05	5.16	3.57	6.91	5.74
FR	0.18	0.11	12.49	7.21	13.87	11.77
IR	0.19	0.17	11.67	10.35	15.27	14.85
IT	0.13	0.12	8.11	7.87	14.26	9.85
NL	0.38	0.31	28.08*	24.69*	30.23*	29.56*

Notes:
1. Trace and λ-max stand for the trace and the maximum eigenvalue statistics, respectively (Johansen 1988).
2. An asterisk indicates rejection of the null hypothesis of no-cointegration at the 5 per cent level. Critical values at the 5 per cent level: for λ-max = 14.1 and for the trace = 15.4 (Osterwald-Lenum, 1992).
3. D and ND stand for dummies and no-dummies, respectively. The dummies used for each system take the value one for the periods:
    BE: October 1981, February 1982, June 1982, August 1993;
    FR: October 1981, June 1982, March 1983, April 1986, August 1993;
    IR: October 1981, June 1982, March 1983, August 1993;
    IT: October 1981, June 1982, July 1985, September 1992;
    and zero otherwise.

Granger causality runs from the opposite direction is easily accepted ($\chi^2(1) =0.26$). This finding establishes the validity of a strong GDH in the case of the Netherlands.

Third, the next question is whether the non-cointegration finding of the other bivariate systems under consideration has remained unaltered throughout the sample period. This is a valid question to ask, for the EMS has gone through different phases since its creation (1979). A period of frequent realignments (early 1980s), followed by a period of relative tranquillity, was succeeded by a turbulent period leading to a widening of the fluctuation bands from ±2.25 per cent since its inception to ±15 per cent (August 1993). It is, therefore, proper to question the time invariance of the causality and cointegration features of the interest rates under consideration. To investigate the issue, we have estimated the five bivariate VAR(1) models recursively, and examined the time profile of the maximum eigenvalue of the matrix π – for each bivariate system. Such estimates are presented in Figures 3.1a–e as curves I. There it can be seen that these estimates have remained roughly stable at low levels (in most cases around

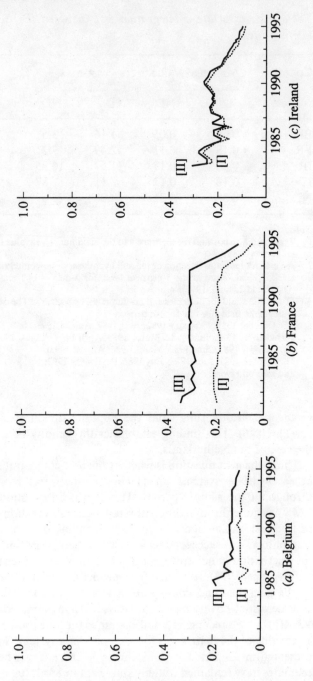

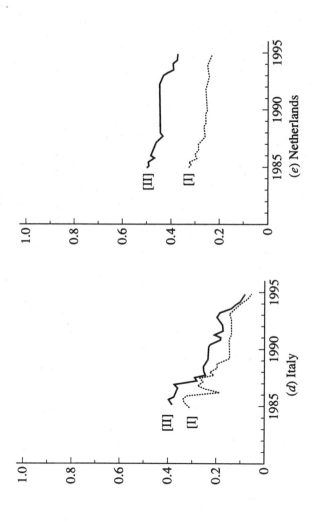

Note: (I) and (II) refer to the recursive estimates of the maximum eigenvalue, without and with dummies, respectively.

Figure 3.1 Recursive estimates of the maximum eigenvalue in the bivariate systems

0.2) until August 1993, when they declined further. This means that the non-cointegration property characterizing all bivariate VAR(1) models, except that for the Netherlands, is time invariant. Moreover, the 'cointegrability' of these systems has decreased after the widening of the fluctuation bands, indicating the laxity of linkages of short-run interest rates within the EMS. A notable exception is, again, the Netherlands: the respective maximum eigenvalue estimates have not declined. This suggests that the Dutch monetary authorities did not consider increasing the degree of their monetary autonomy, despite the fact that the new institutional arrangements had allowed them to do so. The case of Italy is slightly different. The Italian interest rate seems to have been cointegrated with the German rate, until about mid-1982, when the bilateral exchange rate for the DM against the Italian lira rose by 7 per cent. This finding reinforces our point (Section 2, methodological step 3), that any failure to reject the null hypothesis of no cointegration should be interpreted with care, if it is known that distinct once-off breaks have occurred within the sample period under consideration. That is, before accepting without reservation the non-cointegration results, we must ensure that the non-rejection of the null is not due to deterministic breaks in the series. Sequential tests for identifying potential break dates have been made and are described in an Appendix.[2] These tests enable us to reject the null hypothesis of structural invariance, exactly at the economically interpretable dates of realignments. To that end, we have repeated the cointegration tests by including dummy variables in the bivariate VAR(1) models. The respective results re-confirm the null hypothesis of no cointegration (Table 3.2). However, the inclusion of dummy variables, for the relevant realignment dates, has increased throughout the size of the maximum eigenvalue of the long-run matrix $\Pi = \mathbf{A} - \mathbf{I}$. This is seen in Figures 3.1a–e, where the recursive estimates of the maximum eigenvalues, in the presence of dummies, are reported as curves II. Hence, the realignments have contributed to the non-cointegrability of the systems in question, although they are not solely responsible for that.

The overall conclusion emerging from our bivariate analysis is that the ERM does not seem to have induced linkages between the interest rates of the individual EMS countries and Germany. The only exception appears to be the Netherlands, for which non-cointegration is easily rejected. This finding is hardly surprising, for in the history of the EMS there has not been a single realignment in which the Dutch guilder has not been revalued *pari passu* with the DM against the other EMS currencies.

On the other hand, non-cointegration between the rest of the EMS rates and the German one, could merely be the result of a gradual convergence of the interest rates of the individual EMS countries towards the German rate

(Caporale and Pittis 1993). This indicates that no co-movement or long-run relationship should be expected to prevail in a sample dominated by a 'convergence period'. This point is often neglected by the majority of the relevant studies.

Fourth, we have demonstrated (Hassapis et al. 1996) that causality inference in incomplete systems and, hence, cointegration is strongly affected by the omission of a third variable, which may even cause both preexisting variables. As already mentioned, the US interest rate, i_t^{US}, is an obvious candidate for such a variable, since the US monetary policy has likely affected the respective policies of the EMS and other countries. Estimation results from the trivariate VAR(1) models along with their misspecification tests are reported in Table 3.3. Again, no departure from the underlying model assumptions is detected, and the Schwarz information criterion suggests that, for all countries, the first-order models are preferable to higher-order models. Interestingly enough, the α_{11} estimates appear to be significantly lower than one for all countries under consideration. This implies that Granger causality is expected to run from either Germany ($\alpha_{12} \neq 0$) or the US ($\alpha_{13} \neq 0$) or both to each individual EMS country. In addition, in all cases, the estimates of α_{22} also appear to be smaller than unity, although they are greater in size than the respective α_{11} estimates. This suggests that either each EMS interest rate, i_t^*, or i_t^{US}, or both should cause the German rate, i_t^{GE}. Finally, in all cases, the α_{33} estimates are indistinguishably different from one. This result is pointing towards no Granger causality running from any EMS country and/or Germany to the US.

Since Granger causality has been informally detected to be present in all trivariate systems, the latter are expected to be cointegrated. Formal cointegration tests reveal that each EMS country's i_t^* is cointegrated with i_t^{GE} and i_t^{US} in a trivariate framework, with the dimension of the cointegration space being equal to one (Table 3.4). This, however, does not necessarily imply that all three variables in each system enter the cointegrating vector $\mathbf{b} = [b_{11}, b_{21}, b_{31}]'$. For example, assume that the long-run relationship among the interest rates in question, is given by

$$b_{11}i_t^* + b_{21}i_t^{GE} + b_{31}i_t^{US} = 0 \qquad (3.3)$$

There is no *a priori* guarantee that all elements of vector $\mathbf{b}$ are different from zero. For example, assume that $b_{21} = 0$. In such a case, the one cointegrating vector, detected by the Johansen tests, reflects a long-run relationship between i_t^* and i_t^{US}. Testing for such hypotheses is of paramount importance in the context of the questions raised in this chapter and

Table 3.3 *Trivariate analysis: VAR(1) in levels*

Statistic	BE	GE	US	FR	GE	US	IR	GE	US	IT	GE	US
α_{11}	0.541 (0.083)			0.793 (0.064)			0.711 (0.065)			0.798 (0.045)		
α_{12}	0.225 (0.062)			0.102 (0.051)			0.146 (0.076)			0.055 (0.041)		
α_{13}	0.251 (0.052)			0.061 (0.042)			0.246 (0.067)			0.246 (0.048)		
α_{21}		-0.312 (0.063)			-0.275 (0.056)			-0.187 (0.046)			-0.1 (0.035)	
α_{22}		0.812 (0.041)			0.892 (0.041)			0.872 (0.054)			0.875 (0.048)	
α_{23}		0.198 (0.031)			0.169 (0.038)			0.146 (0.042)			0.162 (0.033)	
α_{31}			0.038 (0.125)			0.018 (0.088)			0.089 (0.055)			0.027 (0.066)
α_{32}			-0.021 (0.092)			-0.091 (0.063)			-0.072 (0.062)			-0.012 (0.074)
α_{33}			1.000 (0.075)			0.978 (0.055)			1.000 (0.055)			1.000 (0.068)

P-values for misspecification tests

Statistic	BE	GE	US	FR	GE	US	IR	GE	US	IT	GE	US
AR(4)	0.566	0.473	0.756	0.634	0.472	0.653	0.356	0.398	0.225	0.448	0.755	0.165
N	0.334	0.706	0.053	0.875	0.703	0.068	0.387	0.102	0.043*	0.178	0.968	0.187
ARCH	0.915	0.914	0.985	0.911	0.854	0.452	0.088	0.941	0.812	0.199	0.099	0.179
LIN	0.456	0.798	0.712	0.698	0.952	0.607	0.275	0.280	0.240	0.456	0.198	0.616
SIC (4)	1.26			0.39			2.13			1.19		
SIC (3)	0.71			−0.21			1.63			0.78		
SIC (2)	0.41			−0.03			1.39			0.62		
SIC (1)	−0.22			−0.51			0.93			0.09		

Note: See Table 3.1.

45

Table 3.4 Trivariate cointegration tests

Countries	Max eigenvalue	λ-max	Trace
BE	0.54	48.11*	51.63*
FR	0.37	28.88*	39.23*
IR	0.55	42.35*	51.71*
IT	0.59	53.55*	56.85*

Note: Critical values for λ-max and for trace are 21.0 and 29.7, respectively (Osterwald–Lenum 1992).

can be conducted by means of likelihood ratio tests (Johansen 1988; Hassapis et al. 1996). Table 3.5a reports the results from testing for zero restrictions on the elements of both the cointegrating vector **b** and the loading matrix $\mathbf{c} = [c_{11}, c_{21}, c_{31}]'$ for the whole sample. A rather provocative result emerges from this exercise: the i_t^{GE} does not enter the cointegrating relationship for any EMS country except Belgium. This automatically precludes the possibility that the previously detected Granger causality is of the type $\alpha_{12} \neq 0$, which is evidence against any type of the

Table 3.5 Testing for zero restrictions on the cointegrating and loading vectors

(a) Sample 1979.2–1994.4

		BE	FR	IR	IT
H_0: $c_{11}=0$	$\chi^2(1)$	25.771	7.175	20.392	29.135
	P-value	(0.000)*	(0.007)*	(0.000)*	(0.000)*
H_0: $c_{21}=0$	$\chi^2(1)$	31.075	20.712	17.865	24.748
	P-value	(0.000)*	(0.000)*	(0.000)*	(0.000)*
H_0: $c_{31}=0$	$\chi^2(1)$	0.012	0.471	2.745	0.005
	P-value	(0.981)	(0.495)	(0.104)	(0.935)
H_0: $b_{11}=0$	$\chi^2(1)$	40.051	18.567	33.143	35.789
	P-value	(0.000)*	(0.000)*	(0.000)*	(0.000)
H_0: $b_{21}=0$	$\chi^2(1)$	13.210	1.553	1.182	0.028
	P-value	(0.000)*	(0.213)	(0.275)	(0.861)
H_0: $b_{31}=0$	$\chi^2(1)$	41.415	16.897	25.856	49.951
	P-value	(0.000)*	(0.000)*	(0.000)*	(0.000)*

Table 3.5 cont.

(b) Sample 1979.2–1991.1

		BE	FR	IR	IT
H_0: $c_{11} = 0$	$\chi^2(1)$	24.287	12.276	16.522	25.258
	P-value	(0.000)*	(0.000)*	(0.000)*	(0.000)*
H_0: $c_{21} = 0$	$\chi^2(1)$	19.465	19.921	10.432	14.672
	P-value	(0.000)*	(0.000)*	(0.000)*	(0.000)*
H_0: $c_{31} = 0$	$\chi^2(1)$	0.319	0.199	0.215	0.653
	P-value	(0.572)	(0.655)	(0.604)	(0.418)
H_0: $b_{11} = 0$	$\chi^2(1)$	37.742	25.113	28.654	32.711
	P-value	(0.000)*	(0.000)*	(0.000)*	(0.000)*
H_0: $b_{21} = 0$	$\chi^2(1)$	14.815	5.837	4.659	6.734
	P-value	(0.000)*	(0.015)*	(0.022)*	(0.012)*
H_0: $b_{31} = 0$	$\chi^2(1)$	32.637	11.134	18.568	38.313
	P-value	(0.000)*	(0.000)*	(0.000)*	(0.000)*

(c) Sample 1979.2–1988.4

		BE	FR	IR	IT
H_0: $c_{11} = 0$	$\chi^2(1)$	13.598	7.283	9.313	4.876
	P-value	(0.000)*	(0.007)*	(0.002)*	(0.027)*
H_0: $c_{21} = 0$	$\chi^2(1)$	19.831	37.92	15.059	16.472
	P-value	(0.000)*	(0.000)*	(0.000)*	(0.000)*
H_0: $c_{31} = 0$	$\chi^2(1)$	1.649	0.058	0.511	2.687
	P-value	(0.199)	(0.808)	(0.474)	(0.101)
H_0: $b_{11} = 0$	$\chi^2(1)$	24.446	14.943	11.345	11.607
	P-value	(0.000)*	(0.000)*	(0.000)*	(0.000)*
H_0: $b_{21} = 0$	$\chi^2(1)$	10.335	15.581	9.339	12.519
	P-value	(0.001)*	(0.000)*	(0.002)*	(0.000)*
H_0: $b_{31} = 0$	$\chi^2(1)$	56.849	34.639	38.994	28.664
	P-value	(0.000)*	(0.000)*	(0.000)*	(0.000)*

Note: * The asterisks denote rejection of the full hypothesis.

GDH. Moreover, the hypothesis $\alpha_{31} = 0$ cannot be rejected for any of the systems under consideration. This in turn implies that the i_t^{US} is weakly exogenous in all systems, when the elements of the cointegrating vector are considered (Johansen 1992). The results in Table 3.5a suggest that matrix

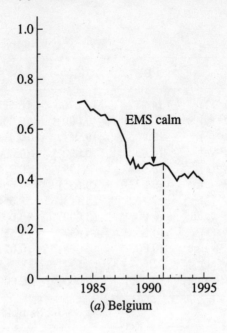

(*a*) Belgium

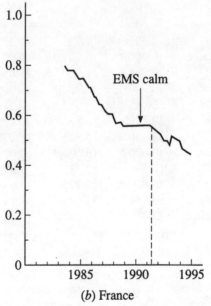

(*b*) France

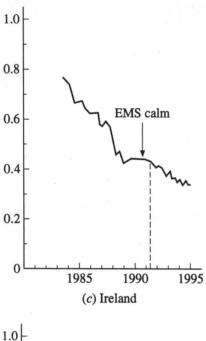

(c) Ireland

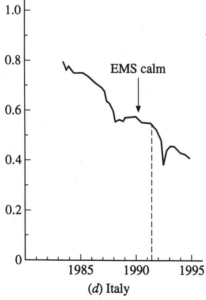

(d) Italy

Figure 3.2 *Recursive estimates of the maximum eigenvalue in the trivariate systems*

A, which describes the causality linkages of interest, takes a different form for Belgium on the one hand, and for France, Ireland and Italy on the other. In particular, we write:

Matrix **A** for Belgium   Matrix **A** for France, Ireland, Italy

$$\begin{bmatrix} \alpha_{11} & \alpha_{12} & \alpha_{13} \\ \alpha_{21} & \alpha_{22} & \alpha_{23} \\ 0 & 0 & 1 \end{bmatrix} \qquad \begin{bmatrix} \alpha_{11} & 0 & \alpha_{13} \\ \alpha_{21} & 1 & \alpha_{23} \\ 0 & 0 & 1 \end{bmatrix}$$

In all cases, the i_t^{US} seems to cause all i_t^*'s but is not caused by them. This finding contradicts the findings by Kirchgaessner and Wolters (1993) and Artus et al. (1991). Concerning the intra-EMS linkages, the case of Belgium is more 'normal'; it reflects a symmetric functioning of the monetary policies of Belgium and Germany. The other three cases are rather 'strange': the i_t^{GE} appears to be caused by rather than cause the interest rates of France, Ireland or Italy. This result may be counter-intuitive at a first glance. However, the concurrence of (i) the escalation of the i_t^{GE} due to the Bundesbank's tight monetary policy following the German reunification; (ii) the increasing uncertainty as regards the future of the EMS (the British pound and the Italian lira withdrew from the ERM in September 1992); and (iii) the resulting widening of the EMS fluctuation bands in August 1993, seem to have induced, as already mentioned, a higher degree of monetary autonomy to the system. That turbulent period might have affected the causality linkages of the interest rates under consideration. Indeed, the dynamic properties of all trivariate systems have been significantly affected since the beginning of 1991. This can be seen in Figures 3.2a–d, where recursive estimates for the maximum eigenvalue of the systems under consideration are presented. The evidence indicates that the long-run properties of the systems seem to have been considerably stable during the 1987–91 period. None the less, a distinct drop of the maximum eigenvalue has occurred in the first quarter of 1991. Since that date the maximum eigenvalue for all systems has exhibited an erratic behaviour. It is natural then to try to investigate the causality linkages among the interest rates under consideration for the time span 1979.2 to 1991.1. The results from testing for zero restrictions in both the cointegrating vector and the vector of the loading factors are reported in Table 3.5b. The evidence suggests that the i_t^{GE} enters into the cointegrating vector of all systems under consideration. In addition, the hypothesis that the US rate is weakly exogenous with respect to the cointegrating vector

($c_{31} = 0$) cannot be rejected. Hence, matrix **A** takes the same form for all systems, that is,

$$
\mathbf{A} = \begin{bmatrix} \alpha_{11} & \alpha_{12} & \alpha_{13} \\ \alpha_{21} & \alpha_{22} & \alpha_{23} \\ 0 & 0 & 1 \end{bmatrix}
$$

The empirical analysis reveals the following. First, the i_t^{US} causes all European rates, including i_t^{GE}, but is not caused by any one of them. This finding contradicts earlier results (Katsimbris and Miller 1993) according to which i_t^{GE} and the three EMS (Irish, Italian and Dutch) interest rates Granger cause i_t^{GE}. Second, the EMS has been functioning as a rather symmetric system, since causality between Germany and the rest of the EMS countries has been found to run in both directions (see also De Grauwe 1989; and Katsimbris 1993). This result is in disagreement with the estimates given by authors arguing in favour of the strong version of the GDH (for example Katsimbris and Miller 1993; and Karfakis and Moschos 1990). These studies suggest that i_t^{GE} causes the EMS rates, but is not caused by them. Is such a discrepancy attributed to differences in sample sizes used? The present study uses quarterly data extending up to 1994, whereas the previous ones use monthly data that do not go beyond 1988.11. However, the difference between the evidence provided here and in the earlier studies is too large to be attributed solely to sample size considerations. In fact, by reestimating our systems for the period covered by the earlier studies we obtained results (Table 3.5c) similar to ours for the 1979.2–1991.1 period (Table 3.5b).

The most important difference between this study and the previous ones concerns the econometric methodology. Earlier studies (for example, Katsimbris and Miller 1993) do not examine the interest rate linkages among EMS countries, Germany and the US in a trivariate context. Instead, they carry out their analyses in separate bivariate frameworks. But causality and cointegration analysis in incomplete systems may lead to totally erroneous conclusions. Moreover, when they estimate bivariate systems in error correction form, they impose specific restrictions on the error correction terms, thus implicitly imposing untested restrictions on the cointegrating vectors. Last but not least, testing causality hypotheses in cointegrated systems via F-tests may also lead to erroneous inferences; because the F-statistics do not follow standard asymptotics, unless there is a sufficient degree of cointegration arising from the variables, whose causal effects are being tested. In the present case, the evidence points towards only one cointegrating vector, thus violating the necessary condition for standard asymptotics.

4   Summary and conclusions

In this chapter we have reexamined the validity of GDH. In this respect, we have extended the familiar bivariate VAR systems environment to trivariate VAR systems, and allowed for the possibility of the US monetary policy to affect the monetary policies of the EMS countries.

In the case of the bivariate VAR systems, we have investigated three possibilities: the strong version of the GDH; the symmetry hypothesis; and the monetary autonomy hypothesis (Section 3). Next, we have dealt with trivariate VAR systems in which the US interest rate was added to account for the possibility of US monetary policy influences on the monetary policies of the EMS countries. In this new environment we have studied additional variations of the GDH, namely, the strong, semi-strong, and weak (types 1 and 2) versions, and introduced the US Dominance Hypothesis. These possibilities have enabled us to examine whether the US interest rate affects directly each of the individual EMS rates, or indirectly via its effect on the German rate.

The empirical evidence stemming from the short-term interest rate systems seems to support the symmetry hypothesis within the EMS, and the US Dominance Hypothesis, according to which: (i) the German rate affects each of the EMS rates and is affected by them, and (ii) the US rate affects the EMS rates, both directly and indirectly through its effect on the German rate.

References

Akaike, H. (1973), 'Information Theory and the Extenuation of the Maximum Likelihood Principle', in B.N. Petrov and F. Csaki (eds), *2nd International Symposium on Information Theory*, Budapest: Akailseoniai-Kiudo, pp. 267–81.
Artis, M.J. and D. Nachane (1990), 'Wages and Prices in Europe: A Test for the German Leadership Hypothesis', *Weltwirtschaftliches Archiv*, **126**, 59–77.
Artus, P., S. Avouyi-Dovi, E. Bleuze and F. Lecointre (1991), 'Transmission of US Monetary Policy to Europe and Asymmetry in the European Monetary System', *European Economic Review*, **35**, 1369–84.
Baldwin, R. (1991), 'Discussion', *Economic Policy*, **12**, 89–91.
Banerjee, A. and G. Urga (1995), 'Looking for Structural Breaks in Cointegrated Systems', mimeo.
Biltoft, K. and C. Boersch (1992), 'Interest Rate Causality and Asymmetry in the EMS', *Open Economies Review*, **3** (3), 297–306.
Caporale, G.M. and N. Pittis (1993), 'Common Stochastic Trends and Inflation Convergence in the EMS', *Weltwirtschaftliches Archiv*, **129**, 207–15.
Caporale, G.M. and N. Pittis (1995), 'Causality and Forecasting in Incomplete Systems', mimeo.
De Grauwe, P. (1989), 'Is the European System a DM Zone?', Carnegie-Rochester Conference Series on Public Policy CEPR Discussion Paper, No. 297.

Engle, R.F. and C.W.J. Granger (1987), 'Cointegration and Error Correction: Representation Estimation and Testing', *Econometrica*, **55**, 251–76.

Fischer, S. (1987), 'International Macroeconomic Policy Coordination', National Bureau of Economic Research (NBER) Working Paper, No. 2244.

Giavazzi, F. and A. Giovannini (1987), 'Models of the EMS: Is Europe a Greater Deutsche Mark Area?', in R. Bryant and R. Portes (eds), *Global Macroeconomics: Policy, Conflict and Cooperation*, London: Macmillan.

Giavazzi, F. and M. Pagano (1988), 'The Advantage of Tying One's Hands. EMS Discipline and Central Bank Credibility', *European Economic Review*, **32**, 1055–82.

Gros, D. and N. Thygesen (1988), 'Le SME: Performance et perspectives', *Observations et Diagnostiques Economiques*, **24**, 55–80.

Hassapis, C., N. Pittis and K. Prodromidis (1996), 'Unit Roots and Granger Causality in the EMS Interest Rates: The German Dominance Hypothesis Revisited', Athens University of Economics and Business, Department of Economics, Discussion Paper Series.

Johansen, S. (1988), 'Statistical Analysis of Cointegration Vectors', *Journal of Economic Dynamics and Control*, **12**, 231–54.

Johansen, S. (1992), 'Cointegration in Partial Systems and the Efficiency of Single Equation Analysis', *Journal of Econometrics*, **52**, 389–402.

Karfakis, J.C. and D. Moschos (1990), 'Interest Rate Linkages Within the European Monetary System: A Time Series Analysis', *Journal of Money, Credit and Banking*, **22**, 388–94.

Katsimbris, G.M. (1993), 'Interest Rate Linkages Within the European Monetary System: A Multivariate Analysis', *Journal of Multinational Financial Management*, **2** (3–4), 95–105.

Katsimbris, G.M. and S.M. Miller (1993), 'Interest Rate Linkages Within the European Monetary System: Further Analysis', *Journal of Money, Credit and Banking*, **25**, 771–9.

Kirchgaessner, G. and J. Wolters (1993), 'Does the DM Dominate the Euro Market? An Empirical Investigation', *Review of Economics and Statistics*, **75** (4), 773–8.

Kremers, J.J.M. (1990), 'Gaining Policy Credibility for a Disinflation: Ireland's Experience in the EMS', *IMF Staff Papers*, **37**, 116–45.

Lutkepohl, H. (1991), *Introduction to Multiple Time Series Analysis*, Berlin-Heidelberg: Springer-Verlag.

Miller, M. and A. Sutherland (1991), 'The Walters Critique of the EMS – A Case of Inconsistent Expectations?', *Manchester School of Economic and Social Studies*, **59**, 23–37.

Osterwald-Lenum M. (1992), 'A Note with Fractiles of the Asymptotic Distribution of the Likelihood Cointegration Rank Test Statistics Four Cases,' Oxford Bulletin of Economics and Statistics, **50**, 361–78.

Perron, P. (1989), 'The Great Crash, the Oil Price Shock and the Unit Root Hypothesis', *Econometrica*, **57**, 1361–401.

Robertson, J.C. (1993), 'Misspecification Testing in Systems of Equations', Unpublished PhD thesis, Virginia Polytechnic Institute and State University.

Russo, M. and G. Tuilio (1988), 'Monetary Coordination within the EMS: Is There a Rule?', IMF Occasional Paper, No. 61.

Schwarz, G. (1978), 'Estimating the Dimension of a Model', *Annals of Statistics*, **6**, 461–4.

Sims, C.A., J.H. Stock, and M.W. Watson (1990), 'Inference in Linear Time Series Models with Some Unit Roots', *Econometrica*, **58**, 113–44.

Smeets, H. D. (1990), 'Does Germany Dominate the EMS?', *Journal of Common Market Studies*, **29**, 37–52.

Spanos, A. (1986), *Statistical Foundations of Econometric Modelling*, Cambridge: Cambridge University Press.

Spanos, A. (1990), 'Unit Roots and Their Dependence on the Conditioning Information Set', *Advances in Econometrics*, **8**, 271–92.

Toda, H.Y. and P.C.B. Phillips (1994), 'Vector Autoregression and Causality: A Theoretical Overview and Simulation Study', *Econometric Reviews*, **13**, 259–85.

Von Hagen, J. and M. Fratianni (1990), 'German Dominance in the EMS: Evidence from Interest Rates', *Journal of International Money and Finance*, **9**, 358–75.
Walters, A. (1990), *Sterling in Danger*, London: Fontana.
Weber, A.A. (1991), 'Reputation and Credibility in the EMS', *Economic Policy*, **12**, 58–102.
Wyplosz, C. (1989), 'Asymmetry in the EMS: International or Systemic?', *European Economic Review*, **33**, 310–20.

4 Expected devaluations in the ERM
*Leo Michelis and Christos C. Paraskevopoulos**

1 Introduction

The Exchange Rate Mechanism (ERM) of the European Monetary System (EMS) is a multilateral exchange rate regime in which the exchange rate of each participating currency is allowed to fluctuate within fixed bands defined around bilateral central parities relative to each participating currency. In this setting a realignment corresponds to an adjustment of the bilateral central rates.

A proper understanding of the causes of realignments in the ERM is crucial for the stability of the EMS and also for the credibility of economic policies of the participating countries. Credible ERM target zones (that is, fixed exchange rate bands without realignments) have been viewed by markets as an indicator of general price stability in the EMS and, in fact, constitute a necessary condition for a country joining the Economic and Monetary Union (EMU) as envisioned in Stage III of the Maastricht Treaty. Regarding the participation of a country in the EMU, the Maastricht Treaty (1992) stipulates 'respect of nominal fluctuation margins of ERM for at least two years without severe tensions and without devaluing against any other Member State currency'.

In the empirical literature there are several well-developed methods of measuring expected realignments or devaluation expectations and hence target-zone credibility. These include raw interest rate differentials, the simplest test of Svensson (1991) which adjusts interest rate differentials for minimum and maximum expected depreciation within the exchange rate bands, and the drift adjustment method which adjusts the interest rate differentials by the expected rate of depreciation within the band (Bertola and Svensson 1993). In addition, consideration of the behaviour of forward rates provides an alternative way of studying target-zone credibility (Bartolini and Bondar 1991).

* An earlier version of the chapter was presented at the International Conference on Economic Integration in Transition, Athens, Greece, 21–24 August, 1996, the Allied Social Science Associations (ASSA) annual meetings, San Francisco, 5–7 January, 1996, and the Applied Econometrics Workshop at the University of Western Ontario, London, Ontario, Canada, Spring 1996. We wish to thank the conference and workshop participants for their conmments; John Sharp for his assistance in data collection; and York University (Atkinson College, Grant in Aid Research) for partial financial support. The usual disclaimer applies.

Despite the progress on the problem of measuring devaluation expectations, it has proved a difficult task to explain them empirically. By and large most macroeconomic fundamentals which are important in conventional models of exchange rate determination fail to explain expected devaluations in the ERM. In a recent comprehensive study of the ERM participants, Rose and Svensson (1994) relate realignment expectations, using the drift adjustment method, to macroeconomic variables. They find that the only variable that systematically affects realignment expectations is inflation differentials relative to Germany. Foreign exchange reserves and a proxy for monetary variability also matter but not in all the cases considered. Furthermore, macroeconomic fundamentals cannot account for the currency crisis of September 1992.

The research for this chapter was largely motivated by the work of Rose and Svensson. Given the poor performance of existing empirical models of realignment expectations, we extend the set of explanatory variables in the hope of finding a better fit of the data. Among the additional variables are dummy variables to capture the potential effects of political events such as the removal of foreign exchange controls in the countries participating in the ERM and the German Unification which we proxy also by real interest rate differentials. We also incorporate a dummy variable to investigate the effects of self-fulfilling speculative attacks thought to have been encouraged by the conditions for nominal convergence laid down by the Maastricht Treaty. Finally, the rate of unemployment is included as an explanatory variable of devaluation expectations as a means of incorporating the effects of worsening economic conditions in Europe since the early 1990s. Persistent and rising levels of unemployment increase the economic costs of austerity policies and may erode their credibility (Drazen and Masson 1994). Eventually such policies may have to be abandoned even by 'tough' governments. In anticipation of future policy shift, traders may attack the currencies of these countries before the policy shift actually occurs.

In what follows we restrict our analysis to two initial participants of the ERM: Italy and France. Following the existing literature we treat Germany as the centre of the EMS so that exchange rates and other relevant variables will be considered relative to German values. Italy is chosen because it is the only EMS country with overt signs of deteriorating international competitiveness. To control for these we are led to consider France which had no significant competitive difficulties in the EMS and even had strong macroeconomic fundamentals leading up to the crisis of September 1992 (see Eichengreen and Wyplosz 1993).

The rest of the chapter is organized as follows. Section 2 gives a more complete theoretical account of the variables that are included in our empirical model of expected devaluations. Section 3 lays down the model and defines the relevant variables. Section 4 reports on the empirical results and the conclusions are presented in the last section. The sources of the data used are contained in Appendix 4A at the end of the chapter.

2 Determinants of devaluation expectations

Since its inception in March 1979, the EMS has been characterized by two distinct phases. The Old EMS spanning the period up to January 1987 and the New EMS, extending from January 1987 until the present; more precisely up until the currency crisis of September 1992. The Old EMS has been characterized by capital controls and relatively frequent realignments (twelve in total) reflecting primarily persistent inflation differentials across EMS countries. The New EMS has been a period of gradual removal of foreign exchange controls with complete elimination among ERM participants by June 1990 and infrequent realignments achieved partly through the September 1987 Basle–Nyborg Agreement. Aside from the currency crisis of 1992 it seemed as if realignments had become a thing of the past in the New EMS. In fact only one realignment took place during this period, on 8 January 1990, coinciding with the narrowing of the Italian fluctuation bands from ± 6 per cent to ± 2.25 per cent. The financial crisis of 1992, however, proved otherwise.

In this section we explore several potential determinants of devaluation expectations under the broad categories of economic fundamentals, political events and speculative considerations.

2.1 Economic fundamentals

Conventional models of exchange rate determination provide close links between exchange rates and macroeconomic fundamentals. First, simple flexible-price monetary models relate exchange rates to levels of economic activity and monetary aggregates (for example, see Backus 1984). Furthermore, sticky-price models incorporate the role of inflation as well (Dornbusch 1976; Franker 1979). Second, balance of payments crises models emphasize the importance of the level of foreign exchange reserves and the state of a country's balance of payments (Krugman 1979). If a country runs persistent balance of payments deficits it will exhaust its foreign exchange reserves and eventually it will be forced to abandon fixed exchange rates.

Real exchange rate movements can also have an important influence on exchange rates. Large and persistent misalignments of real exchange rates can precipitate balance of payments crises in which the perception that a currency is overvalued can lead to capital flight and exhaustion in a central bank's foreign reserves. In such cases, orderly realignments can ease the pressure in a quasi-fixed exchange rate system and at least partially restore a country's international competitiveness.

2.2   Political events

Certain political events in Europe in the recent experience of the EMS may have exerted important influence on the ERM system and may have contributed to the 1992 financial crisis. Prominent among these is the gradual removal of foreign exchange controls and their complete elimination in most ERM participant countries by 1 July 1990 as mandated by the Single European Act. With free capital mobility, holding the line on the fixed parities of the ERM may became more difficult. For instance, given the more accommodating monetary policy of Italy compared to Germany, large quantities of financial capital can flow freely between the two countries in anticipation of the lira's devaluation, thereby threatening the lira/DM parity and the stability of the EMS. Eichengreen and Wyplosz (1993) report similar pressures on Britain's exchange rate in 1992.

A second political decision was the German Economic and Monetary Union (GEMU) following the election of 3 October 1990. The GEMU is often cited in the literature as representing an asymmetric shock in the EMS which required a revaluation of the Deutschmark. Even though Germany favoured revaluation, it was strongly opposed by other EMS members because it meant a devaluation of their currencies. According to this interpretation, the currency crisis of 1992 was a market-imposed correction of the GEMU shock on the ERM parities. However, this interpretation may not provide a good explanation of the crisis since this occurred almost two years after German Unification.

The third and perhaps most important political event was the ratification of the Maastricht Treaty (MT) on 7 April 1992. Even though discussions about the creation of the EMU had intensified as early as September 1987, the signing of the MT made explicit the conditions under which a country may qualify for participation in the EMU. Regarding the monetary aspects of the MT the following nominal convergence criteria were laid down:

1.   inflation rate not higher than 1.5 per cent above the average of the three countries with the lowest inflation rates;
2.   government deficits and debt not exceeding 3 per cent and 60 per cent of the GDP, respectively;
3.   long-term interest rate not in excess of 2 per cent of the three countries with the lowest inflation rates;
4.   no devaluation of currency in two years preceding the entrance into the union.

Why is the MT important? The main reason is that the MT may have created incentives for inviting speculative attacks.

2.3   Speculative considerations

Speculative attacks can be of two distinct types: self-fulfilling speculative attacks which, if they occur, cause a shift in economic policies regardless of the level of current fundamentals (Obstfeld 1986) and speculative attacks grounded either in current fundamentals or in inevitable shifts of policies in the future (Krugman 1979 and Eichengreen and Wyplosz 1993), respectively. The MT can be linked directly to self-fulfilling speculative attacks because it makes exchange rate stability a precondition for EMU participation. A successful speculative attack by violating condition (4) above for nominal convergence would disqualify a country from EMU participation, thereby eliminating the incentive of a country's policymakers to pursue tough policies. The only option then left for a government is to adopt more accommodating policies.

The MT can also be related to speculative attacks resulting from inevitable future shifts in monetary policy caused by rising unemployment. Viewed as an additional constraint on policy members, the MT coincided with worsening economic conditions in Europe. Doubts about the viability of the Treaty became official following the negative outcome of the Danish referendum in June 1992. Given high unemployment rates, it became clear that policies of austerity consistent with the MT will have to be abandoned in the future. In turn, this may have created favourable grounds for speculative activity on the ERM parities.

3   The model

To construct an empirical model of expected devaluations we must first decide on an appropriate measure of expected devaluations. Assuming uncovered interest parity (UIP), we use the interest rate differentials adjusted by an estimate of the expected rate of depreciation within the band as a proxy for expected devaluations.[1] To illustrate the drift adjustment method briefly, consider the decomposition of the log exchange rate s into the log central parity c and the log deviation from central parity x:

$$s_t = c_t + x_t. \qquad (4.1)$$

Using (4.1), the one period expected devaluation of the exchange rate can be decomposed into the expected change of the central parity and the expected change in the deviation from the central parity:

$$E_t(\Delta s_t) = E_t(\Delta c_t) + E_t(\Delta x_t) \qquad (4.2)$$

where Δ is the difference operator and E_t denotes conditional expectation based on information available at time t. Using the right-hand side of (4.2) in the usual UIP condition and manipulating the resulting expression, it is easily seen that

$$E_t(\Delta c_t) = i_t - i_t{}^* - E_t(\Delta x_t) \qquad (4.3)$$

where i_t and $i_t{}^*$ are the one period domestic and foreign interest rates, respectively.

In our empirical regression model of expected devaluations, the left-hand side of (4.3) is the dependent variable which we proxy with the variable

$$y_t = i_t - i_t{}^* - d_t \qquad (4.4)$$

where d_t is an estimate of the $E_t(\Delta x_t)$ obtained as the fitted value from the regression of Δx_t, on a constant, x_t, i_t and $i_t{}^*$.

Let $X_t = (X_{1t}, X_{2t}, X_{3t}, X_{4t}, X_{5t},)$ and $(Z_{1t}, Z_{2t}, Z_{3t}, Z_{4t}, Z_{5t}, Z_{6t})$. We can then write the regression model as

$$y_t = X_t\beta + Z_t\gamma + \epsilon_t \qquad (4.5)$$

where y_t is given by (4.4), β and γ are unknown regression coefficients and ϵ_t is a random error term assumed to be orthogonal to all the variables in X_t and Z_t.

Equation (4.5) represents our extended model of devaluation expectations in the ERM. Setting $\gamma = 0$, one obtains the standard model which relates expected devaluations to the main macroeconomic fundamentals.

The model in (4.5) was estimated by OLS twice: once using the Italy/Germany (IL/DM) data and on another occasion using the France/Germany (FF/DM) data. In both cases the relevant main macroeconomic variables were extracted from the IFS (International Financial Statistics) tape series at quarterly frequencies. The Italy/Germany statistical analysis involved 55 observations: 1979:1 to 1992:3 when Italy dropped out of the ERM arrangement, and the France/Germany analysis involved 65 observations from 1979:1 to 1994:4.

The following is a complete list and definitions of the independent variables (regressors) in the model. Below, the word differential means differential relative to Germany.

X_1:   deviations of s_t from c_t
X_2:   inflation differentials
X_3:   log of foreign exchange reserves differential measured in DM
X_4:   trade balance differential

X_5:   log of money supplies (M1) differential measured in DM

Z_1:   log of $1 + t^*$ where t^* is the number of periods since last realignment

Z_2:   dummy variable equal to 1 after the Basle–Nyborg Agreement and zero otherwise

Z_3:   dummy variable equal to 1 during the period of no foreign exchange controls and zero otherwise

Z_4:   dummy variable equal to 1 after the GEMU shock and zero otherwise

Z_5:   dummy variable equal to 1 after the MT ratification and zero otherwise

Z_6:   percentage unemployment rate (French or Italian).

All these variables, except X_1 and Z_1 can be rationalized by the arguments in Section 2.[2] Following Chen and Giovannini (1993), X_1 and Z_1 are included to capture institutional aspects of the ERM system, and to incorporate learning and reputation effects, respectively. Also below we report results when the dummy in Z_4 is replaced by the real interest rate differential and when political dummies are included in the estimated model to capture the 'type' of political regime in Italy and France.

4   Empirical results

Tables 4.1 and 4.2 report the empirical results for the IL/DM expected devaluations when the GEMU is proxied by a dummy variable and the real interest rate differential between the two countries, respectively. The reason for using the latter is that the GEMU coincided with tight monetary and expansionary fiscal policies in Germany; a policy mix that contributed to rising real rates in Germany and the rest of Europe. Furthermore, in each case, model (4.5) was extended by two additional regressors: a political dummy and its interaction with unemployment in Italy. The political dummy, D_1, was set equal to one for the period 1984:1 to 1987:4 and zero otherwise. This period coincided with rising inflation in Italy and an interest rate differential with respect to Germany that turned positive and rising steadily thereafter in 1987–88 (OECD, Economic Surveys). Thus D_1 is intended to capture a 'weak' policymaker in Italy. The two tables report the dependent and independent variables together with their estimated coefficients and t-ratios. In Table 4.1 the variables that are statistically significant at the 5 per cent level are the deviation of the exchange rate from the central parity, the inflation differential, the log of the foreign exchange reserves differentials, unemployment, political dummy and the interaction variable between the political dummy and unemployment. It is interesting to note that unemployment enters the

Table 4.1   Three-month IL/DM expected devaluations, $Z_4 = GEMU$ proxied by dummy variable

Independent variable	Coefficient	t-ratio
C	−12.59	3.96
X_1	−30.63*	−3.64
X_2	0.48*	4.44
X_3	−3.15*	−3.02
X_4	0.00	0.53
X_5	4.48	1.67
Z_1	−0.22	−0.56
Z_2	0.57	0.60
Z_3	−1.64	−1.58
Z_4	1.25	1.05
Z_5	1.41	1.06
Z_6	14.35*	3.12
D_1	1.35*	4.99
D_1Z_6	−1.43*	−3.27

Diagnostics	Extended model	Standard model
No. of observations	55.00	55.00
R-squared	0.86	0.70
R-squared	0.81	0.66
R-ratio	18.48	21.99
DW	1.65	0.57
Log likelihood	−71.60	−92.00

Notes
*   Statistically significant at the 5 per cent level.
Dependent variable: $y_t = i_t − i_t{}^* − d_t$.

estimated relationship with a correct positive sign, in that higher unemployment is associated with larger adjusted interest rates differentials and therefore larger expected devaluations for the IL/DM exchange rate. Further, the unemployment variable is the most statistically significant variable among all the other variables in this estimated regression model. The political dummy variable also has the correct sign and is statistically significant, indicating that the public's perception of a weak government in Italy contributed positively to that country's expected devaluations of its currency. However, the interaction variable between the political dummy

Table 4.2   *Three-month IL/DM expected devaluations, Z_4 = GEMU proxied by real interest rate differential*

Independent variable	Coefficient	t-ratio
C	10.50	−6.77
X_1	−3.80	−0.47
X_3	−1.00	−1.09
X_4	0.00	1.85
X_5	3.97	1.74
Z_1	0.31	1.03
Z_2	0.04	0.05
*Z_3	−2.14*	−2.75
Z_4	0.06	0.76
Z_5	0.53	0.46
*Z_6	−3.36*	−4.63
*D_1	−1.19*	−6.02
*D_1Z_6	0.72*	2.66

Diagnostics	Extended model	Standard model
No. of observations	55.00	55.00
R-squared	0.89	0.70
R-squared	0.86	0.66
F-ratio	28.48	21.99
DW	1.86	0.57
Log likelihood	−63.84	−92.00

Notes
* Statistically significant at the 5 per cent level.
Dependent variable: $y_t = i_t - i_t^* - d_t$.

and unemployment is statistically significant but with a negative coefficient. The diagnostics part of the table provides some summary statistics
for the extended model and the standard model obtained by estimating the
empirical model with the X-regressors alone. Using the adjusted R-squared
criterion, it is clear that the extended model provides a better fit of the data
than the standard model. Also the low value of the Durbin–Watson (DW)
statistic in the standard model indicates that it is severely misspecified.
Furthermore the standard model has a lower log likelihood value than the
extended model.

Table 4.2 reports results with the regressor Z_4 now being the real interest rate differential between Italy and Germany. To avoid multicollinearity problems, the inflation differential was dropped from the regression model in this case. The diagnostics in Table 4.2 are similar to those in Table 4.1 with the extended model being superior to the standard model. However, the estimated coefficients and their significance are different in this case. None of the standard macroeconomic variables is statistically significant now, the removal of foreign exchange controls, unemployment and political dummy are statistically significant but with the wrong sign, but the interaction variable is significant and with the correct sign; a weak government combined with higher unemployment is a likely cause of expected devaluations of the Italian lira.

Tables 4.3 and 4.4 report results for the FF/DM expected devaluations analogous to those in Tables 4.1 and 4.2. In addition, three political dummy variables are introduced here to describe the 'type' of the French policymaker. Following Drazen and Masson (1994), we distinguish three phases of the French policy stance. These correspond to the subperiods 1979:1–1982:4, 1983:1–1986:4 and 1987:1–1994:4 and are modelled by three separate dummy variables D_1, D_2 and D_3, respectively. Each dummy variable equals unity in the relevant subperiod and zero otherwise.

The first subperiod is characterized by a 'weak' policymaker and is identified by the election to power of the socialist government of François Mitterrand that followed strongly expansionary policies initially with little commitment to fixed parities. Hence in this subperiod higher unemployment should be associated with higher interest rate differentials and therefore higher expected devaluations. The second subperiod corresponds to a 'tough' policymaker since France shifted to much tighter fiscal and monetary policies and a commitment to a strong franc. Because the French government wished to establish a reputation for toughness, we should expect a negative relationship between interest rate differentials and unemployment in this subperiod. The third subperiod is again characterized by a 'tough' policymaker but persistently high unemployment rates raised legitimate concerns that restrictive policies could not be maintained. This is an instance of the insight provided by Drazen and Masson that announced tough policies may lack credibility if they coincide with adverse economic conditions such as high unemployment. Consequently in this subperiod we should expect a positive association between expected devaluations and unemployment.

Clearly the above discussion implies a changing relationship between unemployment and expected devaluations in France. Accordingly, to investigate this possibility three multiplicative dummy variables are incorporated in the empirical model and their estimated coefficients and t-ratios are reported in the two tables. Table 4.3 contains empirical results when the

Table 4.3   Three-month FF/DM expected devaluations, $Z_4 = GEMU$ proxied by dummy variable

Independent variable	Coefficient	t-Ratio
C	−1.00	−0.14
D_1	−14.07	−1.67
D_2	29.10*	2.58
X_1	−36.55	−1.97
X_2	−0.42	−1.46
X_3	−4.37*	−3.09
X_4	0.00	0.15
X_5	7.63	1.58
Z_1	0.12	0.24
Z_2	−1.29	−0.79
Z_3	−1.95	−1.56
Z_4	1.08	0.56
Z_5	−1.19	−0.80
$D_1 Z_6$	2.64*	4.49
$D_2 Z_6$	−2.47*	−3.01
$D_3 Z_6$	0.33	0.50

Diagnostics	Extended model	Standard model
No. of observations	64.00	64.00
R-squared	0.83	0.62
R-squared	0.78	0.59
F-ratio	15.45	18.52
DW	2.05	1.02
Log likelihood	−111.74	−137.41

Notes
* Statistically significant at the 5 per cent level.
Dependent variable: $y_t = i_t - i_t^* - d_t$.

GEMU shock is modelled by a dummy variable. In this case, the only variables that are statistically significant and have the correct sign are the foreign exchange reserve differential and the unemployment rate in the first two subperiods. The unemployment rate has the correct sign in the third subperiod also, but it is not statistically significant. As expected, an increase in the French log foreign exchange reserve position relative to Germany reduces devaluation expectations of the FF/DM central parity.

*Table 4.4   Three month FF/DM expected devaluations, $Z_4 = GEMU$
proxied by real interest rate differential*

Independent variable	Coefficient	t-ratio
C	−2.83	−0.99
D_1	2.74	0.78
D_2	20.46*	5.16
X_1	−12.49	−1.63
X_3	−1.10	−1.78
X_4	0.00*	2.23
X_5	7.05 *	4.19
Z_1	−0.08	−0.38
Z_2	−0.33	−0.49
Z_3	−0.69	−1.40
Z_4	0.75*	15.71
Z_5	−0.94	−1.55
D_1Z_6	0.62*	2.39
D_2Z_6	−1.47*	−4.91
D_3Z_6	0.55*	2.12

Diagnostics	Extended model	Standard model
No. of observations	64.00	64.00
R-squared	0.97	0.62
R-squared	0.96	0.59
F-ratio	113.57	18.52
DW	1.76	1.02
Log likelihood	−56.62	−137.41

Notes
* Statistically significant at the 5 per cent level.
Dependent variable: $y_t = i_t - i_t^* - d_t$.

The sign pattern of the estimated unemployment coefficients in the three
subperiods is also consistent with the predictions of the Drazen and
Masson theory. In the first and third subperiods, high unemployment is
associated with a widening of the adjusted interest rate differential between
France and Germany, reflecting increasing concern about realignment of
the FF/DM central rate. In the second subperiod, however, higher
unemployment is associated with lower interest rate differential. This is
consistent with the 'tough' policy stance of the French authorities who

were attempting to gain credibility with their strong franc policy. The diagnostics section of Table 4.3 shows that the extended model provides a better fit of the France/Germany data than the standard model. In the standard model, the adjusted R-squared coefficient is only 56 per cent, but in the extended model it is 78 per cent. The DW statistic is 2.05 in the extended model but only 1.01 in the standard model, reflecting misspecification of the latter model.

Table 4.4 provides information when the GEMU shock is proxied by the real interest rate differential and the inflation differential is removed from the estimated regression to avoid multicollinearity problems. In this case, the log money supply differential is statistically significant and has the correct sign. Higher levels of the log money supply differentials are associated with higher expected devaluations of the FF/DM central rate. The real interest rate differential is an important determinant of devaluation expectations as well. As expected, its coefficient is positive and its t-ratio is 15.71 which is highly statistically significant. The sign pattern of the unemployment in the three subperiods is the same as in Table 4.3, but now unemployment in the third subperiod is also statistically significant. The diagnostics in Table 4.4 show that modelling the GEMU with the real interest rate differential improves substantially the fit of the extended model. The adjusted R-squared coefficient in this case is 96 per cent compared to 78 per cent in Table 4.3. The DW statistic is reduced from 2.05 to 1.76 but it still provides evidence against serial correlation in the error term of the estimated regression. Further, the log likelihood function attains a value of -56.61 in Table 4.4 compared to -111.74 in Table 4.3.

5 Conclusion

In this study, we have attempted to investigate the determinants of devaluation expectations in the ERM of the EMS. Our extended model incorporates not only the standard macroeconomic variables used in the existing empirical literature on devaluation expectations but also variables motivated by political considerations and by the literature on speculative attacks. These include dummy variables for the Basle–Nyborg Agreement, the removal of foreign exchange controls, the Maastricht Treaty, and the GEMU shock which we also proxy by the real interest rate differential. In addition, political dummies and their interaction with unemployment were included in the model to investigate the potential effects of the type of policymaker and state of the economy on devaluation expectations.

The extended model was estimated using quarterly data for Italy and France relative to Germany. The empirical results indicate that the extended model outperforms the standard model in explaining devaluation expectations in the ERM. The variable that is consistently statistically significant for all the cases we considered is the level of unemployment and its interactions with the type of policymaker in France or Italy. The GEMU, when proxied by the real interest rate differential, is also an important determinant of devaluation expectations for the FF/DM exchange rate. In this case, the money supply differential is a significant variable in explaining devaluation expectations as well.

The main conclusion to be drawn from the empirical findings of this chapter is that unless policy makers in the EMS adopt policies aimed at reducing the persistently high unemployment levels, the credibility of the ERM will be eroded and the likelihood of achieving the EMU will be low. This is the case for even among the 'core' countries of the system such as France and Germany.

Notes

1. The assumption of UIP has been rejected in a larger number of empirical studies. However, as noted by Rose and Svensson (1991) there is empirical support of UIP for the franc/DM exchange rate during the ERM period. Also Svensson (1992) shows that in exchange rate target-zone models the exchange risk premium should be insignificant.

    In the statistical analysis we experimented also with the raw interest rate differentials. The two methods delivered similar results but the drift adjustment method was marginally better in terms of goodness of fit. For this reason we opted and report results for the latter method only.

2. The real exchange rate and real income differential were included in some estimated regressions and they were found to be statistically insignificant. For this reason we do not report results on these variables.

References

Backus, D. (1984), 'Empirical Models of the Exchange Rate: Separating the Wheat from the Chaff', *Canadian Journal of Economics*, XVII, 824–46.

Bartolini, L. and A. Bondar (1992), 'Target Zones and Forward Rates in a Model with Repeated Realignments', *Journal of Monetary Economics*, 30, 373–408.

Bertola, G. And L.E.O. Svensson (1993), 'Stochastic Devaluation Risk and the Empirical Fit of Target-zone Models', *Review of Economic Studies*, 60 (3), 689–712.

Chen, Z. and A. Giovannini (1993), 'The Determinants of Realignment Expectations Under the EMS', National Bureau of Economic Research Working Paper No. 4291, Cambridge, MA.

Dornbusch, R. (1976), 'Expectations and Exchange Rate Dynamics', *Journal of Political Economy*, 84, 1061–76.

Drazen, A. and P.R. Masson (1994), 'Credibility of Policies Versus Credibility of Policy-makers', *Quarterly Journal of Economics*, August, 735–54.

Eichengreen, B. And C. Wyplosz (1993), The unstable EMS', *Brooking Papers on Economic Activity*, 1, 51–125.

Frankel, J. (1979), 'On the Mark: A Theory of Floating Exchange Rates Based on Real Interest Differentials', *American Economic Review*, 69 (4), 610–22.

Krugman, P. (1979), 'A Model of Balance of Payments Crises', *Journal of Money, Credit and Banking*, 11, 311–25.

Maastricht Treaty (1992), *Treaty on Economic Union*, Luxembourg: Office for Official Publications of the European Communities.

Obstfeld, M. (1986), 'Rational and Self-fulfilling Balance of Payments Crises', *American Economic Review*, LXXVI, 72–81.

Rose, A.K. and L.E.O. Svensson (1991), 'Expected and predicted realignments: The FF/DM Exchange Rate During the EMS', Institute of International Economic Studies Seminar Paper No. 485, IIES, Stockholm.

Rose, A.K. and L.E.O. Svensson (1994), 'European Exchange Rate Credibility Before the Fall', *European Economic Review*, **38**, 1185–216.

Svensson, L.E.O. (1991), 'The Simplest Test of Target Zone Credibility', *IMF Staff Papers*, **38**, 655–65.

Svensson, L.E.O. (1992), 'The Foreign Exchange Risk Premium in a Target Zone with Devaluation Risk', *Journal of International Economics*, **33**, 21–40.

Svensson, L.E.O. (1993), 'Assessing Target Zone Credibiltiy: Mean Reversion and Devaluation Expectations in the ERM, 1979–1992', *European Economic Review*, **37**, 763–802.

Appendix 4A

The data used in this study were obtained from the following sources.

1. International Financial Statistics: exchange rates, foreign exchange reserves (DM million), trade balances (DM million), money supplies (DM million), interest rates (3-month T-bill rate), price indices (CPI).
2. Organization for Economic Cooperation and Development: Quarterly Labour Statistics (1995): unemployment rates.
3. Svensson (1993): central rates c_t.
4. Authors: $X_t = s_t - c_t$, $Z_1 = \log(1 + t^*)$, dummy variables.

Note that foreign exchange reserves, trade balances and money supplies were converted to DM from ECU using the ECU/DM exchange rate.

5 Stability of a monetary union: theoretical considerations

George D. Demopoulos and
*Nicholas A. Yannacopoulos**

1 Introduction

The theory of optimum currency areas (OCAs) attempts to define the domain for a single currency.[1] Lerner (1944) dealt with this issue and emphasized the importance of free factor mobility for the establishment of a currency area, a criterion that was later adopted by Mundell (1961).

Mundell (1961) observed that the costs of a monetary union stem from asymmetric shocks and that free factor mobility acts as an absorber of these shocks. However, he goes one step further by stressing the fact that if factors of production are mobile across national boundaries, a flexible exchange rate becomes unnecessary and possibly harmful. Mundell defines an OCA as an area of free factor mobility.

McKinnon (1963) stressed the importance of openness in connection with the exchange rate regime. The idea that the benefits of a monetary union rise with openness (openness is defined as the value added of trade in total output) needs elaboration. The usual argument for the greater significance of the exchange rate adjustment in order to equilibrate trade rests on the lower propensity to import.

The balance of these two considerations, that is, the free factor mobility and the openness of the economies, defined, in the older literature, the optimum domain of a currency area. To these considerations one must add fiscal integration, that is, the extent to which policy at the federal level can serve as an alternative to the use of monetary policy to foster asymmetric shocks. The need for fiscal integration is justified on analytical and historical grounds. It is justified on analytical grounds because the closer the fiscal integration, the smaller will be the net effect which a shift in export demand will have on the balance of payments and thus on real exchange rates. It is justified on historical grounds because the domain of a single currency has generally had the same boundaries as its central political and fiscal system (McKinnon 1995; Goodhart 1995).

The criticism has emphasized two weaknesses of the theory of OCAs up

* We would like to thank Professors V. Alexander and G. Karras for their helpful comments on an earlier version of this chapter.

to the 1990s. First, the criteria for the determination of an OCA (factor mobility, openness, and fiscal integration) were incomplete and partial as they stressed only some of the elements present in the adjustment process under the various exchange rate regimes. Therefore, a formal synthesis was necessary. Second, and more important, the absence of a formal model for the determination of the optimum domain of currency areas divorced from the policy aspects (Melitz 1995a).

A formal synthesis of the various criteria was attempted in an expository paper by Krugman (1990). He treated the costs and the benefits of a monetary union as a function of openness. He postulated that benefits are an increasing function of openness, while costs are a decreasing function of it. The point at which the two curves cross each other determines the optimal degree of openness, that is, the degree of openness that is consistent with an OCA. Krugman's diagram, which was adopted by a number of authors (Artis 1994; De Grauwe 1994), does not determine an OCA. It constitutes however a formal synthesis of the approaches by Mundell (1961) and McKinnon (1963) as it is clear in De Grauwe's exposition where the costs and the benefits curves are drawn for a given degree of factor mobility.

The first suggestion for a formal model for an OCA was made by Krugman and Obstfeld (1991), where the costs and benefits of a currency area are treated as a function of its size. As the currency area expands, the benefits from adopting a single currency increase while the costs increase at an increasing pace as new countries subject to their own macroeconomic adjustment problems join the currency area. The OCA occurs when marginal costs equal marginal revenues.

This suggestion was taken up by Demopoulos and Yannacopoulos (1995) who gave a geometrical interpretation of the Krugman and Obstfeld model (1991). They suggested that under the conditions referred to in this model the monetary union cannot survive (it is unstable) because every member can improve its position by withdrawing from it. The stability property suggested by Demopoulos and Yannacopoulos is analogous to the core concept of the game theory.

The most complete formal model of a monetary union is due to Melitz (1995b). Melitz adopts a marginal analysis to the problem which is similar to the analysis suggested by Krugman and Obstfeld. However, he treats the possible expansion of a given currency area as a continuous variable ranging from zero to one: zero if there is no expansion beyond the existing national borders, and one if all sources of competition and trade are included in the union. Again, the OCA occurs when the marginal benefits from the expansion of the currency area equal the marginal costs. At the point at which the OCA is determined, the welfare function pertaining to a currency area is maximized. Melitz concludes, however, that the determination of an OCA is 'not an optimisation exercise in the usual sense. It requires concertation' (Melitz 1995b, p. 294).

There is no doubt that the adoption of a single currency (the formation of a currency area) requires a formal agreement.

The first question we seek to answer is whether the conditions of the determination of an OCA as given by the marginal analysis are consistent with the conditions that guarantee a stable agreement between the members of a currency area. Stability (and therefore the survival of a monetary union) is achieved when any subset of monetary union members cannot improve upon its position by withdrawing from the monetary union.

We develop this argument by outlining a formal model of a monetary union based on the principles of marginal analysis as suggested by Krugman and Obstfeld (1991) and Melitz (1995b). We find that under conditions of rising marginal costs there will be no economic motive for the formation of a monetary union, and if a union is formed, for example by decree, it will be unstable since any subgroup (subcoalition) of countries can improve upon its allocation by abandoning the union. Hence, the suggested marginal analysis fails to determine an OCA.

The second question is the determination of the stability of a currency area. Since the concept of stability outlined previously is analogous to the concept of the core in the cooperative game theory, we study the formation of a monetary union in the context of this theory. In other words, we seek to determine the economic conditions for the existence of the core. We find that under conditions of increasing marginal costs the core does not exist and therefore the monetary union is not viable.

The rest of the chapter is organized as follows. In Section 2, we outline a formal model of a monetary union based on the principles of marginal analysis. In Section 3, we discuss the theory of monetary unions in the context of the cooperative game theory. In the final section we summarize the conclusions.

2   A marginal approach to the theory of monetary unions

By a monetary union we mean a set of sovereign countries having a common currency and a common central bank. The starting-point for a discussion of the issues of the theory of monetary unions is supplied by the theory of optimum currency areas that seeks to determine the optimum domain for a single currency. This theory makes the plausible assertion that a monetary union is more desirable the more structurally similar are the economies participating in it. Since participation in a currency area brings benefits and costs, optimality can be evaluated on a costs–benefits basis. The argument is illustrated in Figure 5.1. Following Krugman (1990)

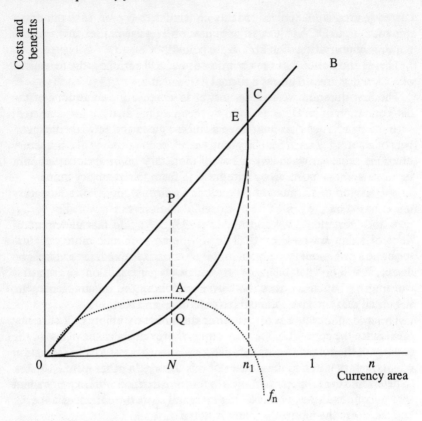

Note: 0*N* = optimum currency area.

Figure 5.1   The 'conventional' model of monetary unions

and Krugman and Obstfeld (1991), we choose the unit interval (0,1) along the horizontal axis of Figure 5.1, and we assume that to each point of the interval corresponds a particular country. There is a degree of freedom in choosing how to place the various countries along the (0,1) interval. We use that degree of freedom by aligning the countries in order of decreasing openness of their economies. Thus, we place towards the origin countries with a relatively greater share in international trade. Conversely, we place towards unity countries with a relatively small share in international trade. On the vertical axis we measure the costs and benefits to the monetary union.

The benefits curve of the monetary union is shown in Figure 5.1 as 0B. The upward slope of the curve is justified by the argument that the benefits derived from the use of a single currency (and therefore from the elimination of transaction costs and the consequent enhancing of the roles of money as a unit of account and as a medium of exchange) will be greater, the larger the single currency area (Mundell 1968). It is postulated for simplicity that the 0B curve is a straight line, implying that the marginal benefits to the union, derived from its geographical expansion, remain constant.

The costs of a monetary union are due to the inability of the member countries to use their monetary policies to accommodate local macroeconomic shocks (asymmetric shocks). These asymmetric shocks are due to the differences in the economic structure of participating economies in the monetary union (that is, differences in technology, preferences and factor endowments), which lead to their specialization according to the principle of comparative advantage.[2] The existence of a single currency (and of a common central bank) deprives the member countries of their ability to use the exchange rate as a policy tool in order to cope with these shocks. Therefore, the likelihood of macroeconomic adjustment problems grows at an increasing rate as the union is extended geographically to include a greater variety of structurally dissimilar countries subject to asymmetric shocks.[3] The costs curve of the monetary union, reflecting the likelihood of macroeconomic adjustment problems, is shown as 0C in Figure 5.1. It is drawn on the assumption of a given degree of structural similarity of the currency area members. Its upward slope is justified by the fact that the costs of a monetary union increase with decreasing openness of the countries participating in the union, given the importance of nominal exchange rate adjustments for the relatively closed economies.

The optimum size of the union (the optimum currency area) is $0N$ and occurs at the point where the marginal benefits from adopting a single currency equal the marginal cost resulting from the loss of economic stability to the union. The curve $0An_1$, termed the net benefits curve, gives the difference between total benefits and total costs. This difference is maximized when the number of countries is $0N$. Beyond this point, the net benefits to the monetary union are declining, and beyond n_1, become negative.

The factor limiting the optimum currency area in this model is the increasing marginal costs (reflected in the slope of the 0C curve), arising from the appearance of asymmetric shocks.[4] Therefore, the existence of asymmetric shock absorbers (relative price and wage flexibility, and/or free factor mobility) may render the 0C curve relatively more flat, and therefore the geographical extension of the optimum currency area is larger. In the limit (that is, if free factor mobility and relative price flexibility were fully effective in absorbing the asymmetric shocks) the 0C curve would become horizontal, and therefore the marginal costs from the geographical expansion of the monetary union would be zero. Similarly, if all countries participating in a monetary union were structurally identical, the shocks in the union would be symmetric rather than asymmetric, and therefore the OC curve would be horizontal. It is clear that in all these cases there would be no maximum position of net benefits of the union, implying that the net benefits curve would be a straight line with an upward slope, as the OB curve. But if the monetary union never runs into increasing costs, there would be no economic limit for it to extend its operations, and hence it would always pay the union to be expanded geographically. A factor that may provide a limit to its expansion in this extreme case is the political factor. Another limit for the expansion of the monetary union is the cost of information about the worth of all possible coalitions that can be formed and the cost arising from the formation of the various coalitions (see below).

This model determines the optimum number of countries that may form a monetary union.[5] It does not describe the course of actions these countries have to take to achieve this outcome. Obviously, this presupposes a binding agreement on the part of the interested countries, that is, the formation of a coalition.[6] We now pose the following question: is such an agreement aiming at the formation of such a coalition possible? Another way to put this question is by assuming that the countries concerned have formed a monetary union (for example by decree) and asking whether it can survive. Survival means that the monetary union offers to its member countries higher benefits than they could get otherwise in any subcoalition.

The model reveals that under conditions of rising marginal costs, survival is impossible because a subgroup (subcoalition) of countries always has an incentive to break away from the monetary union. That is, under conditions of rising marginal costs there will be no economic motive for the formation of a monetary union, and if a union is formed by decree it will be unstable since any subgroup (subcoalition) of countries can improve upon its allocation by abandoning the union. Therefore, the suggested marginal analysis fails to determine an optimum currency area. In the next section, we attempt to answer the question of the stability of a currency area in the context of cooperative game theory.

3   The monetary union as a cooperative game
Obviously, the formation of the monetary union presupposes a binding agreement on the part of the interested parties, that is, the formation of a grand coalition, consisting of the N countries that form the optimum currency area. We are justified therefore in looking at the monetary union as a cooperative game with transferable payoff.

3.1   Elements of a monetary union cooperative game

A cooperative game (with transferable payoff) consists of:[7]

1. A finite set of N countries $[N = 1, 2, \ldots, n]$ forming part of a single currency area. Any subset of N (including N itself and all the one subset elements) is called a coalition. In particular, the coalition of the N countries (that is, the coalition of the countries that form a monetary union) will be called a *grand* coalition. Obviously, there are among the n countries, $2^n - 1$ coalitions possible, including the trivial coalitions consisting of a single country.

2. A function v which assigns to a coalition the minimum benefit which may ensure to itself, irrespective of the behaviour of the others. This function, called a 'characteristic function', has the following properties:

$$v(\phi) = 0 \tag{5.1}$$

$$v(S \cup T) > v(S) + v(T) \quad \text{whenever } S \cap T = \phi \tag{5.2}$$

The first property states that the null set obtains nothing. The second property, known as superadditivity, states that if two separate sets of countries form a larger coalition $S \cup T$, then they can do at least as well as the sum of what they can do separately.

It will be assumed that the benefit $v(S)$ of a coalition S depends only on the elements in S (that is, we assume that the game is symmetric). Given the assumption of symmetry we can map the characteristic function in relation to the number of countries included in a coalition. The symmetry is justified on the following ground: the introduction of a single currency improves the quality of money as a medium of exchange by reducing transaction costs. Therefore, as the monetary union expands, that is, as the size of the coalition S increases the cost of exchange is getting smaller leading to an expansion of the trade within the currency area and to an increase of consumption per head (Melitz 1996). Therefore, we may reasonably treat the benefits of a monetary union as a function of its size.

The following example illustrates: Consider a three-person cooperative game with $N = 1, 2, 3$, and the following characteristic function:

$v(\phi) = 0$
$v(1) = v(2) = v(3) = 0$
$v(12) = v(13) = v(23) = 3$
$v(123) = 3$

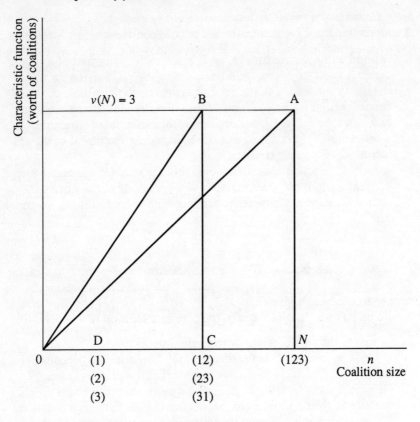

Figure 5.2   The characteristic function of a symmetric game

The game is symmetric because coalitions of the same size have the same worth. It is then possible to map the characteristic function in relation to the number of countries included in a coalition as shown in Figure 5.2. We can see from this figure that the coalition of the size $0N$ (three-country coalition) is AN (three units of 'utility'), and therefore the slope of $0A$ gives the per country benefit to be obtained, that is, $(AN/0N) = (3/3) = 1$. Similarly, the worth of the coalition of the size $0C$ (two-country coalition) is BC (three units of 'utility'), and therefore the slope of $0B$ gives the per country benefit to be obtained, that is, $(BC/0C) = (3/2) = 1.5$. Finally, the worth of the coalition of the size $0D$ (one-country coalition) is zero. In this particular example, a three-country coalition cannot be formed, because a two-country coalition can guarantee for its members greater benefits than the three-country coalition (see below).

3.2 Chances of forming an agreement; the core of the game

The next question is to evaluate the chances of forming an agreement between all countries interested in the formation of a monetary union. It can be stipulated that in the case of two countries the following two conditions must be satisfied for any reasonable (and stable) agreement:

1. *Condition of individual rationality* This condition states that it would be irrational for a single country to agree to a joint outcome under which it receives a lower payoff than it would assure itself by its own individual efforts.
2. *Condition of group rationality (Pareto optimality requirement)* This condition states that any agreement should be efficient in the sense that no alternative agreement is feasible that yields higher payoffs simultaneously to both countries.

An agreement that satisfies the conditions of individual and group rationality is called a *core*. In a situation with three or more countries, a third limitation should be added in defining the core that stipulates that a core outcome has to give each coalition as much as this coalition could obtain on its own. In other words, the core as a solution to a cooperative game states that no subcoalition of countries ends up by preferring a benefit vector to that resulting from overall cooperation (Owen 1982).

More formally, let $w = (w_1, w_2, \ldots, w_n)$ be a benefits vector, that is, an arrangement that gives country i the benefit w_i ($i = 1, 2, \ldots, n$). This benefit vector is an allocation if it satisfies the following conditions:

$$w_i > [(i)] \quad \text{for every } i \in N \text{ (condition of individual rationality)} \quad (5.3)$$

$$\sum_{i \in N} w_i = v(N) \quad \text{(condition of group rationality).} \quad (5.4)$$

A set of allocations is called a core if they cannot be improved upon by any coalition. A coalition of countries S is said to improve upon a given allocation w_i if it exists another allocation y_i such that:

$$y_i > w_i \quad \text{for every } i \in S \quad (5.5)$$

$$\sum_{i \in N} w_i = v(S). \quad (5.6)$$

Any allocation that can be improved upon cannot be considered as a reasonable equilibrium to a monetary union because the coalition S would always have an incentive to split off from it. In this case the core is empty. If a core exists, that is, if the core contains all the reasonable outcomes accruing to the members of a monetary union, then the union is stable. Since every coalition of countries gets some parts of the benefits accruing to the monetary union as a whole, no country has an incentive to split off. Therefore, the existence of the core in a monetary union game is a necessary condition for its survival.

3.3   Conditions for the existence of the core in a monetary union

In the symmetric game considered here, a core exists, that is, a country has no incentive to split off from the monetary union, if and only if:

$$v(S) \leq (s/N)v(N) \qquad (5.7)$$

where s denotes the number of the countries participating in the coalition S. This result has a simple geometrical interpretation (Ponssard 1981). The characteristic function has to lie below the straight line 0A in Figure 5.2, the slope of which specifies how much the grand coalition (a monetary union in our case) can promise to its members. If the characteristic function lies below the straight line, the benefits that the various subcoalitions can promise to their members are less than these members can obtain by joining the grand coalition (the monetary union), and therefore no member of the grand coalition has an incentive to break off; the core then exists. Otherwise, the core is empty. In the cooperative game illustrated in Figure 5.2, the core is empty because point B (at point B corresponds the benefits of all two-country coalitions) lies above the straight line 0A.

In our present purpose the characteristic function specifies the benefits that any coalition S can obtain for its members under the technical restrictions of the model of the monetary union, regardless of the actions of those outside the coalition. And since the benefits accruing to the members of the monetary union are given by the net benefits function (see Section 2), its shape will play an important role in the determination of the stability of a monetary union. Starting from the simple example outlined in Section 2, we shall construct different game theoretic models reflecting different structural conditions of the countries that form a monetary union.[8]

Case a   Consider the 'conventional' model of a monetary union outlined in Section 2, where we have assumed that a set of countries having different degrees of openness form a monetary union. In Figure 5.3 the net benefits function $f(n)$ corresponds to the part 0A of the benefits curve of Figure 5.1. The geometry of the $f(n)$ is justified, as we have already seen, by the fact that as the number of countries joining a monetary union increases (that is,

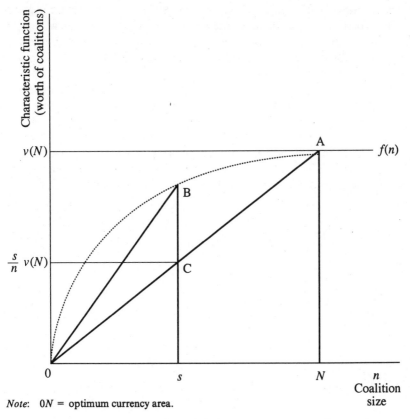

Note: $0N$ = optimum currency area.

Figure 5.3   *The 'conventional' model of a monetary union: the core is empty*

as the size of the coalition increases) the benefits of the monetary union increase but at a decreasing rate. Accordingly, the benefits function is concave as shown in Figure 5.3.

A typical characteristic function of a game of this type is shown in Figure 5.3. Obviously, in this game the core is empty because its characteristic function lies above the straight line 0A. For example, a coalition with s members has worth sB, and therefore it can promise to its members a higher per country benefit than they can obtain participating in the monetary union. In fact, the slope of the straight line 0B that gives the per country benefit of a coalition of the size s, is higher than the slope of the straight line 0A, that gives the per country benefit that the grand coalition can offer to its members; and, since the benefits curve is concave it follows that the per country benefits that coalitions of different sizes can promise to their members will always be higher than the per country benefit that the grand coalition can offer to its members. Therefore, no monetary union can survive under the assumptions of the 'conventional' model. This result is summarized in the following proposition.

Proposition 1 If the net benefits function is strictly concave the monetary union does not posses a core. Therefore the union is not viable.

Case b   Consider the case of N [$N = 1, 2, \ldots, n$] where the benefits from the expansion of a monetary union dominate its possible costs. As we have already seen in Section 2, in this case the net benefits curve $f(n)$ is a straight line starting from the origin (see Figure 5.4). This monetary union has a

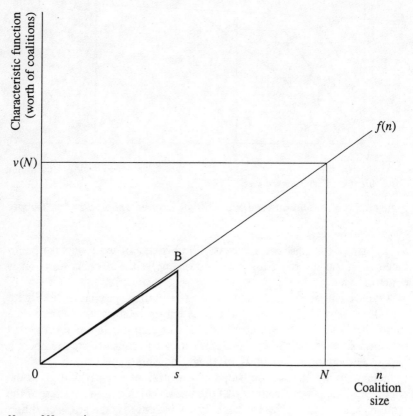

Note: $0N$ = optimum currency area.

Figure 5.4   A model of a monetary union with a single core

single core and therefore it is viable. For example, the worth of the coalition of the size s is sB, and therefore the per country benefit that this coalition can afford to its members is the same with the per country benefit that the grand coalition (the monetary union) can guarantee for its members. Therefore no subcoalition has an incentive to break away from the monetary union.

Case c The benefits from the expansion of the monetary union dominate costs, but we now assume that the net benefits function increases at an increasing rate as the monetary union expands geographically (see Figure 5.5). The net benefits curve is convex implying that there is a decrease in net benefits, when the number of countries participating in the monetary union

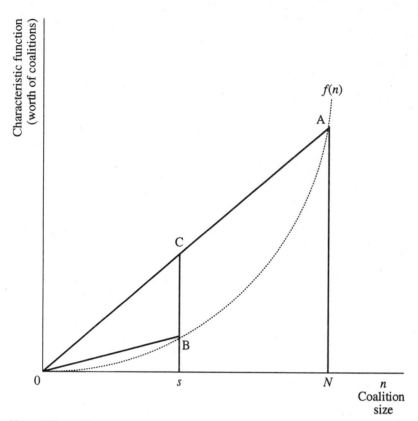

Note: $0N$ = optimum currency area.

Figure 5.5 A model of a monetary union with a large core

is small. Since the net benefits curve is strictly convex, it lies below the 0A straight line (see Figure 5.5) and therefore the per country benefits that coalitions of different size can promise to their members will always be less as compared with the per country benefits available in the whole game. A core then always exists. For example, a coalition of the size *s* has worth *s*B, and it can guarantee for its members smaller benefits than the benefits that the monetary union as a whole can guarantee for its members (the slope of 0B is less than the slope of 0A, in Figure 5.5). From cases (b) and (c) we derive the following proposition.

Proposition 2   If the net benefits function is convex or strictly convex the monetary union possesses a core. Therefore the union is viable.

Case d   In Figure 5.6 we give an example of a generalized net benefits function. This net benefits function exhibits increasing returns for the coalition of the size *s*, and decreasing returns beyond *s*. A core exists for coalitions less than *s*. If the size of the coalition increases beyond s the core disappears.

4   Conclusions

This chapter has outlined a formal model of a monetary union based on the principles of marginal analysis. We have found that the conventional marginal analysis cannot determine the optimum currency area because under conditions of increasing marginal costs no country has the intention of joining a monetary union. A monetary union formed, for example, by decree under those conditions could be unstable because any country or coalitions of countries could have the intention of breaking away from it in order to secure for their members higher benefits at a lower marginal cost.

We then looked at the necessary conditions for the determination of the stability of a monetary union utilizing concepts from the cooperative game theory. That is, we have looked at the existence of the core of the game. If a core exists, that is, if the core contains all the reasonable outcomes accruing to the members of a monetary union, then the union is stable.

We have found that in the conventional model of a monetary union where we assume that a set of countries with varying degree of openness form a monetary union, the core does not exist since it reflects rising marginal costs due to reduced economic stability as the union is extended to include more closed economies for which nominal exchange rate adjustments have a greater significance. Therefore, no monetary union can survive under the assumptions of the conventional model.

On the other hand, the core exists and the monetary union is viable under conditions of increasing returns to the coalition, implying that it

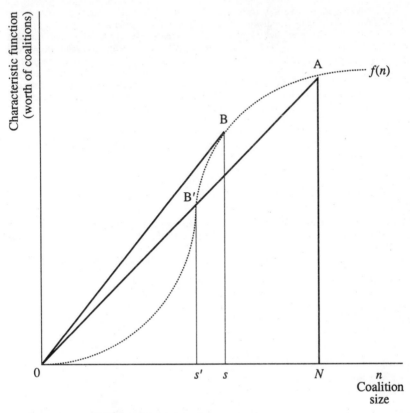

Figure 5.6   A more general net benefits function

consists of structurally similar economies. This is so because the incremental return to the coalition from adding a new member exceeds the already existing return per member.

Notes

1. This presentation of the OCA theory abstracts from monetary policy issues. Monetary issues are emphasized in Tavlas (1993).
2. The costs discussed in this model are referred to the costs which are internal to the union. Melitz (1995b) remind us that a monetary union is not isolated from the rest of the world. Therefore, he suggests that we have to take into account also the costs that stem from sources outside of the union. Melitz's consideration does not affect our analysis.
3. The criterion of similarity of the economies participating in a monetary union is reflected in what Vaubel (1976, 1978), von Hagen and Neumann (1994), and De Grauwe and Heens (1993) have called the variability of the real exchange rate.
4. The likelihood of asymmetric shocks will be greatly reduced in the case of a union in which the participating economies were structurally similar and/or the relative prices of the final

commodities and factors of production were flexible. If it is assumed that the participating economies are structurally dissimilar and the degree of price and wage flexibility is low, free factor mobility may help to absorb the asymmetric shocks (Lerner 1944; Mundell 1961). However, Vaubel (1976) emphasizes that factor mobility, diversification, fiscal integration and openness are all reflected in the criterion of the real exchange rate variability.

5. At the point at which the OCA is determined, the welfare function pertaining to a currency area is maximized. Melitz (1995b, p. 294) concludes that the determination of an OCA is 'not an optimisation exercise in the usual sense. It requires concertation'.
6. The formation of coalitions requires a political decision. The role of political factors leading to a successful monetary integration is emphasized by Mintz (1970).
7. By transferable payoff (utility) we mean that if payoff is in monetary units, and A pays B one monetary unit, B's gain is the same as A's loss.
8. See also Shapley and Shubik (1967).

References

Artis, M. (1994), 'European Monetary Union', in M. Artis and N. Lee (eds), *The Economics of the European Monetary Union: Policy and Analysis*, Oxford: Oxford University Press, pp. 346–67.

De Grauwe, P. (1994), *The Economics of Monetary Integration*, Second edn, Oxford: Oxford University Press.

De Grauwe, P. and H. Heens (1993), 'Real Exchange Rate Variability in Monetary Unions', *Recherches Economiques de Louvain*, **59**, 105–17.

Demopoulos, G.D. and N.A. Yannacopoulos (1995), 'A Note of the Theory of Monetary Unions', Discussion Paper No. 66, Athens University of Economics and Business.

Goodhart, C.A.E. (1995), 'The Political Economy of Monetary Union', in P.B. Kenen (ed.), *Understanding Interdependence: The Macroeconomics of the Open Economy*, Princeton, NJ: Princeton University Press, pp. 448–505.

Krugman, P.R. (1990), 'Policy Problems of a Monetary Union', in P. De Grauwe and L. Papademos (eds), *The European Monetary System in the 1990s*, London: Longman. Reprinted in P.R. Krugman (1992), *Currencies and Crises*, Cambridge, MA: The MIT Press, pp. 185–203.

Krugman, P.R. and M. Obstfeld (1991), *International Economics: Theory and Policy*, New York: Harper Collins.

Lerner, Abba P. (1944), *The Economics of Control*, New York: Macmillan.

McKinnon, R.I. (1963), 'Optimum Currency Areas', *American Economic Review*, **53**, 717–25.

McKinnon, R.I. (1995), 'Panel: One Money for How Many?', in P.B. Kenen (ed.), *Understanding Interdependence: The Macroeconomics of the Open Economy*, Princeton, NJ: Princeton University Press, pp. 88–97.

Melitz, J. (1995a), 'The Current Impasse in Research on Optimum Currency Areas', *European Economic Review*, **39**, 492–500.

Melitz, J. (1995b), 'A Suggested Reformulation of the Theory of Optimal Currency Areas', *Open Economies Review*, **6**, 281–98.

Melitz, J. (1996), 'The Theory of Optimum Currency Areas, Trade Adjustment, and Trade', *Open Economies Review*, **7**, 99–116.

Mintz, N. (1970), *Monetary Union and Economic Integration*, New York: New York University Press.

Mundell, R.A. (1961), 'A Theory of Optimum Currency Areas', *American Economic Review*, **51**, 657–65.

Mundell, R.A. (1968), *International Economics*, London: Macmillan.

Owen, G. (1982), *Game Theory*, New York: Academic Press.

Ponssard, J.P. (1981), *Competitive Strategies*, Amsterdam: North-Holland.

Shapley, L.S. and M. Shubik (1967), 'Ownership and the Production Function', *Quarterly Journal of Economics*, **LXXXI**, 88–109.

Tavlas, G.S. (1993), 'The "New" Theory of Optimum Currency Areas', *World Economy*, **6**, 663–85.

Vaubel, R. (1976), 'Real Exchange-rate Changes in the European Community: The Empirical Evidence and its Implications for European Currency Unification', *Weltwirtschaftliches Archiv*, **112**, 429–68.

Vaubel, R. (1978), 'Real Exchange-rate Changes in the European Community: A New Approach to the Determination of Optimum Currency Areas', *Journal of International Economics*, **8**, 319–39.

von Hagen, J. and M.J.M. Neumann (1994), 'Real Exchange Rate Variability Within and Between Currency Areas: How Far Away is EMU?', *Review of Economics and Statistics*, **76**, 236–44.

PART II

POLICY AND POLITICAL ASPECTS OF EUROPEAN INTEGRATION

6   Value-added tax and the internal market in the EU: comparison of the transitional and the definitive VAT systems

Theodore A. Georgakopoulos

1   Introduction

The creation of the single European internal market in 1993 involved, among other things, the abolition of fiscal controls at intra-union borders and made necessary the change in the VAT system on intra-union transactions, which could no longer be taxed at the border in the country of destination, as was the case before. The transitional system, which was adopted in 1993, provided for the transfer of taxation of intra-union supplies from the border to the interior of the member countries. In particular, intra-union supplies to persons subject to VAT are zero rated in the country of supply (the origin country) and they are effectively taxed when resold in the market of the acquisition country (the destination country) by the intra-union buyer.[1] On the contrary, sales to final consumers crossing borders, as well as to certain exempt persons with a relatively small intra-union turnover, are taxed in the country of origin. Special provisions have been adopted in some cases (for example, distance sales, sales to public bodies, sales of transport means and goods subject to harmonized excises), where substantial divergencies in tax rates between the member countries, as exist today, could severely interfere with competition and cause wide misallocation of resources.

The above hybrid destination/origin system was to be replaced in 1997 by a definitive VAT system based on the origin principle, whereby all intra-union supplies will be taxed in the country of origin and the tax will be set against the buyer's tax liability in the country of destination. The European Commission was supposed to have submitted a proposal concerning the details of this new system by the end of 1994 (see European Commission 1992) but no such proposal has been put forth as yet. Instead, Commissioner Mario Monti has recently forwarded to the other members of the Commission a communication providing for a longer-run programme for the introduction of a new VAT system, which is suited to the demands of the single market (see European Commission 1996). The new system will provide for a single place of taxation of all transactions of each taxable person and for the allocation of the revenues among the member countries not by the tax system itself, which introduces considerable complications, but on the basis of domestic consumption in each member country. Such a system will require very extensive harmonization measures, concerning tax rates, the right to deduct, exemptions, the tax treatment of small firms and of the other special schemes, as well as uniform application rules, collective responsibility and greater cooperation between tax administrations.

This chapter, which was written before the new Commission document, compares the two systems (the transitional and the definitive one), in the context of the existing provisions of the 6th Directive, by scrutinizing the main pros and cons of each. Four major issues, which form the core of the discussions, are carefully considered. Two of them are allocative, one is revenue, and consequently income, redistributive, while the last is administrative. The first allocative issue concerns the extra financial burden that the transitional system is supposed to place on domestic sales, which are taxed at the time of supply, compared with intra-union supplies which go untaxed until their first resale in the country of destination. The second allocative issue concerns the tax discrimination between intra-community sales and domestic sales or imports from third countries, which will take place, under the origin principle, as a result of tax rate divergencies between the member countries. The third issue concerns the inter-country revenue transfers and the associated problems that will follow the introduction of the definitive VAT system, since intra-union supplies will be taxed and the revenues be paid to the authorities of the country of origin, while they will be credited against the buyers' tax liability from domestic sales, in the destination country. The final issue concerns the administrative problems faced by the tax authorities and by business of both the origin and the destination country, under the transitional system. These issues are analysed and evaluated in turn, and some conclusions concerning the desirability of each system are offered.

2 The financial burden of domestic and intra-union supplies under the transitional and the definitive VAT systems

One important criticism of the transitional system is that it provides a favourable tax treatment to intra-community sales and discriminates against domestic sales. The argument is simple. Since intra-community sales, under the transitional system, are zero rated in the country of origin and remain free of tax until they are resold in the domestic market of the destination country, whereas domestic sales are taxed at the time of supply, VAT places a financial burden on the latter and favours the former, thereby distorting conditions of competition and resource allocation. On the contrary, it is said, the definitive VAT system will treat all sales equally, since intra-union supplies will also be taxed at the time of the supply and

will therefore not distort conditions of competition and resource allocation.

The above argument is wrong. It is not true that the transitional system
places a financial burden on domestic supplies, thereby favouring intra-
community sales. VAT does not place any net financial burden on a
domestic transaction. What it really does is that it places a burden or
assures a gain to one of the transactors, which is exactly balanced by an
equal gain or burden of the other transactor. Whether it is the buyer or the
seller who bears the burden or gets the gain depends on the time lapse
between the date of the supply and the date of submission of the first
periodic return compared with the credit given by the seller. If the former is
longer than the latter, the buyer bears a financial cost (since he/she has to
pay tax before he/she can credit it) and the seller has a financial gain (since
he/she gets the tax revenues before he/she has to pay it to the government).
On the other hand, if the former is shorter than the latter period, the seller
bears a financial cost (since he/she has to pay tax before he/she raises it
from the buyer) while the buyer gets a gain (since he/she can credit tax
before he/she pays it). In all cases however, the gain/burden of the one
party is exactly balanced by the burden/gain of the other party so that no
net burden is placed on the domestic transaction. The market mechanism
can, by appropriate price changes, compensate the losers and extract the
total gain from the gainers thereby restoring pre-VAT conditions of
competition.

On the contrary, it is the definitive VAT system which will discriminate
the burden against or in favour of intra-union supplies and will distort
conditions of competition. This appears to be somewhat strange, since the
definitive VAT system treats intra-union and domestic supplies equally
and is therefore supposed to place the same financial burden on both. Yet,
as in the case of the transitional system, VAT will not place any net burden
on domestic supplies, since the burden/gain of one transactor will be
balanced exactly by the gain/burden of the other transactor. On the
contrary, in the case of intra-union supplies, the burden/gain of the one
transactor will usually differ from the gain/burden of the other transactor
so that conditions of competition will usually be distorted. It is only in
some special cases, such as, for example, when the tax periods are of equal
length and interest rates are the same in the member countries, that the
definitive system will be neutral. Such conditions, however, are not present
in the EU, at the moment. If either the tax periods and/or interest rates
differ, the definitive VAT system will usually discriminate against or in
favour of intra-union, compared to domestic, supplies and will therefore
distort conditions of competition and resource allocation (for details, see
Georgakopoulos 1996a). However, as I have shown in a recent paper, this

extra burden/gain, is not, in general, very big to provide a strong argument against the definitive system (ibid.).

3   The transitional and the definitive VAT systems and the allocation of resources under unequal tax rates

A second important issue that bears on the decision to change the VAT system on intra-community supplies is the impact on resource allocation, when tax rates differ among the member countries. This is a question that has been heavily discussed in the literature since the publication of the Neumark Report in the early 1960s (for a selection of studies, see European Commission 1963; Dosser 1967; Shibata 1967; Whalley 1989; Berglas 1981; Georgakopoulos 1992; Georgakopoulos and Hitiris 1992). The traditional view that the origin principle causes resource misallocation when tax rates differ among the member countries has been shown to hold true only in an otherwise optimal world. On the contrary, in a second-best world, as is the situation in an economic union, where the tariff on trade with third countries has already distorted the optimal allocation of resources, the origin principle can improve rather than harm this allocation (see Georgakopoulos 1989 and Georgakopoulos and Hitiris 1992). It is only under very restrictive conditions that the two principles are equivalent (see Georgakopoulos 1992).

However, one must notice here that, in the case of VAT, rate differences between member countries do not affect the allocation of resources in the case of supplies to taxable persons, who have the right to deduct input tax.[2] It is only in the case of supplies to persons not having the right to deduct input tax, for example, final consumers crossing borders, distance sales, exempt persons (small businesses, farmers, public bodies, traders in exempted activities) and so on, that the origin principle causes reallocation of resources, which can, however, as I have shown in a recent paper, again be beneficial in the second-best world of an economic union (see Georgakopoulos 1994).

The above theoretical findings, based on the assumption that high-tax country producers can, if necessary, shift their sales to the world market and get the world price, have little relevance to the real world where such an assumption does not really hold true. In such circumstances, the origin principle can severely distort sales to persons not having the right to deduct input tax and cause wide resource misallocation, when tax rates differ widely among the member countries. This is indeed the case with the EU countries where substantial differences exist in tax burdens today. These differences are not only due to differences in the size of the two nominal rates adopted (the standard rate and the reduced rate) which, as shown in Table 6.1, differ substantially (10 percentage points for the standard and 7

Table 6.1   VAT rates applying in the EU member countries

Country	Reduced rate	Standard rate	Zero rate
1. Austria	10	20	—
2. Belgium	1/6	20.5/12	0
3. Denmark	—	25	0
4. Finland	12	22	—
5. France	2.1/5.5	18.6	—
6. Germany	7	15	—
7. Greece	4/8	18	—
8. Ireland	2.5	21.5/12.5	0
9. Italy	4/9	19/13	—
10. Luxembourg	3/6	15/12	—
11. Netherlands	6	17.5	—
12. Portugal	5	16	—
13. Spain	3/6	15	—
14. Sweden	12	25	—
15. United Kingdom	—	17.5	0

percentage points for the reduced rate), but also to the special transitional derogations that have been granted to some member countries. Indeed, as Table 6.1 indicates, four countries (Belgium, Denmark, Ireland and the UK) continue to use zero rate on a number of domestic supplies; four member countries (Belgium, Ireland, Italy and Luxembourg) use inter-mediate rates, lower than the limit of 15 per cent set by the 6th Directive for the standard rate); six member countries (Belgium, France, Greece, Italy, Luxembourg and Spain) use two reduced rates, one of which is below the lowest limit of 5 per cent set by the 6th Directive; while Denmark and the UK have not introduced a reduced rate and Ireland uses a reduced rate lower than 5 per cent. With the UK zero rating children's clothes and Denmark subjecting them to 25 per cent, the application of the definitive regime, without any specific arrangements, can clearly create severe distortions of competition and resource misallocation.

However, one must stress here that the problem of resource misalloca-tion due to tax rate divergencies between the member countries, connected with supplies to persons not having the right to deduct input tax, is also present in the transitional VAT system and has been met by special arrangements for certain transactions where serious problems could otherwise arise. Such arrangements concern distance sales, sales to public bodies, supplies of transport means, supplies of goods subject to special excises and so on. Although some of these arrangements have created certain problems in practice, for example the necessity for appointing business representatives in member countries where distance sales exceed a certain amount per year, they could serve equally well or badly in the definitive VAT system for at least some time until considerable approximation of rates is achieved. The argument that the definitive VAT system will severely distort conditions of competition and cause wide misallocation of resources, unless rate divergencies among the member countries are severely reduced, is not therefore relevant here. Both the transitional and the definitive VAT systems cause the same problems of competition and resource misallocation when tax rates differ among the member countries, and these problems could, in the definitive VAT system, be met by broadly similar arrangements that are employed in the transitional system.

4   Inter-country revenue transfers under the origin principle
A third important issue connected with the transition to the definitive VAT system is the problem of revenue transfers between the member countries. The transitional system ensures that VAT revenues accrue to the country of destination which is considered to be entitled to get it. On the contrary, under the definitive VAT system, revenues will be transferred from member countries with a deficit in intra-union trade to member countries with a surplus in intra-union trade and from low-tax to high-tax member countries. This is a very important problem for some EU member countries, for example, Greece and Portugal, whose intra-union supplies constitute only 40 per cent and 70 per cent of their acquisitions, respectively. The losses of these countries will perhaps be even larger than suggested by the relation between intra-union supplies and acquisitions, since the proportion of their supplies subject to the low-tax rate is larger than the corresponding proportion of their acquisitions subject to this rate and the opposite is true for the proportions of trade subject to the standard VAT rate. In the case of Greece, for example, only about 20 per cent of its acquisitions are subject to the low-tax rate, while the corresponding proportion for its supplies is 34 per cent. Finally, both countries levy relatively low tax rates (below EU average) so that there will be no revenue compensation from the use of high rates. Recent estimates for Greece, based on detailed Intrastat data of intra-union trade, show that Greece will experience a net loss of revenues of the order of 20 per cent of the total revenues from VAT and more than 7 per cent of the total central government tax revenues (see Georgakopoulos et al. 1996). Revenue losses will also be experienced by Spain and the UK, which have deficits in their intra-union trade balances and they do not levy comparatively

large tax rates. Finally, losses may be experienced by France, whereas all other countries are expected to be net revenue gainers from these inter-country revenue transfers.

The problem now is how the revenue gainers would compensate the losers so that no net revenue transfers take place. Two alternative mechanisms (approaches) are widely discussed in the literature and in public administration offices: (i) the microeconomic approach, and (ii) the macroeconomic approach. The former provides for the collection of special data relating to intra-union trade and the corresponding tax revenue transfers, while the latter is based on the exploitation of existing macroeconomic data, for example, intra-community (Intrastat) trade data, total consumption, GDP, and so on.

Under the first approach, intra-union traders will be asked to state periodically the size of intra-union trade by member country or in total for all other member countries, as well as the tax charged on supplies or paid for acquisitions. These data will be dealt with by national tax authorities to calculate their revenue claims and obligations on the basis of which the final clearance will take place. A number of issues arise here such as, for example, the time length within which these data will be collected and the clearances be carried out; the nature of the clearance (bilateral or Com-munity-wide); use of advance payments to bridge the gap between tax receipt and clearance; currency to be used for clearance purposes and related problems; and so on. These issues, as well as other less important ones, have been and are still debated and views seem to differ substantially.

In its initial proposals for the harmonization of value-added tax, in view of the single European internal market, in 1987, the European Commission proposed the use of the microeconomic approach, with the data collected and processed by the national administrations and the clearances made by a central Community clearance procedure every month (see European Commission 1987). The German origin committee, on the other hand, proposes that data collection be made by national administrations every three months, on the basis of which preliminary payments will be made, according to the estimates of the origin country, the estimates of the destination country not being taken into account at this point (see Federal Ministry of Finance 1994). Final clearances will be made every year, when the estimates of the destination country will also be taken into account and, if the two estimates differ by more than an agreed percentage, an average of the two will be used for the clearance. In contrast to the European Commission, the German committee proposes bilateral clearances and advance payments to bridge the gap between tax receipt by the origin and repayment to the destination country. Other weaker administrations, which are bound to meet with more difficult problems in collecting and processing all the detailed information necessary for the operation of the microeconomic approach, seem to prefer longer periods. The Greek origin committee, for example, suggests that if the microeconomic approach is finally adopted, although not recommended, clearances be made every year after the submission of the annual recapitulative return, so that the administrative cost be reduced (see Ministry of Finance 1996). Like the European Commission, it also suggests that clearances be made by a central community institution, and not bilaterally, while, like the German committee, it also suggests advance payments and goes further to propose that balances should bear interest.

Coming to the macroeconomic approach, this is based on the exploitation of existing macroeconomic data, such as trade data, consumption or GDP data and so on. The macroeconomic approach has been suggested by the European Commission in its 1989 proposals for harmonization of the VAT systems in the member countries, in view of the strong objections of member states in its 1987 proposals (see European Commission 1989). The German committee considers the use of the macroeconomic approach as the proper one for the long-run solution of the problem, but suggests the use of the microeconomic approach in the short run. Weaker administrations, like the Greek one, are strongly in favour of the macroeconomic approach, in view of the high administrative cost of collecting and processing the necessary data for the application of the microeconomic computations. Commissioner Monti, in his recent proposals, also suggests the use of the macroeconomic approach, with consumption being used as the basis for revenue allocation.

In my view, the macroeconomic approach is to be preferred: it is simpler and much less expensive in its use and gives equally, and perhaps more, accurate estimates of the revenue transfers. Concerning the basis of the computation, the use of the trade data give more accurate estimates, but such data do not cover services, for which no comparable data exist. The use of consumption suggested by the Commission has the advantage of allowing the change in the place of taxation, something not allowed by the trade data, which require the tax to be levied at the place where the supply takes place. A combination of the two approaches can, as I have argued in a recent study for the Ministry of Finance, provide a better solution to the problem (see Georgakopoulos et al. 1996). Rather than collecting microeconomic data at very short intervals, which is administratively very expensive, one can collect such data at much longer intervals, say every five years. The estimates of the inter-country revenue transfers concerning the base year should be transformed as percentages of a macroeconomic variable, for example, total trade or consumption, on the basis of which estimates for the following four years could easily be derived. Given that the structure of trade and/or consumption does not change substantially within such relatively short periods and provided tax rates remain constant (otherwise corrections could be made), very satisfactory estimates can be derived. Recent estimates of Greece's losses for the years 1993 and 1994, using average VAT rates levied on the country's total intra-union trade for 1992 and the trade aggregates for these years, were quite close to the estimates derived on the basis of detailed data of intra-union trade in these years (ibid.).

5 Administrative problems of the transitional VAT system

An important administrative argument against the transitional and in favour of the definitive VAT system is that the former meets with considerable administrative problems in both member countries (the supplying country and the acquiring country). Intra-union suppliers meet with considerable difficulties in proving that zero-rated sales are really intra-union and not domestic supplies, while tax administrations also have difficulties in checking evasion via sales in the domestic market characterized as intra-union sales in the books and not taxed (see European Commission 1996). Intra-union buyers, on the other hand, have no incentive to declare to tax authorities their acquisitions from other member countries (as there is no input tax to be deducted), which makes it difficult for tax authorities to control subsequent domestic supplies and check evasion. On the contrary, if intra-union supplies are taxed at the origin country, intra-union buyers will have an incentive to declare their acquisitions from other member countries in order to be able to deduct input tax.

This argument is clearly correct but its importance seems to have been overstated. It is not true that the introduction of the origin principle on intra-union supplies will automatically reduce tax evasion. A basic condition for the automatic built-in mechanism of VAT to deter tax evasion is that tax authorities can check domestic supplies satisfactorily. If the probability of detecting tax evasion in the subsequent domestic supplies is small, intra-union buyers will have no reason to declare their acquisitions from other member countries. They would rather prefer to pay input tax than declare them, since the latter would allow tax authorities to check their domestic supplies better, thereby paying VAT on the value added in subsequent stages, as well as income tax. It is only when the probability of being detected is large that intra-union buyers would have some incentive to declare their purchases from other member countries and deduct input tax. As a result, member countries with weak tax administrations, where evasion is high, should not place such a big emphasis on this factor as a way of controlling evasion. On the contrary, evasion may increase under the origin principle, since checking of false invoices issued in other member countries and used to deduct input tax will be more difficult than under the existing regime.

6   Conclusions

The preceding analysis gives rise to the following conclusions.

First, the argument that the transitional VAT system places an extra financial burden on domestic as compared to intra-union supplies, thereby distorting conditions of competition and causing resource misallocation, whereas the definitive VAT system is neutral between the two sources of supply, is not correct. On the contrary, it is the transitional VAT system which is neutral between domestic and intra-union supplies, while the definitive VAT system will, most probably, discriminate the financial burden between them. However, the financial burden or gain of intra-union supplies will, most probably, not be substantial and it will tend to fall as inflation and interest rate differentials will fall in the process of closer economic and monetary integration.

Second, the argument that the introduction of the definitive VAT system, will, in the presence of the existing wide tax burden divergencies between the EU member countries, cause serious distortions of competition and resource misallocation, is not relevant here. Both the transitional system, with the destination principle in force, and the definitive VAT system, with the origin principle in force, will cause the same problems of competition and resource allocation and these problems can, with the same degree of success or failure, be met, in the definitive system, by similar special arrangements that are in force in the transitional VAT system.

Third, the argument that the definitive VAT system will cause wide revenue redistribution among the member countries, which will make necessary the use of costly mechanisms of compensating the revenue losers at the expense of revenue gainers is correct, but its power has perhaps been very much exaggerated. It appears that the use of the macroeconomic approach, properly designed, or even the combination of the microeconomic and the macroeconomic approaches along the lines suggested in this chapter, can give quite satisfactory results, without excessively high administrative costs.

Fourth, the argument that the definitive VAT system will allow the automatic built-in mechanism of this tax to reduce fraud also seems to have been overly exaggerated, since its power depends on the ability of member countries to control domestic supplies, which may be limited in countries with weak tax administrations where tax evasion is substantial. Moreover, a new source of evasion opens up in the definitive VAT system with the possibility of wide use of false invoices to deduct input tax.

Overall, it appears that, within the existing framework set by the 6th Directive, there are no powerful economic or even administrative arguments suggesting the transition to the definitive VAT system, apart from the political argument of treating intra-union supplies in the same way as domestic supplies, although in economic terms, this, in fact, constitutes unequal treatment. Therefore, it appears that a wider look at the problems caused by VAT in the single internal market, along the lines suggested by Commissioner Monti's report, rather than a direct shift to the definitive VAT system in the context of the 6th Directive, is necessary.

Notes

1. Intra-union buyers must declare their purchases from other member countries, as well as the VAT that should have been paid at the border, but this tax can be credited as input tax so that no tax is paid at this point. The tax on intra-union acquisitions is therefore effectively paid at their next sale in the domestic market where no input tax on intra-union purchases can be credited again.
2. This is, of course, so, provided the buyer in one member country is allowed to deduct the actual amount of VAT charged by suppliers in other member countries from his/her tax liability in his/her own country and then charge his/her sales at its own country's tax rate, which will, most probably, be the case with the definitive VAT system in the EU.

References

Commission of the European Communities (1963), *The EEC Reports on Tax Harmonisation*, International Bureau of Fiscal Documentation.

Dosser, D.G.M. (1967), 'Economic Analysis of Tax Harmonisation', in Carl S. Shoup (ed.), *Fiscal Harmonisation in Common Markets*, New York: Columbia University Press, pp. 1–144.

European Commission (1985), *Completing.the Internal Market*, White Paper, COM (85), final.

European Commission (1987), *Commission Communication on the Completion of the Internal Market: The Introduction of a VAT Clearing Mechanism for Intra-community Sales*, COM (87), 323 final/2.

European Commission (1989), *On the Completion of the Internal Market and the Approximation of Indirect Taxes*, Commission Communication to the Council and Parliament, COM (89), 260 final.

European Commission (1991), Council Directive 91/680/EEC, of 16 December 1991, Supplementing the Common System of Value-added Tax and Amending Directive 77/388/EEC with a View to the Abolition of Fiscal Frontiers.

European Commission (1992), Council Directive 92/77/EEC, of 19 October 1992, Supplementing the Common System of Value-added Tax and Amending Directive 77/388/EEC.

European Commission (1994), *Report of the Commission to the Council and the Parliament Concerning the Functioning of the Transitional VAT System on Intra-union Transactions*, COM (94), 515.

European Commission (1996), *A Common System of VAT: A Programme for the Single Market*, COM (96), 328.

Federal Ministry of Finance (1994), *Report of the Country of Origin*, Bonn: Commission.

Georgakopoulos, T. (1989), 'Harmonisation of Commodity Taxes: The Restricted Origin Principle', *Journal of Public Economics*, **31**, 137–9.

Georgakopoulos, T. (1992), 'Trade, Trade Distortion and Paetto Inefficiencies Under the Restricted Origin Principle', *Public Economics*, **41**, 381–90.

Georgakopoulos, T. (1994), 'The Harmonisation in the European Union. The Distinction/Origin Principle', Athens University of Economics and Business, Discussion Paper No. 5.

Georgakopoulos, T. (1996a), 'The Financial Burden of Domestic and Intra-union Supplies Under the Transitional and the Definitive VAT System in the EU' (mimeo available).

Georgakopoulos, T. (1996b), 'Inter-country Revenue Transfers Under the Definitive VAT System in the EU: The Micro- and Macro-approaches Compared' (mimeo available), 'Destination, Origin and Restricted Origin Principles', *Public Economics*, **16**, 377–87.

Georgakopoulos, T. and T. Hitiris (1992), 'On the Equivalence of the Destination and the Restricted Origin Principle', *Economic Journal*, pp. 351–5.

Georgakopoulos T., I. Loizides and B. Giachalis (1996), 'Revenue Implications of the Origin Principle in the EU: The Case of Greece' (mimeo available).

Greek Ministry of Finance 1996; Report of Commission of the Definitive VAT system in the EU, Autumn 1YP6. (Greek).

Institute of Fiscal Studies (1988), *Fiscal Harmonisation – An analysis of the EC proposals*, London: IFS.

Pearson, M. and S. Smith (1988), '1992: Issues in Indirect Taxation', *Fiscal Studies*, **9**, 25–35.

Shibata, M. (1967) 'The Unions' in C.S. Shoup (ed.) *Fiscal Harmonisation in Common Markets*, New York: Columbia University Press, pp. 145–264.

Whalley (1929) 'Uniform Domestic and Economic Integration', *Public Economics*, **11**, 13–21.

7 Greek agriculture under the CAP: the experience of the first fifteen years
Nicholas C. Baltas

1 Introduction

Agriculture is a vital element not only in the rural economy but also in the wider national economy of Greece. Greece's agriculture occupies the first place in terms of its share in GDP, population and balance of trade among the member states of the European Union (EU). Specifically, Greece's agriculture contributes in terms of GDP, the active population and its value exports 14.21 and 31 per cent, respectively, against 3.6 and 9 per cent at an average level in the EU.

Notwithstanding these characteristics, Greek agriculture suffers from major structural problems. Small and fragmented landholdings, insufficient rural infrastructure, an inefficient marketing system and weak farmers' bargaining power are just a few of the factors that contribute to the formation of high-cost production structures and hinder the development of Greek agriculture. The overall result of these problems is that farm incomes have remained very low compared with incomes elsewhere in the Greek economy and those of the farm sectors of other EU member states.

The accession of Greece into the European Community in 1981 resulted in the immediate implementation of the Common Agricultural Policy (CAP) and the gradual (within 5 years) removal of tariffs on the trade of agricultural products with other member countries. Consequently, the institutional framework within which Greek agriculture had developed in the post-war period changed radically and the regulating ability of the Greek state was significantly limited (Maraveyas 1994).

The question which we will try to answer in this chapter is to what degree the change in the institutional framework of the development of Greek agriculture, due to the implementation of the CAP[1] and the freeing of trade in agricultural products within the Community, affected Greek agriculture. Specifically, after a short review of agricultural policy in Greece before accession and the changes made during the transition period, an attempt is made in this chapter to assess quantitatively and qualitatively developments in key indicators of Greek agriculture. Moreover, the agricultural sector's prospects are examined in view of the reform of CAP, the implementation of the Uruguay Agreement and the Central and East European Countries Agreements with the EU.

2   Agricultural policy in Greece before and after accession

The main mechanisms through which pre-accession Greece supported her agricultural sector included a guaranteed minimum price system, with or without intervention, direct income support to farmers, input subsidies, import restrictions and export promotion measures, favourable credit terms, and so on.

1. *Guaranteed minimum prices*   Minimum prices schemes, which applied to the main crop products, were based on the rationale that they: (i) safeguarded farmers' incomes against fluctuations and (ii) provided signals for the government's wish to promote (or to discourage) particular crops. These schemes, however, differed widely among the various products. For cereals, tobacco, olive oil, and so on, minimum farmgate prices were applied through market intervention mechanisms, according to which the state intervention agency has an open-ended obligation to buy in at the fixed price any quantities of various crops offered by farmers.

    For some products, such as rice and tobacco, besides price fixing which was not always an effective measure, production was restricted through acreage quotas. Since Greece's accession to the EC in 1981, all such barriers have been removed.

    For other products, for example, tomatoes for processing and sugar beet, contracts were made between farmers and processors. For cotton, a deficiency payment system was applied.[2] For perishable commodities, such as fruit and vegetables, minimum prices were guaranteed only for the quantities sold to processors and exporters. The latter were subsidized provided they bought from the farmers at the minimum guaranteed prices. In the case of some fruit and vegetables, for example, peaches and oranges, a withdrawal mechanism was occasionally implemented as a means of market stabilization. With the exception of milk, for which a minimum price was used, no minimum farm prices were guaranteed for livestock products.

2. *Subsidies to farmers*   Direct subsidies were granted to farmers mainly for products to which intervention was not applied (cotton) or was applied (wheat, tobacco, olive oil, and so on) and also to shepherds of less-favoured and/or mountainous areas and isolated islands.

3. *Input subsidies*   Input subsidies were an important means of supporting the agricultural sector in Greece before accession. Subsidization of input prices started with fertilizers in 1953 and was later extended to

animal feed, pesticides and improved seeds. The deficits from the subsidized input prices were covered by the budget. Electricity was also supplied at lower prices and subsidies for the purchase of machinery were granted. Subsidies were also provided for processing and marketing facilities. The policy of low input prices, originally aimed at improving the productivity of the sector through technological advances, eventually became a cost-reducing device.

4. *Import restrictions and export restitutions*   Besides the measures used in the domestic market, various means for curtailing imports and promoting exports were also employed. On the import side, and in conjunction with tariffs and other duties and levies, licensing was the main measure employed. All of them were relatively low compared with the import restrictions imposed by the CAP. On the export side, restitutions were the most important means.

5. *Favourable credit conditions*   Favourable credit terms (plentiful credit with long payoff periods at subsidized interest rate) provided a strong means of supporting the agricultural sector.

Following the accession of Greece to the EC, the national policy was replaced by the CAP. Although the accession agreement provided for a five-year transition period for most of the products, prices equalized with the common CAP prices within a two-year period. Intervention buying-in to support market prices, direct subsidies to farmers and exports restitutions to close the gap between Community and world market prices, have been kept in place, albeit at higher levels. Subsidies on inputs were gradually abolished. Import duties levied on products for which a common policy existed were adapted to the common EC tariff rates at the time of accession (extended to seven years for peaches and tomatoes), while for the remaining products tariffs were gradually adjusted within a five-year period and are only applied to imports from third countries. It should be noted that the import restriction schemes implemented by the preexisting policy was generally low compared with that adopted by the CAP. Certain products, known as basic products (cereals, beef meat, dairy products) and to some extent olive oil, are highly protected by variable levies, while the protection for Mediterranean products[3] is realized mainly through tariffs and is relatively low or non-existent particularly after the Uruguay Round Agreement. However, the total average protection from tariffs and variable levies was increased from 15 per cent of gross value added in agriculture before accession (1979) to 30 per cent after accession in 1985 (Georgakopoulos 1988). Farmers' subsidies were harmonized within the same period as prices, so that, in fact, farmers have received the full subsidies provided by the CAP since 1982. Finally, the favourable credit terms were gradually abolished. On one hand this is due to the economic stabilization programme (designed to bring about a reduction in budget deficits and internal and external borrowing) initiated by the Greek government in the mid-1980s and on the other to the liberalization of the banking system since the late 1980s.

3 Support of agricultural incomes

Greece's accession to the EU has led to a significant increase of national and EAGGF transfers to the agricultural sector (Table 7.1). Although the national expenditures increased in absolute terms they decreased as a percentage of gross value added in agriculture. On the contrary, receipts from the EAGGF rose in both absolute and relative terms, leading to a substantial increase of agricultural incomes. While the total support of agricultural incomes was 16.3 per cent of gross agricultural value added in 1980, it reached 49.7 per cent in 1994. Of this, the national contribution was 9.7 per cent and the remaining 40 per cent from the EAGGF Guarantee Section. These percentages make clear the huge contribution of the CAP in support of Greek farmers' incomes.

In order to evaluate the total income gain to the Greek farmers, in addition to the financial gain in the form of direct or indirect subsidies, the income gain from external protection must be calculated. This gain results from the increased prices, compared to world prices, which are enjoyed by the Greek farmers due to the external protection provided by the CAP. This income gain comes chiefly from the EAGGF Guarantee Section budget, a smaller part from the national budget and the remaining part is borne by EU consumers.

It is clear that the income of Greek farmers depends upon the price support mechanisms and upon the external protective measures of the CAP, so much so that, in certain areas of Greece, in which agriculture is still the largest source of income, the continuation of the CAP support mechanisms seems to be a precondition for the survival of the entire local economy.

Subsidies for the basic agricultural products are shown in Table 7.2. It is noticeable that the degree of protection for most of the agricultural products follows an upward trend, with the exception of soft wheat and beef meat. For certain products, such as sugar, olive oil, tobacco, sheep- and goatmeat, the increase in protection was impressive.

4 Agricultural production and productivity

The volume of agricultural production increased by an average annual rate of 0.8 per cent during the 1980–94 period (Table 7.3). Real prices of final agricultural output increased significantly in the first years after accession

Table 7.1 Financial support from national and EU sources to the Greek agricultural sector (billion drachmas)

Year	Gross value added in agriculture	Expenditure from the EAGGF guarantee sector		National expenditure		Total expenditure	
		Amount	As percentage of gross value added in agriculture (%)	Amount	As percentage of gross value added in agriculture (%)	Amount	As percentage of gross value added in agriculture (%)
1980	205	—	—	40.8	16.3	40.8	16.3
1981	303	9.0	3.0	85.2	28.1	94.2	31.1
1982	381	44.6	11.7	80.1	21.0	124.7	32.7
1983	414	76.3	18.4	65.5	15.8	141.8	34.2
1984	539	84.1	15.6	73.4	13.6	157.5	29.2
1985	665	120.9	18.2	114.3	17.2	235.2	35.4
1986	753	187.8	25.0	117.5	15.6	305.3	40.6
1987	801	204.8	25.6	113.1	14.1	317.9	39.7
1988	945	217.1	23.0	127.9	13.5	345.0	36.5
1989	1129	286.7	25.4	160.5	14.2	447.2	39.6
1990	1141	373.4	32.7	216.3	19.0	589.7	51.7
1991	1619	476.8	29.5	204.0	12.6	680.8	42.1
1992	1574	528.0	33.5	195.0	12.4	723.0	45.9
1993	1596	709.0	44.4	225.7	14.1	934.7	58.5
1994	1924	768.0	40.0	187.5	9.7	955.5	49.7

Source: Ministry of Agriculture.

Table 7.2   Financial support to the basic agricultural products (as percentage of their gross value added)

Products	1978	1980	1981	1982	1985	1992
1. Cereals	29.6	18.9	13.0	19.2	8.2	21.3
(wheat)	(28.8)	(14.2)	(4.4)	(18.5)	(12.2)	—
2. Sugar	40.9	88.6	56.2	46.7	85.5	—
3. Fruit and vegetables	7.3	9.0	8.1	22.2	23.0	17.6
4 Wine	3.0	5.2	2.4	20.3	35.5	9.9
5. Olive products	8.7	—	9.0	18.3	15.1	100.6
(olive oil)	(9.3)	—	(10.4)	(11.6)	(15.4)	(122.3)
6. Industrial crops	23.4	29.1	22.8	66.3	56.7	75.2
a. Tobacco	32.5	42.8	18.0	89.4	74.0	109.8
b. Cotton	11.8	11.4	29.1	32.1	39.7	59.1
7. Meat	2.5	—	—	0.2	1.5	12.9
a. Beef	10.0	—	—	0.8	3.0	4.5
b. Sheep–goat	—	—	—	—	2.3	33.5
c. Others	0.1	—	—	—	—	—
8. Dairy products	1.7	—	—	0.2	1.1	0.9

Sources: Ministry of Agriculture; Georgakopoulos and Zanias (1995).

and then followed a downward trend which became more pronounced after the reform of the CAP[4] in 1992.

The value of agricultural output follows a similar evolution to that of producer prices. With regard to the evolution of the index of relative prices received and paid by farmers, an upward trend appears now, which becomes steeper after 1985 (Figure 7.1). This trend is reversed after 1994, a development which Greece shares with other EU countries. It is also worth mentioning that per capita agricultural income has substantially improved despite some cyclical fluctuation in agricultural production. Specifically, the index of real per capita agricultural income has risen from 73.6 in 1980 to more than 100 in 1994. This was due to the rapid increase of subsidies granted through the support mechanisms of the CAP, as can be seen in Table 7.2. These subsidies are incorporated into the producer prices and thus increase the value of the agricultural product and, consequently, of agricultural incomes. Moreover, agricultural income per person employed in farming as a percentage of income enjoyed by the average Greek worker has risen from 56.6 per cent in the early 1980s to 71 per cent a decade later (Georgakopoulos and Zanias 1995).

Table 7.3 Evaluation of agricultural production, prices and value added, volume and prices of intermediate consumption, terms of trade and agricultural income (average 1989–1991 = 100)

Year	Volume index of final agricultural production	Price index of final agricultural product		Value index of final agricultural product		Volume index of intermediate consumption in agriculture	Price index of intermediate consumption in agriculture		'Terms of trade' index in agriculture[1]	Agricultural income[2] index
		Nominal	Real	Nominal	Real		Nominal	Real		
1980	93.5	20.5	109.6	19.2	102.5	86.2	21.5	114.6	95.5	73.6
1981	94.2	24.8	110.6	23.4	104.2	88.9	26.2	116.8	94.7	77.9
1982	96.0	30.1	107.3	28.9	103.0	90.5	30.1	107.4	99.9	80.0
1983	92.1	35.5	106.1	32.7	97.7	93.6	37.2	111.2	95.3	72.7
1984	94.7	43.9	109.1	41.6	103.4	93.1	44.4	110.4	98.8	79.0
1985	98.8	51.7	109.4	51.2	108.1	96.2	52.7	111.3	98.3	81.1
1986	97.8	58.8	105.7	57.5	103.5	90.5	61.3	110.3	95.8	80.2
1987	96.5	64.7	101.8	62.4	98.2	95.1	67.5	106.2	95.8	80.7
1988	100.8	72.5	98.7	73.1	99.5	96.3	76.2	103.8	95.0	82.0
1989	105.1	81.8	99.1	86.1	104.2	99.6	82.8	100.2	98.9	99.6
1990	90.9	99.7	99.9	90.6	90.8	100.0	98.8	99.0	100.8	85.8
1991	104.0	118.5	101.0	123.3	105.0	100.4	118.4	100.9	101.1	114.5
1992	101.7	121.3	90.0	123.5	91.5	102.0	135.1	100.2	89.8	92.5
1993	100.4	130.0	84.9	130.6	85.2	106.3	145.4	94.9	89.4	91.1
1994	104.1	147.2	86.8	153.3	90.4	107.4	157.1	92.6	93.7	101.1

Notes:
1. It derives as the ratio of the nominal price index of final agricultural product to the price index of intermediate consumption in agriculture.
2. It derives as the ratio of value added at constant prices per annual work units.

Source: Eurostat.

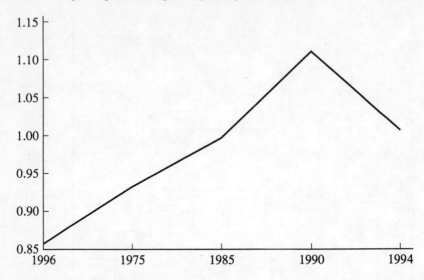

Source: National Statistical Service of Greece.

Figure 7.1   Ratio of prices received and paid by farmers (1985 = 100)

Despite the small increase in total agricultural output, the production of some agricultural products increased significantly after accession. This can be attributed to various factors, the most important of which is the different degree of support provided by the mechanisms of the CAP. Thus, production of hard wheat, cotton and sugar beet rose significantly because of the efficient level of support provided by the CAP (Table 7.4), while the increase in maize can be traced to the doubling of yields following the introduction of hybrid seeds in the late 1970s and early 1980s (Baltas 1987). In contrast, production of soft wheat, barley and tobacco[5] (after the reform of the CAP) fell because of the decreasing degree of support, while beef production decreased because of the implementation of the Monetary Compensatory Amounts (MCAs) mechanism which came to an end at the beginning of 1993. Finally, production of other products such as wine, olive oil, sheepmeat, and so on remained relatively constant.

Average labour productivity in agriculture shows an upward trend compared to the other sectors of the economy. Specifically, during the 1980–94 period, labour productivity in agriculture increased at constant prices by an average annual rate of 2.6 per cent against 0.2 per cent for the other sectors of the economy, resulting in a narrowing of the gap between the two (Figure 7.2). Despite this increase, labour productivity in Greek agriculture is far behind that of the EU12, since the ratio is 2:1. In any case,

Table 7.4 Volume of production and producer prices for basic agricultural products

Products	Volume (1980–81)	Prices 1980	Volume (1992–93)	Prices 1993	Average annual variation	
	(000 T)	(Dr/Kg)	(000 T)	(Dr/Kg)	Volume	Prices
Soft wheat	2235	9.8	828	43.6	−7.4	12.2
Hard wheat	714	13.9	1251	46.9	4.4	9.8
Barley	782	9.4	451	42.5	−4.1	12.3
Maize	1392	9.4	2191	46.5	2.9	13.1
Wine	546	10.0	522	79.7	−0.4	17.3
Olive oil	287	97.8	285	639.7	−0.1	15.5
Tobacco	124	123.0	84	1114.0	−3.0	18.5
Cotton	370	33.0	931	290.0	7.4	18.2
Sugar beet	2108	1.9	2901	11.9	2.5	15.2
Beef	97	147.3	76	987.0	−1.8	15.8
Sheepmeat	80	197.2	82	984.1	0.2	13.2
Pork	144	97.8	147	495.6	0.2	13.3
Goatmeat	39	103.6	47	1107.4	1.4	20.0
Poultry	145	65.9	171	474.7	1.3	16.4
Milk	1710	15.2	185	140.6	0.6	18.7

Sources: Ministry of Agriculture; Georgakopoulos and Zanias (1995).

these improvements in labour productivity are mainly due to the rapid decrease of the agricultural labour force (at an average annual rate of −2.1 for the period).

Individual increases in the yields of some agricultural products are largely attributable to improvements in genetic material and to increased use of fertilizers and other inputs. However, this increase in the use of inputs was not accompanied by structural transformation[6] and technological improvement in the methods of production. This is primarily due to the stagnation of investment, as much on the part of the state as on the part of the farmers themselves. The reasons for the fluctuation of public investment around the level of 2.5 billion drachmas annually (at constant 1970 prices) may be sought in the overall decrease in public investment as a result of the budgetary crisis and the priority given to consumption expenditure in order to ensure social peace and the electoral survival of the governments of the day. The slowdown in private investment to an average annual decrease of 3.7 per cent (at constant 1970 prices), in spite of the increased financial support from the EAGGF, is explained by the tighter credit policies of the Agricultural Bank of Greece, the rising level of

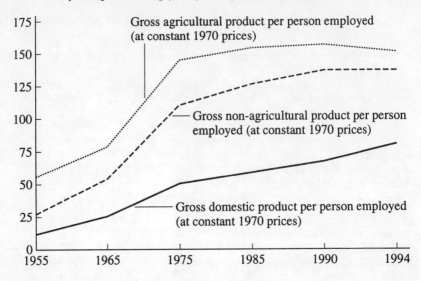

Source: National Accounts and National Statistical Service of Greece.

Figure 7.2   Labour productivity of agricultural and non-agricultural sectors

interest rates in the 1980s, farmers' expectations of a drop in anticipated real incomes and, in some cases, to lower public investment (Baltas 1996). The large increase in real agricultural interest rates is the result of the tight credit policy that was followed and is due on the one hand to the efforts made to cut public deficits and public debt and on the other hand to the gradual liberalization of the banking system following Greece's entry into the EC. It seems likely that demographic factors, such as the ageing of the agricultural labour force and the reluctance of farmers' children to take up farming (characteristically, only one-third of existing farm heads have heirs) have also played a negative role in the large drop observed in agricultural investment.

5   Impact on the trade in agricultural products
Agricultural trade flows were substantially affected as a result of the application of the CAP. The new regime brought about a substantial trade diversion and a shift of imports from third countries to EU countries. This reorientation was associated with higher import prices, which contributed to the trade deficits while they also reinforced the inflationary trends in the economy, especially during the early 1980s. Thus, Greece traditionally had a positive agricultural balance of trade which turned

negative after the accession, representing 5.6 per cent of the total trade deficit (1994).

In particular, while the ratio of exports of agricultural products to imports with the EC was 1.4 prior to the country's accession, this ratio had dropped during the next decade to 0.72 by 1990 (Maraveyas 1994), turning Greece into a deficit country in agricultural products as a result of the freeing of imports from the other member countries and of its inability to improve the farming sector's performance by producing cheaper and better-quality agricultural products that could compete with those of the countries in the national as well as in the world markets.

The trade diversion can also be explained by another reason. Because of competitive disadvantage, Greece runs a deficit, mainly in beef and dairy products. Because of Community preference, since its accession into the EU, Greece has been importing these products from the EU countries at prices considerably higher than world prices. Thus, the variable levies imposed on imports from third countries led to trade diversion and to a heavy redistribution of wealth from Greek consumers to EU producers. Moreover, the increase in the volume of imports, coming from the northern countries, was reinforced by changes in the composition of food consumption in Greece over the last four decades. The shares of meat and milk in total food consumption have increased from 20 per cent in 1950 to 44 per cent in 1990. On the other hand, the shares of traditional Greek products such as bread and olives have been reduced from 26 per cent in 1950 to 11.5 per cent in 1990. This evolution is explained by the fact that milk and meat are products of high income elasticity. In contrast, Greece has a large surplus in fruit and vegetables, which, however, it cannot export at high prices because of the low protection afforded to these products. Moreover, Community preference for these products is very limited because of the preferential agreements which the EU has signed with other non-EU Mediterranean countries.

Nevertheless, the agricultural trade balance with third countries initially improved, thanks to export subsidies by the EAGGF Guarantee Section, before gradually turning negative.

6   Conclusions

Greece's accession to the EU impacted on the agricultural sector in several ways, mainly due to the replacement of the national policies applied prior to 1981 by the CAP. The new policy has improved agricultural incomes through subsidies and the other support mechanisms of the CAP.

Agricultural labour productivity has increased faster than that of the non-agricultural sector, mainly as a consequence of the out-migration of farming population rather than the rise of agricultural output. This was to be expected given that the CAP mechanisms concentrate on price support rather than the improvement of agricultural structures. Moreover, the limited financial sources devoted to structural improvements were often diverted to other purposes (Louloudis et al. 1991). It is also likely that efforts for the structural and institutional modernization of Greek agriculture on the part of the state and farmers' cooperative movement were blunted by the relatively generous income support policy of the CAP.

The implementation of the CAP had a significant impact on the composition of the agricultural products because of the different degree of support provided for various products. Thus, it favoured the typical Mediterranean products (durum wheat, cotton, sunflower seeds, and so on) at the expense of animal products (beef, dairy products), soft wheat, barley, and so on, as a result of increased competition from EU member countries after the liberalization of trade in agricultural products. On the other hand, the traditional surplus in the agricultural trade balance turned into a deficit because of trade diversion and a shift of imports from third countries to EU countries.

The foregoing analysis makes it clear that the agricultural and overall economic policy framework will be significantly different in the future. The convergence criteria of the Maastricht Treaty and further liberalization of the financial system will undoubtedly influence the Greek agricultural sector. Specifically, the liberalization of the banking system, which started in the 1980s, will raise the cost of production, despite the expected reduction in nominal and real interest rates that constitute one of the preconditions for convergence.

Moreover, the reform of the CAP, which started in 1992, will continue and will affect other products in which Greece has a particular interest, such as fruit and vegetables, cotton, olive oil and wine. Thus, although the initial reform had little impact,[7] except in the case of tobacco producers, on critical Greek farm products, this will not hold in the planned future reform. Thus, the future CAP reform in conjunction with the GATT Agreement[8] and the enlargement of the EU with Central and Eastern European countries[9] will lead to an unavoidable reduction in the degree of protection afforded to Greek agriculture. Moreover, the ability to reinforce real agricultural incomes through the devaluation of the green drachma, as happened in the past, has been restricted by the Maastricht Treaty (Baltas 1992).

Following the reform, direct payments became essential to numerous farms, including the most successful ones. Yet, the degree of production efficiency and the weight of the financial charges remained a major determinant of financial results and of the farms' ability to adapt to this new situation. The maintenance of the various compensatory payments beyond the transitory period initially envisaged by the reform is indispensable in order to guarantee the survival of most farms in Greece and the other peripheral countries of the Union. Otherwise, some of the more prosperous EU countries are likely to continue to press for the 'renationalization' of the CAP in order to avoid further reductions in farmers' incomes due to the decreasing protection that the reformed CAP will provide. Given the relatively large size of Greece's agriculture and the inability of the Greek government to provide the necessary subsidies, this prospect will be detrimental to Greek interests. To counter this, the necessary measures will have to be taken for the sector's structural and institutional modernization. This will allow the production of cheaper, better-quality agricultural products, thus improving the international competitiveness of Greek agriculture. Moreover, a new reorientation of agricultural production is required in order to change drastically the ratio of crop to livestock production, which is now approximately 69:31, in favour of the latter. This will improve the degree of self-sufficiency in livestock products, limit exchange outflows and increase the employment and income prospects of the rural population on a permanent basis.

The accompanying measures, particularly the one concerning early retirement for older farmers, appear to be the most positive aspect of the reformed CAP. This is not only because the potential transfers to Greece are large, through the increase of the contribution of the EU's budget, but also because this structural measure, in combination with a restrictive price policy, might mean lower land values which will facilitate land acquisition and lead to larger average farm sizes. In fact, the sector's structural adjustment should create the necessary conditions for maintaining the maximum number of viable farms in the wider rural economy. However, it should be pointed out that more than half of Greek farmers are over 55 years old and nearly half of these have no successors. Also, the weak state of the Greek economy and the gloomy prospects for job opportunities outside agriculture, coupled with the large proportion of 'less-favoured' regions in the farming sector, form a serious obstacle to such an adjustment. In this respect, the increased support for less-favoured regions and the structural measures aimed at the creation of alternative sources of income for people who abandon farming or for part-time farmers assume tremendous importance (Caraveli 1993). Finally, the accompanying measures might promote afforestation and protection of the 'less-favoured' and environmentally sensitive areas, resulting in the maintenance of a minimum but sufficient human population in such areas which will be capable of ensuring the protection of the natural environment and hence the future of the countryside.

Notes

1. The impact of implementation of CAP on Greek agriculture has been examined by various studies such as Georgakopoulos (1988 and 1990), Demoussis and Sarris (1988), Georgakopoulos and Paschos (1990), Zanias (1992), Caraveli (1993) and Maraveyas (1994).
2. Deficiency payments are provided to bridge the gap between the intervention and the world market price.
3. European Agricultural Guidance and Guarantee Fund (EAGGF) expenditure was traditionally dominated by the support provided to the northern member countries of the EU. 'Too much' was produced of 'northern commodities' which received 'above-average protection'. The 'southern commodities' (that is, fruit, vegetables, olive oil, cotton, wine, sheep- and goatmeat and tobacco) have traditionally played a minor role in the history, and certainly in the cost of the CAP. Conversely, CAP expenditure has traditionally been greatest for the northern commodities (that is, milk, sugar, beef and veal). After Spain's and Portugal's accession, Mediterranean commodities (in particular, olive oil, peaches, wine, cotton, tobacco, and so on) have become more noticeable in terms of CAP expenditure.
4. The reform implies a major shift in emphasis from price support to forms of farm support not directly linked to production. The substantial reduction in the prices of agricultural products to make them more competitive both within the Community and on world markets is compensated for by hectare or headage payments based on historic data and thus not directly linked to the quantities produced. In addition, new instruments have supplemented, existing ones namely:

   - implementation of measures to limit the use of the factors of production (set aside of arable land and stocking rate criteria) alongside the retention of earlier supply management measures such as the milk production quotas;
   - introduction of accompanying measures such as promotion of environmentally friendly farming, afforestation and early retirement.

   The reform covers 75 per cent of agricultural production falling under common market organizations (that is cereals, oilseeds, protein crops, tobacco, milk, beef and sheepmeat) and is being phased in over the three marketing years 1993/94 to 1995/96.
5. This reform introduces a quota system for the first time reducing the global maximum quantity and the number of the group of recognized varieties of tobacco from 34 to 8. Greek farmers had significant losses because of the country's relatively large tobacco production (a little less than half of the total EU output). This reduction is significant for certain varieties such as flue-cured tobacco produced in Greece, which fell from 71 526 tonnes in 1992 to 37 921 tonnes in 1993, that is a reduction by 47 per cent. Moreover, since tobacco production is localized, this implies that net per farm losses in some regions were much larger than average.
6. Accession has hardly affected the poor structure of Greek agriculture. Average farm size is 4.35 hectares of arable land, farm fragmentation is prevalent with 5.9 land parcels per farm scattered in different localities, irrigated arable land is 31.6 per cent of the arable and farm employment accounts for 21 per cent of the total. Obviously, the funds directed to structural programmes were unable to bring about significant improvement.
7. The redistributive effects of the CAP reform for cereals are minor. This limited redistribution of support operates to the advantage of the Mediterranean countries where low yields and poor farm size structures are the norm. In the milk sector, the increase of quotas for Greece has a positive effect on milk production and farmers' incomes, while in the beef sector the situation has remained the same. in the sheep–goat sector no significant change occurred in the level of output and farm income. The reform entails substantial consumer gains which are proportionally higher in the south, particularly for the poorer households (Baltas 1995). Zanias and Maraveyias (1996) provide quantitative results on the cohesion impact on the CAP among member states. Greece increased slightly its overall benefits from the operation of the CAP in 1994 – essentially

the first post-reform year – compared to the previous five years. The benefits arise from the direct budgetary payments to producers and Greece's low contribution to the EU budget. Otherwise, Greece loses out from intra-EU trade and nearly breaks even from extra-EU trade. The losses from trade are associated with the lower protection rate for its exports (mainly fruit and vegetables) and the higher ones for its agricultural imports (mainly livestock products).

8. The GATT Agreement on agriculture imposes disciplines on member countries in three separate areas: domestic support, market access and export subsidies. The essence of the agreement on agriculture is as follows:

- *Domestic support* Domestic subsidies in the agricultural sector are to be reduced by 20 per cent over six years (13.3 per cent in developing countries). The calculation is made on the base year 1986–88 using the Aggregate Method of Support (AMS), which takes all products globally. For the European Community, this part of the agreement has never been an issue because the various reforms in CAP since 1988 mean that the Community's current total AMS is already more than 20 per cent below the reference figures for 1986–88. The impact of the CAP reform – notably the substantial cut in cereals support prices – will ensure that the AMS stays well below its target level throughout the coming six years.
- *Market access* All import restrictions are converted to customs tariffs (by 'tariffication'). These tariffs are reduced by 36 per cent over a period of 6 years with a minimum reduction of 15 per cent for each agricultural product and for developing countries by 24 per cent over 10 years, using as base for the calculations the 1986–88 period. In order to ensure at least some degree of market opening in all sectors, the GATT Agreement requires each country to make 'minimum access' provisions. Under these arrangements, import opportunities must be opened for the equivalent of 3 per cent of internal consumptions, rising by the end of the 6-year period. Any country may take steps to limit the imports of a product which is specified as being the subject of a concession in order to prevent markets being damaged by a surge of imports, either in terms of their volume or their low price.
- *Export subsidies* The volume of subsidies exports is to be reduced by 21 and 14 per cent for developing countries over 6 years (base period 1986–90). Budgetary expenditure on export subsidies will simultaneously have to be reduced by 36 and 24 per cent for developing countries over 6 years.

It has been argued that the Uruguay Round Agreement on agricultural trade will not lead to a drastic opening of the EU in the 6-year implementation period. However, for fruit, vegetables and wine, Greek producers are likely to face increased competition in the EU markets.

9. The EU's eastward enlargement will result in an increase of the EU's agricultural population and land by 90 and 39 per cent, respectively. In the six Central and Eastern European countries the share of agriculture in GDP ranges from 4.5 to 21 per cent. Concerning the budgetary implications of the enlargement, various estimates have been made which differ substantially between them, ranging from ECU 5 to 50 billion depending on the assumptions used to develop alternative scenarios. According to EU estimates (CEC 1995), the cost of enlargement will require a 25 per cent increase of the current level of the CAP budget, which is equal to ECU 36 billion.

Regarding the future shape of the CAP in the enlarged EU, the recent intense debate has been polarized between those who argue that it is neither feasible nor desirable to extend the CAP to the prospective entrants and those who say that it is both manageable and acceptable. However, the considerable disparities in structure and performance between the economies of the two regions are likely to create many problems for accession. Budgetary constraints will remain a major issue, forcing a new CAP reform as well as antagonism between the eventual new member states and the existing ones. This probably will be the case especially for the southern EU members, if a major redistribution of the already scarce structural funds is to take place. On the other hand, the complementary character of the Central and Eastern European and the southern EU agricultural sectors will result in an expanded potential market for Mediterranean products. Besides, a new reform of the CAP due to the eastward enlargement will benefit consumers.

Concerning the issue of appropriate adjustment of the Central and Eastern European countries' agricultural policies to the CAP it should be noted that the CAP ensures producer prices which are considerably higher for most products. For the CEECs, this will result in an increase of output for many of their products and a fall in consumption. In addition, raising internal prices above world prices would create a need for applying export subsidies which may not be in line with the GATT Agreement (Moutsatsos and Tikof 1995).

References

Baltas, C.N. (1987), 'Supply Response for Greek Cereals', *European Review of Agricultural Economics*, **14**, 195–220.

Baltas, C.N. (1992), 'The Effects of Adjustment of the Green Drachma to its Current Exchange Rate', *Agricultural Economics*, **7**, 225–43.

Baltas, C.N. (1996), 'Interactions between Agricultural Credit and Private Investment: Empirical Evidence and Policy Implications', in C. Paraskevopoulos, R. Grinspun and T. Georgakopoulos (eds), *Economic Integration and Public Policy in the European Union*, Aldershot, UK: Edward Elgar, pp. 260–72.

Baltas, C.N. (1997), 'The Restructured CAP and the Periphery of the EU', *Food Policy*, **22** (4), 329–43.

Caraveli, H. (1993), 'The Perspective of 1992/93 and Greek Agriculture', *Food Policy*, **18** (5), 394–402.

Commission of the European Communities (CEC) (1995). *Agricultural Strategy Paper*, CSE (95) 607. Brussels, November 1995.

Demoussis, M. and A. Sarris (1988), 'Greek Experience under the CAP: Lessons and Outlook', *European Review of Agricultural Economics*, **15**, 89–107.

Georgakopoulos, T. (1988), 'The Impact of Accession on Agricultural Income in Greece', *European Review of Agricultural Economics*, **15**, 79–88.

Georgakopoulos, T. (1990), 'The Impact of Accession on Food Prices, Inflation and Food Consumption in Greece', *European Review of Agricultural Economics*, **17**, 485–93.

Georgakopoulos, T. and P. Paschos (1990), *Greek Agriculture and the EEC*, Athens: Agricultural Bank of Greece (in Greek).

Georgakopoulos, T. and G. Zanias (1995), 'Primary Production Sector', in A. Kindis, *2004: The Greek Economy at the Turn of the 21st Century*, Athens: Ionian Bank, pp. 465–523 (in Greek).

Louloudis, L., N. Maraveyas and N. Martinos (1991), 'The Social Dimension of the CAP', Congress in Memory of S. Karagiorgas at Panteion University, 27–29 November, Athens.

Maraveyas, N. (1994), 'The Common Agricultural Policy and Greek Agriculture', in P. Kazakos and P. Ioakimidis (eds), *Greece and EC Membership Evaluated*, London: Pinter.

Moutsatsos, D. and M. Tikof (1995), 'The Impact of CAP Reform and the European Union Enlargement on the Trade of Mediterranean Products: A View from Greece', International Centre for Advanced Mediterranean Agronomic Studies Seminar on GATT and Agricultural Trade, Mediterranean Agronomic Institute of Chania, Greece, 3–5 December.

Zanias, G. (1992), 'Farm Price Movements and the Adjustment Problem in Greek Agriculture', *Oxford Agrarian Studies*, **20**, 63–71.

Zanias, G. and N. Maraveyias (1996), 'The Impact of the Common Agricultural Policy (CAP) on Cohesion among EU Member States', International Conference on Economic Integration in Transition, Athens University of Economics and Business and York University, Athens, 21–24 August.

8 Economic integration and development: the case of the EU

Eleni Paliginis

1 Introduction

This chapter will examine the process and outcome of economic integration within the European Union (EU). Economic integration refers to a more advanced cooperation between countries, going beyond the level of free trade. It encompasses the free movement of commodities, labour and capital, the existence of common policies and the gradual withering away of the national state with the partial transfer of sovereignty to a supranational body, in this case the European Union. This transformation of the EU, the most important one in recent years, is expected to have profound effects on all member states. The scope of this chapter is to concentrate on the peripheral countries of the EU (Greece, Portugal, Ireland, Spain), and to examine the effects of economic integration and the possibilities for development and catching up within this new politico-economic environment.

Since its conception in 1957, as the European Economic Community (EEC), the EU has undergone a series of transformations, both widening membership and deepening integration. This process culminated with the creation of the single European market (SEM) in 1992 and the plans for European Monetary Union (EMU) in 1999. Both the SEM and the EMU were strongly influenced by the overall ideological shift of the 1980s, that is, the increasing emphasis on market forces. This was partly balanced by substantial Community assistance to the peripheral countries in the form of *Structural and Cohesion Funds*. The SEM involved the removal of all internal restrictions to the movement of commodities, capital and labour. Unequal industrial structures, weak financial markets and lack of institutional thickness were leaving the EU periphery more exposed to these changes. The assistance from the Community was intended to improve the competitiveness of the periphery and assist the process of catching up.

In Section 2 there will be a discussion of theoretical and empirical work on the growth of the EU; this will be followed by a discussion of the policies and outcomes of European economic integration and a discussion of domestic and EU policies for convergence. A final section summarizes and concludes the argument.

2 Theoretical aspects of growth and convergence in the EU

Although the free movement of goods, labour and capital was one of the original aims of the EEC, this process was only finally concluded in 1992 with the SEM. It represented a most important impetus to industrial restructuring. The openness of the internal market, its protection from outside competition through tariffs, together with the existence of a large, prosperous and sophisticated consuming population, were expected to increase the competitiveness of the European *vis-à-vis* Japanese and US capital. Economic integration was expected to have dynamic effects. Economies of scale could strengthen further the already strong companies, enhancing their competitiveness within a global environment. The potential effects of such integration were estimated using different variations of growth models.

In a Solow-type growth model with a Cobb–Douglas production function (showing constant returns and diminishing marginal productivity), it is shown that, in the long term, growth per person is independent of the rate of investment. As a result of capital accumulation, poor countries tend to grow faster than rich ones until they reach the steady-state growth rate of output and capital. In a variation of this model incorporating technical progress, growth per person is proportional to the rate of growth of *total factor productivity*, TFP.

$$Y = TK^a L^b$$

where $a + b = 1$ and $0 < a < 1$ and $T =$ TFP. Further, as an expansion of TFP will require changes in technology which is exogenously determined, growth is also exogenously determined. As technology was assumed to be universally available, the rate of change of TFP was the same in all countries. In this variation of Solow's model, *convergence* between countries is also feasible as a result of capital accumulation and diminishing returns.

According to Romer's (1986) endogenous growth model there are externalities arising out of the use of capital. Diminishing returns exist, but only at firm level. The existence of externalities to capital implies that capital accumulation will not lead to diminishing returns overall and therefore it could permanently alter the rate of growth. TFP levels and growth rates could differ between countries. There are two important implications of this model. First, as there are no necessarily diminishing returns at a national level, developed economies could experience faster rates of growth than poorer countries, leading to divergence rather than convergence. Second, there is scope for government policies. Policies on education, R&D and subsidies to industries as well as institutional changes could affect permanently the rate of growth, while state or EU policies could reverse the trends towards divergence. Thus, Baumol et al. (1994) argue that whether convergence will take place or not depends on the level of human capital and the ability to assimilate and take advantage of modern technology. Countries satisfying these criteria are a part of the *convergence club*, while for the very poor and backward countries possibilities for convergence do not apply.

In an earlier contribution, Myrdal, in his theory of cumulative causation (1963), discussed the lack of automatic forces leading to convergence between core and periphery. In this model, spatial differences do not disappear over time. Capital and labour tend to migrate towards the prosperous regions. Dynamic economies of scale lead to increasing returns in the developed economies, aggravating the initial disequilibrium between core and periphery. Kaldor (1972) sees that dynamic increasing returns to scale induce higher productivity and rate of growth in the faster-growing economies, making it progressively harder for the others to catch up. According to Kaldor, the engine of growth is the manufacturing sector, as this is the only one which could generate increasing returns.

Cecchini (1988), basing his analysis in a traditional growth theory model, estimated, on behalf of the Commission, the micro and macro effects of the SEM. At the micro level he argued that the elimination of barriers, increased competition and the resulting economies of scale would reduce costs significantly, improve efficiency and increase innovation. At the macro level, by assuming the removal of customs unions, the opening up of procurements and the liberalization of financial services, he found impressive improvements in the medium term. They included an increase in EU GDP by 4.5 per cent, an improvement of public finances by 2.2 per cent of GDP, an increase in employment by 1.8 million and a decrease in unemployment by about 1.5 per cent. These substantial gains were of a once-and-for-all nature. The SEM could influence the level of output but not the rate of growth. Diminishing marginal productivity of capital would force it back into its original rate.

According to an *endogenous growth model*, these estimates could be a serious underestimation of the possible effects of 1992. Following a version of Romer's endogenous growth theory, Baldwin (1989) argued that Cecchini grossly underestimated the potential effects of 1992. As a result of the single market and economies of scale, the output–capital ratio will increase and, given a constant savings rate, there will be an increase in the level of savings, investment and capital stock. Within, this new growth model, Baldwin's estimates of the medium-term potential gains from the SEM are even more impressive, standing at between 3.5 and 9 per cent of EU GDP. Further, with this Romer-type model, it is possible to have a permanent effect on the rate of growth as capital accumulation could keep rising indefinitely. For convergence to take place the periphery will have to grow at a faster rate than the core, and there is nothing in this model to guarantee it. On the contrary, the concentration of centres for R&D and human capital in the core economies, will intensify the tendencies towards divergence.

3   Economic integration of the periphery

The fast industrialization of the nineteenth century and the subsequent Fordist developments in the twentieth century did not encompass the periphery of the EU. They were not only geographically on the periphery of Europe, but they lagged behind in the ongoing economic transformation. Their economies were dominated by a large and unproductive agricultural sector, a fragmented capital, serious structural problems of unemployment or underemployment and a GDP per capita lower than the EU average (Arestis and Paliginis 1993). As a result, the centres of production, banking, finance as well as research and development are entrenched in the core EU. This differentiation between core and periphery poses the question of what is the best way forward for the EU periphery.

The peripheral countries of the EU became full members in the 1980s and this led to a progressive opening of their markets. This liberalization, together with assistance from the EU, was expected to create fast rates of growth, faster than in the core EU, leading eventually to convergence. In a major recent work, Sachs and Warner (1995), discussing generally the problem of convergence, argue that the distinguishing feature between countries which converged and others which failed to do so, was the openness of their economies, that is, the extent to which trade liberalization was achieved. According to this approach, the expected outcome of economic integration for the periphery of the EU was convergence.

A closer examination of the performance of the individual peripheral economies highlights the fact that their progress and integration have followed different trajectories. Ireland's performance was the best, while for the other three the outcomes are mixed. With a rate of growth in 1995 of 5.8 per cent, and an average for the whole period of 4.5 per cent, Ireland is exhibiting a superior performance. Greece's performance has deteriorated since the 1970s (Table 8.1), experiencing an increasing divergence. Portugal and Spain do not show signs of convergence as they are growing at the same rate as the EU (Figure 8.1).

For convergence it is required that the rate of growth is substantially higher than the EU average; on this basis only Ireland satisfies this criterion Sachs and Warner (1995, p. 42) argue that in the period 1970–89 not a single open economy grew less than 2 per cent, Greece being one of the

Table 8.1 GDP and employment growth, 1960–1995

	GDP growth		Employment growth	
	1960–73	1974–95	1960–73	1974–95
Spain	7.3	2.4	0.8	−0.3
Portugal	6.9	2.6	0.02	1.1
Greece	7.7	2.1	−0.5	0.8
Ireland	4.4	4.1	0.09	0.6
EU12	4.8	2.2	0.3	0.2

Source: OECD, *Economic Outlook* (1996).

lowest with 2.38 per cent. None the less, looking at the rate of GDP growth in the period, 1960–73 and 1974–95, this argument does not hold (Table 8.1). In the period 1960–73, when they were all relatively closed economies, they all had, with the exception of Ireland, a rate of growth of GDP per capita higher than in the period 1974–95 and higher than in the EU12.

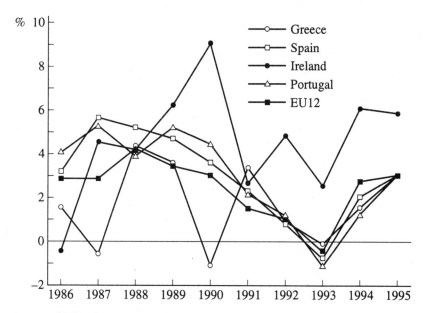

Source: OECD, *Economic Outlook* (1995).

Figure 8.1 Rate of growth of GDP, 1986–1995

From the 1960s onwards, the experience in all these countries is one of relative jobless growth (Table 8.1). The rate of growth in employment was seriously lagging behind growth in GDP.

The main aim of the SEM was to bring a profound transformation in the EU capital and strengthen its competitiveness *vis-à-vis* Japanese and US capital. This involved the restructuring of EU strategic industries such as electronics and information technology. As rational states within the EU were too small for an efficient use of funds, the SEM transcended national boundaries and created a more efficient basis for the conduct of R&D. The new policies aimed to enable winners to emerge. Research projects such as ESPRIT (European Strategic Programme for Research and Development in Information Technology) were examples of the new direction of the EU. As the companies and the research centres involved were disproportionately concentrated in the core EU countries, the expected gains from R&D had a geographical bias.

Expectations about the impending effects of 1992 had itself generated fundamental restructuring in the European capital. An increased flow of foreign direct investment (FDI) as well as a wave of mergers and acquisitions (M&A), the greatest ever across countries in the EU, occurred in the late 1980s. The impact of these policies was very much regional and had a differential effect within both the core and the periphery.

3.1   Exogenous growth

In the EU periphery, countries have adopted two different, but not necessarily mutually exclusive, approaches to development, an exogenously induced growth and a domestically centred one. The first is based on *export-led growth* policies and is influenced by the success of the *Asian Tigers*. The second concentrates in the development of their domestic firms along the line of the experience from 'third Italy'.

There is empirical evidence of a close association between economic growth and the growth of exports (World Bank 1987). Association, of course, does not imply causation and causality tests were inconclusive in this area (Jung and Marshall 1985). Explanations of the benefits accruing to exporting countries were based either on demand-led factors of a Keynesian nature or on supply-side generated effects which enhanced total factor productivity (TFP), and thus growth. The existence of a link between export and growth and the perceived role of multinational enterprises (MNEs), in this context created the wide belief that their experience could be emulated in all other places. More specifically, the potential benefits of MNEs were seen to arise out of an inflow of capital technology and expertise. These helped to bridge the gap between the requirements for development and the lack of endowments of the peripheral countries. High rates of growth, employment, improvements in the balance of payments, training of the local labour force and management are cited as the main advantages of direct investment by MNEs. It is expected that they would become *growth poles* by creating linkages with domestic capital, assisting the acquisition of skills, supporting local R&D and transferring technology, thus setting in motion Myrdal's principle of *cumulative causation*.

From the early 1970s there has been an inflow of FDI in the EU periphery. Expanding domestic markets, protected by high tariff walls, and relatively cheap labour influenced MNEs' behaviour. However, in practice, the lack of linkages with domestic capital and the lack of transfer of skills proved basic weaknesses.

Dunning (1988) in his 'eclectic theory' indicates the main determinants of FDIs as being ownership, location and internalization (the OLI factors). While the OLI factors summarize the reasons behind a company's decision to go multinational, they do not provide an overall explanation of the geographical destination of FDI. Other factors, such as the *institutional thickness* of a country, were seen as being equally important. Institutional thickness refers to a strong institutional presence in the form of financial institutions, development agencies, local authorities and so on, as well as to local, social and cultural factors which could influence growth. All of these together determine economic success (Amin and Thrift 1994).

A substantial distinction is drawn between *cost-driven* companies, which invest in the pursuit of lower production costs, and *performance* companies, which derive their advantages from product excellence and seek the appropriate location for this purpose (Amin and Tomaney 1995). The transfer of new technology, R&D and the enhancement of human capital allow the latter to play an important role in the development of the periphery, particularly if they are integrated with local capital.

The interaction of OLI factors and institutional thickness made the core EU countries very attractive locations for MNEs. The increased globalization of production in the 1980s together with the moves towards the creation of a single European market increased the multinational activities of Japanese and US capital in EU. This could be seen as a result of two main strategies by US and Japanese capital: first, an effort to protect export markets from different forms of trade barriers and second, a desire to rationalize production, as well as gain access to information and technology needed to upgrade and rationalize domestic operations. Neither US nor Japanese capital were particularly interested in low-cost operations.

Between 1986 and 1991, the four peripheral countries have collectively received 14 per cent of the total external FDI in the EU (European Commission 1994). The UK, with 46 per cent of total inward (external)

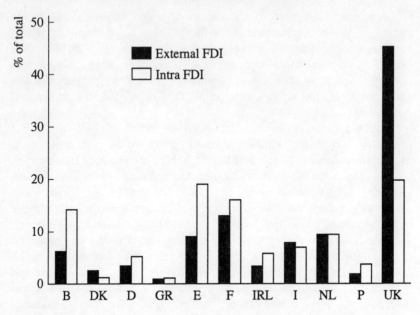

Source: Eurostat.

Figure 8.2   FDI in the EU, by member state, 1986–1991

FDI was the main beneficiary (Figure 8.2). This was despite the fact that total labour cost (wage plus non-wage costs) in 1990 was $6 an hour in Portugal, $8 in Greece, $13 in Spain and Ireland, but $16 in the UK and $24 in Germany.

It is interesting to examine more closely the behaviour of specific peripheral countries with regard to FDIs. It is apparent that Ireland was the most successful in attracting MNEs and enjoys the highest rate of growth in the EU. There was a state-driven policy since the late 1960s geared to attract MNEs to Ireland. Low corporation tax, unrestricted repatriation of profit, the provision of grants and loans as well as a young and well-educated workforce were some of the advantages. Further, both cultural affinities and the English language facilitated the penetration of MNE capital into Ireland. The main areas of operation of such firms were chemicals and the computing industry. The outcome of this penetration was the highest rate of growth, 5.8 per cent, in the EU, in contrast with a 3 per cent average for the EU and 2.8 per cent for the OECD countries. Between 1979 and 1995 the balance of trade swung from a deficit of 17 per cent to a surplus of 19 per cent of GDP, which was the result of an increase in exports from 43 to 70 per cent of GDP and a fall in imports by 10 per

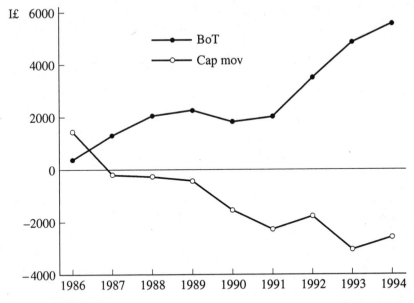

Source: OECD (1996).

Figure 8.3   Ireland's balance of trade and capital movements, 1986–1994

cent; at the same time, gross profit remittances rose from 2.8 to 14.6 per cent of GDP (Walsh 1996). The effects on the balance of payments trade balance and net capital movements are shown in Figure 8.3.

None the less, the success was not without its own problems. The inflow of capital into Ireland created a dual economy: one dominated by foreign capital, exhibiting high productivity and high rates of growth and an indigenous weak capital exhibiting low levels of productivity. State grants generously given to MNEs were depriving local firms of the necessary funds. In addition, there were few linkages between domestic and foreign capital. The expected spin-offs did not occur. MNEs did not operate like a catalyst. Further, the higher rates of unemployment in Ireland, in comparison to Portugal and Greece, may be attributed to the structure of MNEs and their operation in relatively capital-intensive areas. While clothing, textiles and footwear (labour-intensive industries) represent 23 per cent of both the Portuguese and Greek exports, in Ireland these sectors represent only 8 per cent. Chemicals and machinery (capital intensive) represent 46 per cent of exports from Ireland (Barry and Hannan 1995). The result was a rise in unemployment from 7.1 per cent in 1979 to a peak of 17.5 per cent in 1987 to 13.5 per cent in 1995, pointing to a severe case of hysteresis and the creation of dependence on MNEs.

The Culliton Report (1992) on Industrial Policy in Ireland (not implemented) aimed to establish a better balance between inward and domestic capital by switching some of the state expenditure on grants from the MNEs to the promotion and assistance of clusters of local firms.

Spain's and Portugal's incorporation into the EU in 1986 led to an increase of FDI, mostly from the EU countries. As Spain is the largest peripheral country, FDI was mostly of a *market-seeking* nature, concentrating in the already developed regions such as Madrid, Catalunya and Valencia where cost of labour was already relatively high. None the less, although labour cost increased by 30 per cent between 1986 and 1992, wages were still lower than in the core EU countries (Gual and Martin 1995).

The very low wages in Portugal (the lowest in EU) made this country attractive to *cost-reducing* FDI, mainly from the UK, while geographic peripherality and low educational achievements created problems in attracting *performance* firms. This was confirmed in a study by Amin and Tomaney (1995), which showed that most of the MNEs in Portugal, such as recent investment by Ford–VW, GM and Blaupunkt, are greenfield investment of a semi-skilled assembly nature for export purposes. There was almost a total lack of local research facilities and few linkages with domestic capital. The investment incentive for Ford–VW represented Es120 billion out of a total Es450 billion venture.

In the case of Spain and Portugal, increased multinational activity in the late 1980s coincided with a period of expansion in the EU. From 1990 onwards there is a general decline in FDI in peripheral Europe. In Spain, FDI decreased from $13 984 million in 1990 to $8144 million in 1993 (International Financial Statistics 1995). An initial upsurge of FDI in Portugal, following EU membership, was followed by a fall in FDI in the 1990s from $2610 million in 1990 to $1301 million in 1993 (ibid.). This fall was the outcome of both a depression in the EU and the changes in Central and Eastern European (CEE) countries.

In Greece, geographical peripherality and lack of *institutional thickness* are the most important factors, explaining the very small involvement of MNEs in the country. There is an outmoded financial and banking system, a political system based on favouritism and clientelism, a lack of a skilled labour force and frictional unemployment, with very high unemployment among graduates. Growth rates have remained very slow and the performance of the industrial sector has remained weak.

The varied experiences of the peripheral countries of the EU point to the fact that gains could be made by the operation of MNEs in a peripheral country if the operation takes place in a controlled and planned manner. The case of Ireland shows that the state could play a vital role in attracting

MNE capital, but local capital may be starved of funds and a dependent economy could be created.

3.2   *Domestically induced growth*

A domestically induced growth relies on harnessing domestic forces and using small and medium enterprises (SMEs) to generate growth and employment. In this model, development is based on local endowments and thus it does not antagonize local culture and customs.

While Fordism was associated with the large corporation as the engine of growth, in the post-Fordist period smaller and flexible units became viable and could generate employment and growth. The theoretical basis of this approach is the work of post-Fordist theories (Piore and Sabel 1984) and there is a heavy reliance on the experience of the regions of 'third Italy', such as Emilia-Romagna, Modena and others.

Technological changes, from the early 1970s onwards, progressively changed the scope of SMEs. Within this new environment they could respond fast to the increased frequency of market changes by producing customized products and reorganizing both labour relations and distribution networks; they could create 'niches' and exploit their uniqueness. In this sense, their 'smallness' was their advantage. In a globalized environment, they could operate on their own or in conjunction with large domestic companies and MNEs. Subcontracting and production outsourcing has become widespread among larger enterprises in the EU, both at national and international levels (European Network for SME Research 1995). Their knowledge of the 'local', their important networking and their ability to exploit the flexibility of the labour market gave them an advantage. Decentralized forms of organization of production and transfer of control from central to local government were further characteristics of this model. This was heralded as an 'endogenous' form of growth, based on the development of local resources. The outcome of the application of this approach in 'third Italy' was already impressive. In the decade of the 1970s, 65.4 per cent of employment in Emilia-Romagna was in establishments with less than 100 employees against 54.5 per cent for Italy as a whole and, per capita, money income grew annually at 1 per cent more than the Italian average (Brusco 1982).

Within the EU periphery, SMEs do not appear to have played the same role. Although they employ more employees than large-scale enterprises (LSEs), their ability to contribute to exports is small. In Spain, LSEs accounted for 7.3 per cent of all enterprises but 70 per cent of all exports (European Network for SME Research 1995). SMEs are too small and too weak to become *a growth pole*. Within a globally integrated world their role is marginal. In many cases they are the result of economic failure, rather than success.

As a result of shortcomings with both models, a third path of development has been identified. An interaction of indigenous and exogenous opportunities may be the way forward. A state/EU-based assistance of viable and dynamic domestic sectors and assistance only of MNEs with closer linkages to domestic capital and local spin-offs could greatly assist the development of the periphery. This will involve selective assistance of local industries. In the case of Ireland it was suggested that policy should aim to establish clusters of local industries in areas where there was national comparative advantage (Culliton 1992).

4 Policies for the development of the periphery

The development of the periphery depends on domestic and EU policies. Although national policies are still important in shaping the future of a country, globalization and the integration of these economies in the EU have weakened their effect. The globalization of production has led partially to the *hollowing out* of the nation-state. Monetary and fiscal policies, as well as efforts to restructure the industries, could be frustrated. Increasingly, decisions are taken at a supranational level while the openness of their economy and the impact of the SEM, MNEs and the forthcoming EMU point at the importance of decisions at Community level.

Regional policies were the main instrument followed by the EU for the development of the periphery. Structural and Cohesion Funds were used for this purpose. In 1993, the Structural and Cohesion Funds represented 3.3 per cent of GDP for Greece, 1.5 per cent for Spain, 3.1 per cent for Ireland and 3.3 per cent for Portugal. Although these EU contributions are considerable, they have not succeeded in bringing the desired effect as they are quantitatively insufficient and qualitatively not fully appropriate for the industrialization of the periphery. They concentrate on the development of the infrastructure, the development of which is a necessary but not sufficient condition for the industrialization of these countries.

The creation of viable local industry, able to survive in a competitive open world, is important for an autonomous development of the periphery. This requires the modernization of companies. The use of modern technology and appropriate R&D will allow them to innovate, upgrade their products, improve managerial skills and close the productivity gap between core and periphery. R&D does not necessarily involve original research. Peripheral countries, to the extent that they could adopt research to their indigenous needs, could have an advantage over the core countries. 'In technology or organisation, as well as in science, learning and imitating

is typically cheaper and faster than is the original discovery and testing'
(Gomulka 1987, p. 379). The effect of technology is to fuel growth but the
diffusion of it brings ultimately to an end the advantage to the innovator
(Schumpeter 1939). R&D is important for the modernization of the
peripheral economies and thus for convergence, but R&D is too expensive
for EU periphery countries to fund. R&D expenditure (which covers
Science Parks, universities, training programmes and so on) represented
in Greece 0.47 per cent of GDP, in Portugal, 0.5 per cent, Spain 0.87 per
cent and in Ireland 0.91 per cent. The EU12 average was 2 per cent
(European Commission 1994). In peripheral countries neither the state nor
the private sector can afford to fund research. Further the Structural Funds
(SF) do not correct this anomaly. Structural assistance for R&D from the
EU is skewed towards the depressed regions of core countries rather than
the periphery. While 9.3 per cent of SF, are directed towards R&D for
Objective 2 (depressed regions in core countries), Objective 1 (mainly the
peripheral EU countries and a few lagging regions from the developed
ones) receive only 2.7 per cent of SF for this purpose. In particular, R&D
represents 1 per cent of SF in Greece, 2 per cent in Spain, 2.4 per cent in
Portugal and 4 per cent in Ireland. On the other hand, the average
expenditure from the SF for R&D in the core countries is 9.3 per cent.

Similarly, examining the role of the MNEs, it became obvious that they
could assist the developmental process of these countries, but could also
create dependence. The European Commission does not have a specific
policy towards MNEs. Through its policy on tariffs and quotas and the
definition of a minimum local content, it has indirectly influenced their
behaviour but not their location. Policies to assist the location of MNEs in
the periphery, while at the same time providing a regulatory framework for
their operation, are important for the development of the periphery.

5   Conclusions

Economic integration has created mixed effects on the European periphery. Ireland has experienced fast economic growth associated with a
weakening of domestic capital, high unemployment and an increasing
dependence on FDIs. Spain and Portugal have experienced some convergence, while Greece has experienced an actual divergence. Despite the
existence of some differences, there is commonality in their experience and
interesting lessons can be derived from their integration in the EU.

Globalization and the integration of these economies in the EU have
created pressures on their domestic capital. The latter, being weak and
outmoded, finds it very difficult to compete in the world markets and even
to maintain its position in the domestic market. Endogenously induced
growth, although appealing, is likely to play a limited role within a

globalized environment. Exogenously induced growth is also problematic. Geographical peripherality and lack of appropriate institutions inhibit the attraction of MNEs to the peripheral countries, despite their lower wages. Further, the example of Ireland shows that proper state policies are important in attracting MNEs but there is a possibility of competition with local capital and the creation of a dependent parallel economy. The selective development of local, potentially strong, industries, and their interaction with MNEs should be a part of coherent state and EU policies aiming at the development of the EU periphery.

Some of the problems of these economies are difficult to address at a national level. Peripheral countries lack the economic strength and political power to instigate substantive structural changes. The EU could assist in areas such as the modernization of domestic capital and the attraction of MNEs with local linkages. An augmentation of Structural Cohesion Funds together with a more direct policy for the industrialization of the periphery could be the way forward.

References

Amin, A. and N. Thrift (1994), 'Living in the Global', in A. Amin and N. Thrift (eds), *Globalization, Institutions and Regional Development in Europe*, Oxford: Oxford University Press, pp. 1–23.

Amin, A. and J. Tomaney (1995), *Behind the Myth of European Union*, London: Routledge.

Arestis, P. and E. Paliginis (1993), 'Divergence and Peripheral Fordism in the European Community', *Journal of Economic Issues*, Vol. XXVII, **8**, 657–65.

Baldwin, R.E. (I 989), 'The Growth Effects of 1992', *Economic Policy*, **9**, 248–81.

Barry, F. and A. Hannan (1995), 'Multinationals and Indigenous Employment. An "Irish Disease"?', Working Paper 13, University College, Dublin.

Baumol, W., R. Nelson and E. Wolff (eds) (1994), *Convergence and Productivity: Cross-national Studies and Historical Evidence*, New York: Oxford University Press.

Brusco, S. (1982), 'The Emilian Model: Productive Decentralisation and Social Integration', *Cambridge Journal of Economics*, **6**, 167–84.

Cecchini, P. (1988), *The European Challenge, 1992*, Aldershot, UK: Wildwood House.

Culliton, J. (1992), *A Time for Change: Industrial Policy for the 1990s*, Report of the Industrial Policy Review Group, Dublin.

Dunning, J.H. (1988), *Explaining International Production*, London: Unwin Hyman.

European Commission (1994), *Competitiveness and Cohesion: Trends in the Regions. Fifth Periodic Report on the Social and Economic Situation and Development of the Regions in the Community*, Luxembourg.

European Network for SME Research (1995), *3rd Annual Report. The European Observatory for SMEs*. Luxembourg.

Gomulka, S. (1987), 'Catching Up', in J. Eatwell, M. Milgate and P. Newman (eds), *The New Palgrave: A Dictionary of Economics*, Vol. II, London: Macmillan, p. 379.

Gual, J. and C. Martin (1995), 'Trade and Foreign Direct Investment with Central and Eastern Europe: Its Impact on Spain', in R Faini and F. Portes, (eds), *European Union Trade with Eastern Europe*, CEPR, London: pp. 167–201.

International Financial Statistics (1995), International Monetary Fund. Washington.

Jung, W. and P. Marshall (1985), 'Exports, Growth and Causality in Developing Countries', *Journal of Development Economics*, **18**, 1–12.

Kaldor, N. (1972), The Irrelevance of Equilibrium Economics', *Economic Journal*, **82** (328), 1237–55.

Myrdal, G. (1963) *Economic Theory and Underdeveloped Regions*, London: Methuen.
OECD (various years) *Employment Outlook*, Paris: OECD.
Piore, M. and C. Sabel (1984), *The Second Industrial Divide: Possibilities for Prosperity*, New York: Basic Books.
Romer, P. (1986), 'Increasing Returns and Long Run Growth', *Journal of Political Economy*, **94** (5), 1002–37.
Sachs, J. and A. Warner (1995), 'Economic Reform and the Process of Global Integration', *Brooking Papers on Economics*, No. 1, Washington, DC, pp. 1–119.
Schumpeter, J.A. (1939), *Business Cycles*, London: McGraw Hill.
Walsh, B. (1996), 'Stabilization and Adjustment in a Small Open Economy: Ireland 1979–1995', *Oxford Review of Economic Policy*, Autumn, **12** (3), 74–87.
World Bank (1987), *World Development Report*, New York: Oxford University Press.

9 Primary convergence and European monetary integration

*Jiten Borkakoti**

1 Introduction

Economic integration is a process of fusion of economies and, therefore, represents a movement towards free trade. Economic integration can take place in various forms which, in increasing degree of integration, are (i) free trade area, (ii) customs union, (iii) common market and (iv) economic and monetary union. Each form, in principle, is independent in the sense that member countries can voluntarily choose a particular form of integration. In the case of the European Union, however, there appears to be a gradual tendency towards increasing the degree of integration in an evolutionary process. The planned move towards European Monetary Union has led to intense discussion about economic convergence which is seen as a necessary condition for monetary union. Consequently, there is a growing literature on whether the members of the European Union are converging in accordance with the Maastricht criteria. However, these criteria are not only arbitrary in character but are also nominal, and convergence of the economies of the European Union in terms of the Maastricht criteria need not necessarily reflect the true conditions in the real economy. Furthermore, attempts to achieve these criteria simultaneously may also have contradictory effects. For example, a country may have to raise its interest rate in an attempt to keep the exchange rate within the target zone, but an unfortunate consequence of a higher interest rate can be higher levels of unemployment which endogenously increases the government budget deficits as a percentage of GDP. We should also mention that the magic figure of 3 per cent (that is, budget deficits as a percentage of GDP) is not a result of serious scientific studies but rather is a figure arbitrarily chosen as a 'rule of thumb'. In addition, such a fiscal criterion is fudged[1] by excluding government expenditure on gross domestic capital formation.

This chapter argues that convergence of the nominal economic variables, while desirable, is neither necessary nor sufficient for monetary union. What seems to be important is the convergence of the real economy,

* I have benefited from comments by Alvin Birdi, Richard Eckaus and Dirk Willenbockel on an earlier draft of this chapter. Errors that remain are, however, my own responsibility. I wish to thank Andrew Ramsden and Dina Manda for excellent research assistance.

for example, capital accumulation or capital per head. The convergence of the real variables is referred to here as primary convergence, so that monetary or nominal convergence can be referred to as secondary convergence. Primary convergence is desirable in order to avoid certain genuine economic problems (for example, regional unemployment) in the single currency European Union, but again such convergence, although desirable, is neither necessary nor sufficient both in the context of the historical experience of, say, the United States or Great Britain and in the context of the current real situation between the various states of the US or the various provinces of Canada.

Section 2 analyses the argument that monetary union is a natural evolutionary development of economic union and shows how an economic union becomes non-optimal in the absence of a single currency. Section 3 discusses the concept of primary convergence and examines empirically whether primary convergence is taking place in the European Union. Section 4 discusses the feasibility of European Monetary Union, and argues that political will is more important than economic convergence. Lastly, Section 5 contains some concluding remarks.

2   A theoretical analysis of evolutionary economic integration

Assume two countries, namely, A and B, two goods, namely, x and y, and two factors, namely capital (K) and labour (L). The analysis is based on all the standard assumptions of the Heckscher–Ohlin–Samuelson model. Good x is assumed to be relatively K intensive and country A is assumed to be relatively K abundant so that country A exports good x and imports the L-intensive good, y, from country B, the relatively L-abundant country. A historically given world equilibrium exists, the equilibrium terms of trade are determined, and both countries obtain gains from trade. (This can easily be shown by the intersection of two offer curves.) Now, suppose country A begins a non-cooperative game, and imposes a tariff on imports from country B in order to improve its terms of trade. Country A now obtains a higher level of welfare, and the domestic price of the importable good, y, has increased in country A.

However, loss of welfare goads country B to retaliate and it imposes a rate of tariff on imports from A in order to minimize loss of welfare and to neutralize the deteriorating terms of trade such that the original free trade equilibrium price ratio (by assumption) is restored. The non-cooperative game is complete, and both countries find themselves at lower levels of welfare as compared to the free trade levels of welfare. Now each country has succeeded in beggaring the other country. At last, wisdom dawns upon these two countries and they begin to play a cooperative game. They form a Customs Union[2] so that tariff barriers are dismantled, and each country moves up to a higher level of welfare. If there is a third country, the Kemp–Wan theorem[3] confirms that the third country, in principle, is not hurt. It is simply a return to the free trade equilibrium.

Having experienced the benefits of cooperation, these two countries decide to form an economic union (that is, a common market with regional economic regulation) in which factors of production can move freely between the countries. This increases the degree of integration. In order to analyse how this may take place, we need to move from the offer-curve scenario to the production–consumption space with production-possibility curves of countries A and B, and the community indifference curves, depicting internationally identical homothetic tastes. A world equilibrium is obtained when the trade triangles are equal and an international equilibrium price ratio is established. It is necessary to specify that the relative price is the price of good y in terms of good x so that good x is the numéraire of the economic system.

With free mobility of factors of production, the economy essentially becomes one. It is easy to derive the union's production-possibility curve by using a commonplace technique. Juxtapose country B's production block on country A's production block so that the production points coincide. As one slides B's production block along A's production block, the corner of B's production block maps the union's production-possibility curve, say, VV. The union's equilibrium is given at a point where the community indifference curve touches VV. The union's 'autarkic' relative price equals the free trade price, so that, given homotheticity of preferences, the consumption ray remains unchanged. Given that there are only two countries, the union's autarkic equilibrium is obtained.

The mechanical derivation of the union's production-possibility curve is not entirely justified. First, given free mobility, factors of production, may move[4] to the region where it would be more effective. For example, part of capital and labour producing the capital-intensive good x in the labour-abundant country may move to the capital-abundant country which, because of specialization, has certain industry specific advantages. If this is so, the productivity of the migrated factors of production will increase. Thus, there may be further regional specialization. Second, each industry of the union is now somewhat larger so that, for example, R&D resources could be pooled, and this will lead to a higher degree of effectiveness of R&D investment. Thus, the industry's productivity, in general, will be enhanced. If these secondary economic effects are taken into account, then the union's production curve will not remain as VV but will shift outwards. If this potential increase in productivity is realized, then the economy will enjoy a higher level of welfare.

Now how does the economic union become a monetary union to

complete the process of economic integration? In this simple model, there is no money. However, by assumption, the numéraire of both the countries is good x, since the relative price is the price of good y in terms of good x. We can interpret the numéraire good as commodity money so that this model mimics both economic and monetary union in the sense of having a single medium of exchange. We can now pose the following indirect question: what is the likely welfare effect if there is no monetary union? This question is answered by considering two important factors in the absence of a single currency in the economic union. The first is the transaction cost. As reported in Johnson (1996), in the presence of a single currency, the total saving is estimated to be 0.33 per cent of GDP which, for the European Union, is a massive $25 billion. About 50 per cent of the total saving is accounted for by the elimination of the usual spread between the buying and selling rates for foreign currency. Another 14 per cent is accounted for by the elimination of similar charges on banknotes, travellers' cheques and so on. About 25 per cent of the total saving is accounted for by the reduction in firms' management of foreign exchange risks, and the rest is accounted for by the reduction in the cost of cross-border payments. The second is the regional market efficiency in the presence of a single currency. The source of efficiency lies (i) in the ability to make direct comparison of prices so that 'large' price differentials will be competed away, and (ii) in the elimination of the distortionary impact of exchange rate variabilities on product prices in the union.[5] In addition to welfare gains because of the elimination of transaction costs and market inefficiency, there are other indirect benefits. Probably the most important indirect effect is the likely lower interest rates as the EU partners do not have to suffer from high interest rates required to defend their exchange rates. Lower interest rates are also expected because, with a single currency, there will be a single banking market which will be more competitive. These are the indirect benefits. Our simple model gives an efficient production-possibility curve for the union. The costs of not having a single currency are not reflected when there is a numéraire good. Therefore, if the above-mentioned inefficiencies exist, then the economic union will not achieve its full potential so that the equilibrium will lie in the interior of the union production block.

3   Primary convergence of the EU

Primary convergence, as opposed to nominal convergence, refers to cross-country convergence of the real variables as in the new growth theory. The present strategy of the European Union to move to a single currency system is economic convergence. The Maastricht convergence criteria are nominal, but it is desirable to achieve stable exchange rates for a significant period (noting that the medium term is normally taken as a period of 4 to 5 years) in order to establish the euro value of the national currencies. The stability of the exchange rates in the medium to long term is more closely related to the real economy, that is, to the same variables which are considered for convergence in the growth theory. If in the ideal situation, albeit unrealistic, all member countries of the European Union obtain globally stable identical steady states such that the rate of capital (human and physical) accumulation, growth of population and rate of technological progress all grow at the same constant rate everywhere, with identical steady-state capital–labour ratio, then the introduction of the euro will not cause any economic problems because all countries are essentially identical. Taking this pattern of primary convergence as the ideal one, one can examine the actual situation in the European Union. Then, of course, one needs to discuss whether primary convergence is necessary and/or sufficient.

The concept of primary convergence is related to the concepts of convergence in growth theory. For example, Sala-i-Martin (1996), has introduced two main concepts of convergence: One called the β-convergence and the other σ-convergence. Absolute β-convergence[6] can be defined as a dynamic situation when poor countries tend to grow faster than rich countries. If this happens, poor economies catch up with richer ones. This is often known as the 'convergence hypothesis'. The σ-convergence[7] can be defined as a dynamic situation when the dispersion of the real per capita GDP of a group of countries tends to decrease over time. It is shown by Sala-i-Martin (1996) that a necessary condition for the existence of σ-convergence is the existence of β-convergence. Furthermore, a distinction is made between absolute β-convergence and conditional β-convergence. In using the concept of absolute β-convergence, one makes the assumption that the cross-country differences depend on their initial levels of capital. In reality, of course, countries also differ in technology, population growth rates and saving propensities. In such a situation, countries will have different steady states. The growth rate of an economy, then, is positively related to the distance between the actual state and its own steady state. This concept is referred to as the conditional β-convergence. Absolute β-convergence applies only when all economies converge to the same steady state.

We have examined whether the real per capita income is converging by computing the coefficient of variations across countries for three groups of countries EU9, EU10 and EU12, where EU9 excludes Greece, Spain and Portugal, and EU10 excludes Spain and Portugal. As Greece joined the EU in 1981, the figures for EU10 run from 1981 to 1992, and as Portugal and Spain joined in 1986, the figures for EU12 run from 1986 to 1992. Consider

Table 9.1   Per capita real GDP and per capita real capital stock, coefficient of variation for EU9*

Year	Capital stock per capita US$ (1990 = 100)	Gross domestic product per capita US$ (1990 = 100)
1980	0.25202	0.20968
1981	0.23728	0.19833
1982	0.22714	0.18628
1983	0.21547	0.19205
1984	0.20444	0.19517
1985	0.18669	0.20108
1986	0.19790	0.21415
1987	0.21208	0.21669
1988	0.23734	0.20666
1989	0.23734	0.19372
1990	0.24622	0.19198
1991	0.26317	0.18414
1992	0.27973	0.25902

Note: * Belgium, Denmark, France, Germany, Ireland, Italy, Luxembourg, the Netherlands and the UK.

Source: IMF, *International Financial Statistics Yearbook*, 1993.

Table 9.1 where the cross-country coefficient of variation of the per capita real capital stock[8] and the cross-country coefficient of variation of the per capita real GDP are presented for EU9 from 1980 to 1992. For per capita capital stock, it is revealed that primary convergence has occurred from 1980 to 1985, but divergence became empirically prominent from 1985 to 1992. There clearly is a *V*-pattern here. Inclusion of Greece, as seen from Table 9.2, has generally increased the value of the cross-country coefficient of variation of the per capita capital stock, specifically for the years from 1989 to 1992; and the *V*-pattern exists. Inclusion of Portugal and Spain, as seen from Table 9.3, has further increased the value of the cross-country coefficient of variation of the per capita stock from 1986 to 1992. Considering the coefficient of variation of the per capita GDP,[9] the EU9 countries (Table 9.1) do not empirically exhibit a clear trend of economic convergence (with the values of the coefficient marginally going up and down). Inclusion of Greece (Table 9.2) has indicated a trend of divergence, and this trend of divergence becomes more significant if Portugal and Spain (Table 9.3) are included.

Table 9.2   Per capita real GDP and per capita real capital stock, coefficient of variation for EU10*

Year	Capital stock per capita US$ (1990 = 100)	Gross domestic product per capita US$ (1990 = 100)
1981	0.27828	0.19057
1982	0.25464	0.17706
1983	0.23138	0.18426
1984	0.20956	0.19740
1985	0.18347	0.22081
1986	0.18638	0.26647
1987	0.21245	0.28626
1988	0.24957	0.28566
1989	0.28122	0.28337
1990	0.30807	0.29909
1991	0.33624	0.30180
1992	0.36048	0.36435

Note: * EU9 plus Greece.

Source: IMF, *International Financial Statistics Yearbook*, 1993.

Table 9.3   Per capita real GDP and per capita real capital stock, coefficient of variation for EU12*

Year	Capital stock per capita US$ (1990 = 100)	Gross domestic product per capita US$ (1990 = 100)
1986	0.22980	0.34977
1987	0.26208	0.36881
1988	0.29875	0.35653
1989	0.32861	0.35994
1990	0.35347	0.37307
1991	0.37642	0.34060
1992	0.39456	0.42530

Note: * EU10 plus Portugal and Spain.

Source: IMF, *International Financial Statistics Yearbook*, 1993.

It now appears that primary divergence rather than primary convergence is taking place in the EU. We need to analyse whether monetary union will be non-optimal under these circumstances or whether monetary union can take place despite these circumstances without causing severe economic disruption. There is no doubt that the national economic structures of some of the member countries are significantly different not only in terms of composition of GDP but also in terms of the various elasticities, particularly trade elasticities.[10] Probably the most important criterion of monetary union is the convergence of exchange rates. Given that trade elasticities vary and given that exports to the rest of world by the members of the EU is significant, exchange rate volatility is endemic. It is both harmful and useless to try to guide the economy artificially by raising interest rates towards convergence. Exchange rate convergence will take place only via the convergence of the fundamental equilibrium exchange rates, and the convergence of the latter rates are necessarily determined by primary convergence. Table 9.4 reveals that the real effective exchange rates[11] (which pick up the consequences of trade not only with EU partners but also with the rest of the world) are diverging over time. This finding is not surprising because the real effective exchange rates are fundamentally determined by the real sector of the economy. Furthermore, we have

Table 9.4 Cross-country standard deviations of real effective exchange rates (1980 = 100)

Year	EU9*	EU10*	EU12*
1981	5.1256	5.4952	
1982	7.5489	8.6670	
1983	9.4735	9.2452	
1984	10.0170	9.6361	
1985	9.9645	9.3842	
1986	10.9215	10.3424	10.1593
1987	13.1882	12.4825	11.7126
1988	13.1409	12.3239	11.3052
1989	13.4113	12.5520	11.5701
1990	15.7153	14.7079	13.7467
1991	15.1716	14.2354	14.3123
1992	15.2500	14.3948	15.8925

Note: * Excluding Ireland, see note 11.

Source: IMF, *International Financial Statistics Yearbook*, 1994.

Table 9.5   National variation of selected variables

Country	Coefficient of variation, capital stock per capita (US$)	Coefficient of variation, GDP per capita (US$)	Standard deviation: real effective exchange rate (1980 = 100)
Belgium	0.1779	0.2598	8.8598
Denmark	0.1265	0.2251	8.8050
France	0.1488	0.2245	3.2745
Gemany	0.1521	0.2352	9.6966
Greece	0.4069	0.5308	6.1259
Ireland	0.1725	0.2687	—
Italy	0.1396	0.2221	5.5091
Luxembourg	0.1859	0.3504	2.5799
Netherlands	0.1484	0.2729	5.2049
Portugal	0.1112	0.1082	11.4004
Spain	0.2211	0.1842	10.5307
UK	0.1049	0.1679	7.0480

Note: Belgium, Denmark, France, Germany, Ireland, Italy, Luxembourg, the Netherlands and the UK: time series from 1980 to 1992. Greece: time series from 1981 to 1992. Portugal and Spain: time series from 1986 to 1992.

Source: IMF, *International Financial Statistics Yearbook*, 1993.

considered time-series variation of per capita stock of capital, per capita GDP and real effective exchange rate for each country. Table 9.5 presents the computed coefficient of variation of per capita real capital stock and per capita real GDP, and standard deviation of real effective exchange rate for each country. There seems to be significant national time-series variation for all the three variables considered.

In an ideal world, for monetary convergence, one would like to have convergence of the real effective exchange rate. It is a mistake just to look at national exchange rates with reference to the Deutschmark as most countries of the EU carry on substantial international trade with the rest of the world, especially with Japan and North America. It is the convergence of real effective exchange rates which will be of significant importance. But since the convergence of the real effective exchange rates are dependent on primary convergence, it will take a fairly long period of time for such convergence to occur because primary convergence takes time. Sala-i-Martin (1996) reports that the estimated speed of β-convergence (as defined earlier) across the states of the United States is about 2 per cent a year, and convergence across OECD countries is also about 2 per cent. It is, then, a fair guess that EU convergence will not be significantly different from 2 per cent.

4 European Monetary Union

Does it matter if a single currency is introduced despite the EU exhibiting primary divergence rather than primary convergence? A reasonable answer perhaps can be found by examining what has happened over the decades to the primary convergence process of the various states in the United States or to the primary convergence process of the various provinces of Canada. The answer is, of course, indirect, or rather, the answer can be provided only in a reverse way. Despite having a single currency, does primary convergence exist among the provinces of Canada, for example? If the answer is no, then it suggests that convergence of the kind that the EU is looking for is neither necessary nor sufficient for monetary union. That is, it simply indicates that problems of primary convergence always exist, especially in a geographically sprawling country, despite having a single currency.

A much reported work of Poloz (1990) has revealed that the real exchange rates between Canadian provinces are more variable than real exchange rates between France, Italy, the UK and Germany.[12] But Canada's economy is operating quite efficiently, and Canada's provinces have not suffered disastrously from a single currency. The EU is paying a heavy price in terms of the efforts that are being made for the convergence of nominal exchange rates in the form of the Exchange Rate Mechanism (ERM). Thus, it appears that convergence of nominal exchange rates is neither necessary nor sufficient. Furthermore, as argued earlier, primary convergence suggests that the real exchange rates converge, if such convergence is required at all.

However, Eichengreen (1992) found that the real exchange rates among the then EC members (in the 1970s and 1980s) were more variable than the real exchange rates within the United States. There are two points to be noted here: first, Eichengreen considered only four regions in the US – North East, North Central, South and West; second, the data involve aggregation, and the computed variability will inevitably be less than that if actual states, rather than regions, were considered. One would accept that the economic structure of Texas is very different from that of California. When the Silicon Valley prospered in California while Texas got the chill of lower oil prices, there would have been upward pressure on the Californian exchange rate and downward pressure on the Texan exchange rate with an inevitable crisis of an EU-type ERM. This, of course, assumes that Texas and California are two European-type nations with national currencies.

The real exchange rates, under the circumstances, will diverge rather than converge. But with a single currency neither Texas nor California seem to have problems with economic growth and prosperity. Again, the relevance of economic convergence as a condition comes into question.

Monetary union is not something new – a single currency was adopted in 1785 in the United States. There are lessons to be learned from the US experience. First, efficient functioning of the monetary authority is vital. The Federal Reserve System was set up in 1913 and it was realized only in 1933 that twelve Federal Reserve Banks could not pursue independent monetary policy. The German Customs Union was established in 1834, and the monetary union was based on fixed exchange rates. The political union was also based on fixed exchange rates. The political union of Germany in 1871 did not automatically bring about a single currency. The political process helped and the Deutschmark was introduced in 1875. Again, political union between England and Scotland (in 1707) was followed by monetary union. In 1707 the rate of exchange of an English pound was 12 Scottish pounds. Only in 1805 was British monetary union completed, when the exchange rate of one Scottish pound became one English pound. That has survived to the present, even though Scotland has continued to issue Scottish pound notes.

The fear of monetary union today is the likely federal political structure that will be required to oversee the functioning of a single currency, while historically, political union preceded monetary union, and not ill-defined economic convergence. The fear today is that monetary union will lead to an unstoppable movement towards political union. It is the political will which is the most important factor and which will determine whether European Monetary Union will be achieved.

5   Concluding remarks

Using traditional tools of trade theory, it is argued that welfare loss results from not having a monetary union if economic integration has reached the stage of a single market with free movement of goods and factors of production. It is argued that nominal convergence criteria are neither necessary nor sufficient for monetary union. Primary convergence has some clear relevance to the process of monetary union. Primary convergence considers convergence of real variables, for example, capital per head, per capita income or real exchange rates. Empirical evidence suggests that the European Union is primarily diverging. But the history of monetary union in the United States, Germany and Britain suggests that such divergence need not be a deterrent for having a monetary union. Essentially it depends on the political will of the European Union.

Notes

1. The figures of 3 per cent (budget deficit as a percentage of GDP) and 60 per cent (government debt as a percentage of GDP) are not in the main text of the Maastricht Treaty. They are merely 'reference values'.
2. Since we do not have a third country, this simple model cannot distinguish between a free trade area and a customs union. Also note that both countries gain unambiguously because the question of trade diversion does not arise here in the absence of a third country. There is only trade creation here.
3. The Kemp–Wan theorem proves that a customs union, in principle, increases global welfare. In our case, the two countries will continue to have welfare benefit from free trade. If there is a third country, the structure of the common external tariffs can be adjusted so that trade flows with the third country continue at an unchanged level. See Kemp and Wan (1976).
4. See Krugman and Venables (1990) who have carried out an analysis of the movement of production in the context of 'the periphery' and 'the Centre'.
5. In the context of the car industry, the guidelines issued by the EU commission allow a price variation of 12 to 18 per cent for the same model of car, but often, variations of larger than 18 per cent are observed.
6. Let $y_{i,t}$ be the real per capita GDP of the ith country at time period t. Define $R_{i,t,t+T} = \log(y_{i,t+T}/y_{i,t})/T$ is the rate of growth of GDP between t and $t + T$. Now estimate the following regression equation:

$$R_{i,t,t+T} = \alpha - \beta \log(Y_{i,t}) + \epsilon_{it}.$$

If it is found that $\beta > 0$, then the data show absolute β-convergence.
7. If σ_t, is the standard deviation of log ($y_{i,t}$) for a cross-section of i countries. The countries converge if

$$\sigma_t > \sigma_{t+T}.$$

8. Each country's real capital stock is computed by converting each year's gross fixed capital formation into millions of US dollars by using the annual average market exchange rate, and then transforming the values into real terms, by deflating the figures. Various manufacturing price indices are used for various countries because of non-availability of consistent indices. We indicate here after each country the price indices in brackets: Belgium (industrial production), Denmark (home and import goods), France (consumer), Greece (home and import goods), Germany (industrial production), Ireland (manufacturing output), Italy (wholesale), Luxembourg (consumer), the Netherlands (final products), Portugal (consumers), Spain (industrial) and the UK (manufacturing output). The real capital stock is then computed by allowing radioactive depreciation at 10 per cent per annum. For example, in order to compute the real capital stock (K) in 1986, we sum up the following series of real gross capital formation (I), namely

$$K_{1986} = I_{1986} + 0.9 (I_{1985}) + \ldots + 0.1 (I_{1977}).$$

Per capita stock of 1986 is then obtained by dividing K_{1986} by total population.
9. Each country's GDP has been expressed in US dollars. Real GDP in 1990 prices is then found by using GDP deflator. Real per capita GDP is found by dividing real GDP by population.
10. For example, as economic growth takes place, Germany tends to import less but export more, while the UK tends to do exactly the opposite.
11. In Table 9.4, Ireland is excluded although the column headings remain as EU9, EU10 and EU11. This is done only to avoid redefining these notations again. Ireland is not included since her data on effective real exchange rates are not readily available in the 1994 IMF Year Book. If anything, we would guess that standard deviations will increase if Ireland is included.
12. The assumed implication is that the European Union is as good an optimum currency area

as Canada. Also it should be noted that Canadian provinces are structurally very different. For example, Ontario specializes in manufacturing goods while Alberta specializes in primary commodities. France and Germany have a relatively more similar economic structure. The real exchange rate between France and Germany is, then, expected to be more stable.

References

Eichengreen, B. (1992), 'Is Europe an Optimum Currency Area?', in S. Borner and H. Grubel (eds), *The European Community After 1992*, Chapter 8, Basingstoke: Macmillan.

Johnson, C. (1996), *In With the Euro, Out With the Pound*, Harmondsworth: Penguin.

Kemp, M.C. and H.Y. Wan (1976), 'An Elementary Proposition Concerning the Formation of Customs Union', *Journal of International Economics*, **6**, 95–7.

Krugman, P.R. and A.J. Venables (1990), 'Integration and the Competitiveness of Peripheral Industry', in C. Bliss and J.B. De Macedo (eds), *Unity with Diversity in the European Economy: the Community's Southern Frontier*, Cambridge: Cambridge University Press, pp. 56–75.

Poloz, S.S. (1990), 'Real Exchange Rate Adjustment Between Regions in a Common Currency Area', Bank of Canada (unpublished).

Sala-i-Martin, X. (1996), 'The Classical Approach to Convergence Analysis', *Economic Journal*, **106**, 1019–36.

10 Capital flows, foreign exchange reserves and aggregate demand
*Angelos A. Antzoulatos**

1 Introduction

The surprise return of private capital to less-developed countries (LDCs) in the early 1990s was at the time regarded as the herald of a new era for the highly indebted recipient countries, many of which were still suffering from the traumatic experience of the debt crisis. The euphoria did not last for long though. Policymakers and informed observers quickly became apprehensive about the prospect of a sudden capital-flow reversal which could trigger an external financing crisis, threaten the financial systems of the recipient countries and, eventually, lead to another debt crisis (Calvo et al. 1992b and 1993; Dooley 1994; Dooley et al. 1994; Kaminsky and Pereira 1994; Rojas-Suarez and Weisbrod 1995). The similarities with the macroeconomic developments which preceded the crisis of the 1980s were striking; among them, widening current account deficits, partly financed by capital flows, and real exchange rate appreciation in the recipient LDCs; plus a decline in the US interest rates, widely regarded as a major factor motivating the flows (Calvo et al. 1992b). Thus, it is not surprising that the return of private capital to LDCs attracted a lot of attention, as indicated by the numerous studies which analyse the determinants (Calvo et al. 1992b; Calvo and Reinhart 1995; Chuhan et al. 1993) and characteristics of the flows (Culpeper 1994; Gooptu 1993), as well as the policy dilemmas and response of several countries (Carneiro and Garcia 1995; Glick and Moreno 1994; Rosende 1995; Sachs et al. 1995; Spiegel 1995).

Yet, despite all this collective effort, several pertinent questions have not been fully addressed. Among them, why were the widening current account (CA) deficits primarily due to a consumption boom in Latin America (LA)

* I thank George Kaisimbris for insightful discussions at an early stage of the project, and Nilmini Gunaratne and Kevin Kime for assistance in collecting and interpreting the data. I also thank Leonardo Bartolini, Susan Charrette, Gabriel deKock, Linda Goldberg, Erica Groshen, Matthew Higgins, Juann Hung, Carol Osler, Frank Packer; and seminar participants at the Federal Reserve Bank of New York, the Conference on Economic Integration in Transition (Athens, Greece, August 1996) and the European Economic Association 1996 meetings (Istanbul, Turkey) for numerous comments and suggestions which helped immensely in improving the theory section, as well as the analysis and interpretation of the econometric results. Of course, none of them is responsible for any remaining errors. The views expressed here are those of the author and do not necessarily reflect the views of the Federal Reserve Bank of New York or the Federal Reserve System.

and an investment surge in East Asia (Kaminsky and Pereira 1994)? Is the associated decline in LA's savings permanent or temporary? How did other components of domestic demand behave? Why did L.A. countries spend a bigger share of the flows, and save less in the form of reserves, than their East Asian counterparts (Calvo et al. 1992a; Dooley 1994)? Could capital flows not only have allowed higher domestic demand by relaxing a binding external financing constraint, but also induced it in cases where the constraint was not binding?

Addressing these questions bears more than academic relevance. It holds the key to designing and implementing effective policies to cope with capital flows, and to evaluating the likely performance of countries which tap the international financial markets for the first time or after a long absence. Serving as a strong reminder of this need, the surge of capital flows to Central and Eastern Europe, which started in 1992, was accompanied by widening CA deficits, increasing consumption, and real exchange rate appreciation, as in the case of LA earlier in the decade (Calvo et al. 1995). Further, addressing these questions may help draw useful lessons for, if the past can be a guide for the future, the cycle of surges and sudden reversals of capital flows to LDCs will most likely occur again.

Since capital flows relax the external financing constraint LDCs usually face, this chapter addresses the aforementioned questions using the model of a forward-looking but borrowing-constrained individual, who tries to smooth consumption over time. Building upon the theoretical results of Antzoulatos (1994) and Xu (1995), the chapter argues that an increase in the external debt ceiling may induce lower precautionary savings and higher domestic demand even in countries which do not need to borrow. More important, the induced increase in demand should be decreasing in the original ceiling and the accumulated reserves. (As in Edwards (1984) and Wijnbergen (1990), reserves are interpreted as precautionary savings at the country level.)

The model itself can answer some of the aforementioned questions. To begin with, the return of private capital to LDCs, effectively representing an increase in their external debt ceiling, may have induced higher demand (and deteriorating CA deficits) even in countries which were carrying high reserves and, thus, did not need to borrow. Also, LA's lower ceiling prior to the return, a reflection of the debt crisis in the 1980s and the region's poor economic performance relative to Asia, can account for the fact that LA spent a bigger share of the flows than Asia. It can also account for the decline in LA's savings. Consequently, for as long as the perception of a higher-than-before ceiling lasts, it is unlikely that the region's savings will recover.

The credibility of these theoretical answers is enhanced by the empirical results which, in line with the model's predictions, document that LA's domestic demand and components thereof were more sensitive to capital flows and accumulated reserves than Asia's. Moreover, these results are robust to alternative explanations for the consumption booms which are often associated with inflation-stabilization programmes (Calvo 1986), and the surge in consumption and investment associated with credible liberalization (McKinnon and Pill 1994).[1]

The chapter proceeds as follows. Section 2 presents the model, while Section 3 discusses its testable implications. Section 4 starts with some econometric problems related to the unobservable external debt ceiling, and proceeds with the empirical results. Finally, Section 5 summarizes the answers to the questions raised above, paying particular attention to LA's consumption boom, while Appendix 10A.1 describes the data in detail.

2 The model

The prevailing consumption paradigm, the Life-Cycle/Permanent Income Hypothesis model, postulates that people decide how much to consume out of contemporaneous income based on their expected lifetime resources and limited access to borrowing. More formally, a forward-looking individual maximizes the expected value of a time-separable utility function, equation (10.1), subject to a borrowing constraint, inequality (10.2), the asset evolution constraint, equation (10.3), and the usual lifetime budget constraint.

$$\text{Max } E_t \left[\sum_{t=1}^{T} \left(\frac{1}{1+\delta} \right)^{t-1} u(c_t) \right] \quad (0 \leq \delta) \tag{10.1}$$

subject to

$$c_t \leq x_t + U_t \quad (U_t \geq 0) \tag{10.2}$$

$$x_t = R(x_{t-1} - c_{t-1}) + y_t = Rs_{t-1} + y_t \quad (R = 1 + r \geq 1) \tag{10.3}$$

$$c_T = x_T. \tag{10.4}$$

The timing and the nature of his/her decisions are as follows: at the beginning of period t, he/she decides how much to consume, c_t, in order to maximize his/her expected utility over the remaining planning horizon, taking into account expected future income, $E_t y_{t+k} (k \geq 1)$. Consumption at any period cannot exceed the individual's total assets, x_t, plus a debt ceiling, U_t, as described by inequality (10.2). Total assets are equal to savings carried over from the previous period, $s_{t-1} = R(x_{t-1} - c_{t-1})$, plus

realized income, y_t, as described by equation (10.3). For a positive debt
ceiling, savings can be negative and thus x_t can be less than y_t. Consumption at the end of the planning horizon, c_T equals total assets, equation
(10.4), thus ruling out Ponzi schemes. The debt ceiling, the interest rate, r,
and the length of the planning horizon – which can be finite or infinite – are
assumed to be exogenous. In short, optimal consumption, c_t^*, is a function
of current assets, x_t, the debt ceiling, U_t, the time left to the end of the
planning horizon $T-t$, and expected future income, $E_t y_{t+k}$ ($k \geq 1$). To
simplify notation, $T-t$ and $E_t y_{t+k}$ ($k \geq 1$) are dropped from the optimal
consumption function; that is, $c_t^* = c_t^*(x_t; U_t)$.

Despite the lack of an analytical solution for c_t^* under general debt
ceilings and non-quadratic utility function, several of its properties have
been explored. These properties are reflected in Figure 10.1 which exhibits
c_t^* as a function of assets and the debt ceiling, all expressed as fractions of
contemporaneous income. The consumption profiles in Figure 10.1 have
been calculated using Deaton's (1991) two-state income process, as
described in Antzoulatos (1994, p. 194). Their shapes, however, can be

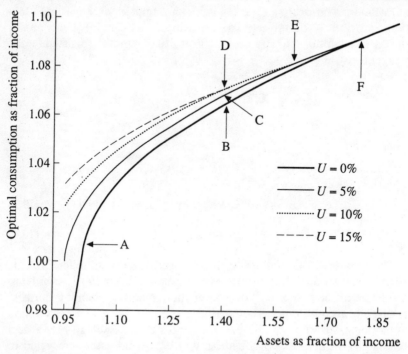

Figure 10.1   Optimal consumption as function of assets and the debt ceiling

verified theoretically by combining the results of Antzoulatos (1994) and Xu (1995).[2] Worth stressing, these shapes rely on some very general assumptons regarding the income process and the utility function. The latter, specifically, is assumed to be continuous, strictly increasing, concave, and three times continuously differentiable with a positve third derivative. A positive third derivative ensures the existence of precautionary savings (Zeldes 1989).

As illustrated in Figure 10.1, $c_t^*(x_t; U_t)$ is continuous, strictly increasing, and concave in assets. (Xu's proof for $U_t = 0$ also applies to $U_t \neq 0$). The 45-degree, straight-line segments of the consumption profiles correspond to the (low) asset levels at which the individual optimally chooses to exhaust his/her credit line and, thus, face a binding constraint (equation (10.2) holds as an equality). At these low asset levels, the desire for higher consumption, determined by his/her preferences and expected future income, dominates the precautionary savings motive. As a result, c_t^* increases one to one with x_t. However, above a critical asset level, $x_t^* = x_t^*(U_t)$, the individual spends progressively less out of each additional unit of assets (for $U_t = 0$, x_t^* corresponds to point A in Figure 10.1). Alternatively, for $x_t > x_t^*$ he/she saves progressively more (dis-saves progressively less when $x_t^* < c_t^* \leq x_t^* + U_t$) as assets increase. These properties can be summarized as:

$$0 < \frac{\partial c_t^*(x_t; U_t)}{\partial xt} \leq 1 \qquad (10.5)$$

$$\frac{\partial^2 c_t^*(x_t; U_t)}{\partial^2 x_t} \leq 0. \qquad (10.6)$$

Figure 10.1 also illustrates that $c_t^*(x_t; U_t)$ is weakly increasing in the debt ceiling (Antzoulatos 1994). More important, c_t^* can be strictly increasing in U_t even when the individual carries high savings and, consequently, does not face the spectra of a binding constraint in the foreseeable future (compare points B, C and D, which correspond to savings carried from the previous period equal to 40 per cent of current income; that is, $x_t = 1.4$). It is the possibility of a binding constraint in the distant future – due to possible, but not certain, negative income shocks – that induces him/her to hold higher precautionary savings (and spend less) at lower debt ceilings. Intuitively, precautionary savings under borrowing constraints can be decomposed into two components (Xu 1995): one, denoted as PS1, which protects against future income downturns, and another, denoted as PS2, which is caused by the borrowing constraint. The latter decreases as

U_t increases, leading to higher c_t^*.

$$0 \leq \frac{\partial c_t^*(x_t; U_t)}{\partial U_t} \leq 1. \tag{10.7}$$

Eventually, at some high enough U_t, denoted as $\bar{U}_t(x_t)$, the borrowing constraint will become irrelevant, PS2 will become zero, and c_t^* will be determined by the individual's expected lifetime resources.[3] $\bar{U}_t(x_t)$ is decreasing in x_t; as assets increase, so do savings – by inequality (10.5) – thus providing a bigger buffer to hedge against negative income shocks. In Figure 10.1 $\bar{U}_t(x_t = 1.4) \approx 10\%$ of current income (point D), $\bar{U}_t(x_t = 1.6) \approx 5\%$ (point E), and $\bar{U}_t(x_t = 1.8) \approx 0\%$ (point F).

Based on the above, the following properties can be shown. First, the slope of $c_t^*(x_t; U_t)$ with respect to x_t is (weakly) decreasing in U_t, as expressed by inequality (10.8). When $U_t \geq \bar{U}_t(x_t)$, (10.8) will hold as an equality. This property is a direct implication of *Proposition 4* in Xu (1995, p. 681) for the general case $U_t \geq 0$. Graphically, it is reflected on the convergence of the consumption profiles as assets increase. Intuitively, it implies that the difference in the consumption levels of individuals who differ only in their debt ceilings will decrease as assets increase. The reason is that, when the constraint is not binding, savings increase along with assets, thus reducing PS2. As a result, the individuals with the lower ceiling, the ones who have to carry higher PS2, spend more out of each additional dollar.

$$\frac{\partial c_t^*(x_t; U_t)/\partial x_t}{\partial U_t} \leq 0. \tag{10.8}$$

Further, the impact of an increase in the debt ceiling progressively decreases as U_t increases (the distance BC is greater than CD). A heuristic proof follows. Let $\bar{x}_t(U_t)$ be the asset level at which PS2 becomes zero for a debt ceiling equal to U_t. (For $U_t = 0$, $\bar{x}_t(U_t = 0)$ corresponds. to point F on Figure 10.1.) Such a level exists as high savings can protect an individual from hitting a binding constraint in the worst-case scenario (Xu 1995). For $x_t \geq \bar{x}_t(U_t)$, it will be $c_t^*(x_t, U_t) = c_t^*(x_t, U_t = \infty)$. Conversely, for $x_t < \bar{x}_t(U_t)$, it will be $c_t^*(x_t, U_t) < c_t^*(x_t, U_t = \infty)$. Next, $\bar{x}_t(U_t)$ is decreasing in U_t, as a higher ceiling provides a bigger buffer to protect against hitting a binding constraint. This, along with the properties that c_t^* is concave in assets and that the consumption profiles converge as assets increase (inequality (10.8)), proves the argument. In mathematical terms,

$$\frac{\partial^2 c_t^*(x_t; U_t)}{\partial^2 U_t} \leq 0. \tag{10.9}$$

By the same reasoning, the impact of an increase in the debt ceiling progressively decreases as assets increase; that is,

$$\frac{\partial c_t^*(x_t; U_t)/\partial x_t}{\partial x_t} \leq 0. \tag{10.10}$$

In general, a *permanent* increase in the debt ceiling will induce a bigger rise in c_t^* than a *temporary* one. For the record, the consumption profiles in Figure 10.1 correspond to debt ceilings which remain constant throughout the planning horizon. Let, for argument's sake, U_t increase for the period t *only* to $U_t = 5$ from $U_t = 0$. This temporary increase will affect c_t^* only at low asset levels at which the $U_t = 0$ constraint is binding, that is, at $x_t < x_t^*(U_t = 0)$. At $x_t > x_t^*(U_t = 0)$, c_t^* will not be affected. However, as the duration of $U = 5$ increases, PS2 will decrease and c_t^* will rise by more. By the same token, if U_{t+k} ($k \geq 1$) is expected to be between zero and five, c_t^* will lie between the consumption profiles which correspond to $U_t = 0$ and $U_t = 5$ in Figure 10.1.

The above properties suggest the regression equation below in which consumption, savings carried over from the previous period, and the debt ceiling are expressed as fractions of current income. Savings is used in place of assets, because x_t is increasing in s_{t-1} (by equation (10.3), $x_t/y_t = 1 + R(s_{t-1}/y_t)$). u_t is the usual error term.

$$\frac{c_t^*}{y_t} = \alpha + \beta \frac{s_{t-1}}{y_t} + \gamma \frac{U_t}{y_t} + u_t. \tag{10.11}$$

It is expected that $0 < \beta \leq 1$ (inequality (10.5)) and $0 \leq \gamma \leq 1$ (inequality (10.7)). Unlike β, γ can be zero as at high debt ceilings an increase in U_t may have no impact on optimal consumption. Also, controlling for U_t, β and γ are expected to be lower for individuals who carry high savings (inequalities (10.6) and (10.10)). Conversely, controlling for x_t (and − by (10.3) − s_{t-1}), β and γ are expected to be lower for those who enjoy a higher debt ceiling (inequalities (10.8) and (10.9)).

3 Implications

3.1 Implications for domestic demand and its components
The chapter interprets foreign exchange reserves as precautionary savings at the country level, and the return of private capital to LDCs as an increase in their external debt ceiling. While the second interpretation is

non-controversial, the first requires some elaboration. In the spirit of the theoretical model outlined above, reserves provide a buffer to smooth domestic demand in case of future declines in foreign currency revenues. A similar interpretation is suggested by Edwards (1984), who treats the reserves-to-GNP ratio as an indicator of international liquidity, and Wijnbergen (1990), who suggests that reserves provide insurance to countries against negative shocks. Needless to say, several sample countries held reserves for other reasons as well, such as, to support their currencies during the implementation of exchange rate-based inflation-stabilization programmes. Fortunately, however, such country-specific reasons can be controlled for by the panel-estimation technique that this chapter employs (see next section).

Nevertheless, the interpretation of foreign exchange reserves as precautionary savings creates a subtle problem. In the model, a positive s_{t-1} implies that the individual is a net saver. Yet, all countries, net debtors and net savers alike, carry positive reserves. This problem can be resolved by interpreting the borrowing constraint (inequality (10.2)), as a cash-in-advance constraint, and $E_t y_{t+k}$ ($k \geq 1$) as expected future income net of scheduled payments associated with existing debt. Under this interpretation, U_t represents the maximum amount a country can borrow in addition to its existing debt. Thus, an increase in U_t relaxes the cash-in-advance constraint and reduces PS2.

Putting all the above together, the conclusions of the previous section can be extended to domestic demand (DD) in two ways. First, by referring to intertemporal models of the current account, as in Wijnbergen (1990). Such models typically postulate that a representative agent faces a decision problem similar to that described by equations (10.1) to (10.4), in which consumption corresponds to DD. Alternatively, the conclusions can be justified by showing that they hold for DD's components.

Calling upon the conceptual framework of a representative consumer, the conclusions are expected to hold for private consumption, C. Dispensing, however, with the omniscient representative consumer creates some practical problems. Simply, individuals care about their personal debt ceiling, not the country's access to foreign funds. They are also unlikely to even know the country's foreign exchange reserves. But to the extent that the availability of more foreign funds to domestic financial institutions increases peoples' debt ceilings, the conclusions of the previous section should hold. The conclusions should also hold even in the case where foreign funds are available to finance exclusively investment or government deficits, as such funds free more domestic savings for consumer loans. Further, an increase in the foreign debt ceiling or in reserves may ease administrative restrictions on imports of consumer goods.

The conclusions are also expected to hold for government consumption, G, as long as the properties of the utility function apply to it. Moreover, a government is more likely than individual consumers to know and care about the impact of its spending on the country's reserves. Finally, investment, I, may rise when the country's external debt ceiling or reserves increase, provided that the associated increase in private and government consumption leads to higher profitability. Of course, investment will also rise when an increase in the ceiling or in reserves supports an expansion of credit to a cash-starved business sector, or eases a binding external financing constraint or administrative restrictions on imports of capital goods.

With these qualifications, the model can answer some of the questions posed in the introduction. That is, the return of private capital to LDCs in the late 1980s may have caused an increase in domestic demand via two channels: by allowing the recipient countries to smooth domestic demand in case of a binding external financing constraint; and by inducing higher demand in countries which carried high foreign exchange reserves and, thus, were not facing a binding constraint. The higher demand, in turn, led to widening CA deficits; everything else equal, an increase in domestic demand leads to a decline in the CA.[4]

3.2 Testable implications

Since relevant series are usually available at an annual frequency only, equation (10.11) is estimated by pooling data for all sample countries in each region, as shown in equation (10.12). In it, the subscript i denotes the country, while α_i is the country-specific intercept (fixed effect). The data come mostly from the International Financial Statistics (IFS) database and are described in Appendix 10A.1. The sample period extends from 1989, the year marking the return of private capital to LDCs (Calvo et al. 1992a; Dooley 1994; Eichengreen 1996), to 1994, the year of the 'peso crisis'.

$$\frac{Z_{i,t}}{Y_{i,t}} = \alpha_i + \beta \frac{S_{i,t-1}}{Y_{i,t}} + \gamma \frac{U_{i,t}}{Y_{i,t}} + u_{i,t}. \qquad (10.12)$$

The common across-regions slopes are expected to be $0 < \beta \leq 1$ and $0 \leq \gamma \leq 1$. Z stands for domestic demand or any of its components. $S_{i,t-1}$ corresponds to total foreign exchange reserves minus gold at the end of the $t-1$ year (line 1/d in IFS). The reserves, which are reported in US dollars, are converted to local currency using the average exchange rate for the t year. In this way, $S_{i,t-1}/Y_{i,t}$ measures the current purchasing power of the reserves carried over from the previous period. Nevertheless, the results are qualitatively the same when the end-of-period $t-1$ exchange rate is used for the conversion.

Besides the restrictions $0 < \beta \le 1$ and $0 \le \gamma \le 1$, the model, along with the recent economic history of the sample countries, implies that both coefficients should be higher for LA than for Asia. Specifically, over the period 1989 to 1994, LA and Asian countries carried on the average approximately equal reserves relative to GDP. The former, however, were most likely facing a lower debt ceiling before 1989. The underlying assumption is that past difficulties in meeting debt-service obligations or outright default, as well as poor macroeconomic management, affect negatively a country's access to the international financial markets.

Briefly, with the exception of the Philippines, Asian countries avoided in the 1980s the debt-servicing difficulties of their LA counterparts. This is documented in Table A1 (p. 41) of the March 1995 *Private Market Financing for Developing Countries*, which lists debt restructuring during the previous decade. In addition, LA countries figure prominently in the protracted negotiations which followed the wave of international debt default of the 1930s (Fernandez-Ansola and Laursen 1995). Finally, if the quality of economic management could be an indicator of perceived creditworthiness, LA's record is much poorer than Asia's: As Mas's witty account of recent currency reforms documents, five LA countries experienced hyperinflation in the 1980s (Mas, 1995, Table 1, p. 485), and seven embarked on a currency reform since 1980 (Mas, 1995, Table 2, pp. 488–9). No Asian country has done either since 1980. Further, the hypothesis that LA countries were facing stricter credit rationing than Asian ones is reflected in the writings of knowledgeable observers (see, for example, Calvo et al. 1993, p. 7).

In essence, the model together with the recent economic history of the two regions can explain why LA spent a bigger share of the flows (higher γ), thus experiencing a larger deterioration of the CA and a bigger decline in savings relative to Asia. It is up to the econometric analysis now to determine whether the model's predictions are satisfied for domestic demand and its components. If they are, they will provide empirical support to the model and thus enhance the credibility of its theoretical answers above.

Before that, however, it should be pointed out that the model's predictions can also be tested intra-regionally. Taking into account that during the sample period Singapore, Taiwan and Malaysia carried very high reserves, deleting them from the sample should result in higher β and γ for Asia (inequalities (10.6) and (10.10)). For the record, the average reserves-to-GDP ratio for these countries exceeded 30 per cent, compared with less than 15 per cent for the remaining sample countries in Asia and LA.

4 Empirical analysis

4.1 Econometric considerations

A positive aspect of the panel estimation approach is that country-specific idiosyncratic factors can be accounted for by the country-specific inter-cepts, α_i, thus allowing β and γ to capture the effect of deviations of $S_{i,t-1}/Y_{i,t}$ and $U_{i,t}/Y_{i,t}$ from their means on the same deviations of $Z_{i,t}/Y_{i,t}$. Examples of such factors are the need to hold high reserves to support a country's currency during the implementation of exchange rate-based inflation-stabilization programmes; and the stage of development, time preferences (parameter δ in equation (10.1)), wealth and consumer access to credit, all of which affect the average consumption-to-GDP ratio. Further, expressing DD and its components as fractions of GDP circum-vents the problem of non-stationarity in the raw series.

But a serious challenge is presented by the measurement of the debt ceiling, $U_{i,t}$. Simply, an observer, regardless of how much informed he/she may be, does not know the maximum amount a country can borrow. He/she only observes the amounts raised in the international financial markets. Let $B_{i,t}$ and $L_{i,t}$ denote the amounts raised in the international bond and loan markets. Leaving aside the severe measurement problems, discussed extensively in World Bank (1988), $B_{i,t}$ and $L_{i,t}$ reflect not only the supply of credit to LDCs, but also the demand for credit by them. There is no way to disentangle the two effects and infer $U_{i,t}$. The strength of the 'supply' effect, however, is manifested in the well-documented reserve accumulation by the recipient countries, an indication that total flows exceeded their CA deficits.

Yet, despite the fact that the debt ceiling is not observable, the model's implications can be tested and the experience of the LA and Asian sample countries can be compared. A sufficient condition is that $U_{i,t}$ is correlated with either $B_{i,t}$ or $L_{i,t}$, or their sum, $B_{i,t} + L_{i,t}$.[5] In more detail, using $B_{i,t}$ as a proxy for $U_{i,t}$ would result in biased coefficient estimates $\hat{\beta}$ and $\hat{\gamma}$, given by:

$$\hat{\beta} = \beta + \lambda\gamma \tag{10.13}$$

$$\hat{\gamma} = \mu\gamma. \tag{10.14}$$

where λ and μ denote the (unknown) regression coefficients of $U_{i,t}$ on $S_{i,t-1}$ and $B_{i,t}$, respectively. As the explanatory value of $B_{i,t}$ for $U_{i,t}$ increases, λ's and β's bias decrease. In the unlikely case where $U_{i,t}$ is proportional to $B_{i,t}$, β's should be zero. Similar conclusions apply to using $L_{i,t}$ and $B_{i,t} + L_{i,t}$ as proxies for $U_{i,t}$.

In the analysis of the empirical results, particular attention is paid to the bias in the estimated coefficients. Here, it suffices to note the results are so strong that the bias does not present a major hindrance for the comparison of LA's and Asia's response to the return of private capital.[6] Given also the loss of efficiency resulting from the use of proxies for $U_{i,t}$, if the analysis produces significant $\hat{\beta}$ and $\hat{\gamma}$, one can reasonably expect that the actual relationship is even stronger.

It should also be noted that, over the sample pedod, LDCs received significant amounts of foreign currency in the form of foreign direct investment (FDI) and equity flows. Both relax the external financing constraint but, unlike bonds and loans, do not create external debt obligations. Asian countries received a much higher proportion of total capital flows in the form of FDI than their LA counterparts. As Calvo et al. (1993, pp. 11–12) document, 44 per cent of the flows to Asia in the early 1990s was in the form of FDI; in LA the FDI share was only 17 per cent. Similar figures for Asian countries are also reported in Glick and Moreno (1994). Further, LA countries received a larger proportion of debt-creating flows in the form of bonds, while their Asian counterparts receive them in the form of syndicated loans. In fact, most Asian sample countries tapped the international bond market in 1993 when it was booming. This pattern in the composition of capital flows suggests that $B_{i,t}$ may be a better proxy for LA's $U_{i,t}$, and $L_{i,t}$ for Asia's – an expectation supported by the empirical results.

4.2 Results

For quick reference, Table 10.1 summarizes the testable implications.

Table 10.2 presents the empirical evidence. Starting from the left, it reports the dependent variable and the proxy for the debt ceiling. The next six columns report the estimated $\hat{\beta}$ and $\hat{\gamma}$ coefficients, the R^2 and DW statistics, the degrees of freedom (DF) and the autocorrelation coefficient of the residuals (ρ) – where applicable – for LA. The remaining six columns report the same information for Asia. The cells for $\hat{\beta}$ and $\hat{\gamma}$ report the estimated coefficients and their t-statistics in parentheses. The latter are calculated using a heteroscedasticity-consistent covariance matrix. Nevertheless, the OLS results are qualitatively the same. One, two and three asterisks (*) denote significance at the 10, 5 and 1 per cent significance level, respectively. Finally, when the residuals exhibit autocorrelation, the estimation method is non-linear least squares, in which the error term is assumed to follow the process $u_{i,t} = \rho u_{i,t-1} + \epsilon_{i,t}$.

Table 10.2 is also subdivided into four panels; one for domestic demand, and three for its components. Each panel has three entries, one for each proxy for $U_{i,t}$. The entry with the highest R^2, presumably corresponding to the best proxy, is highlighted by bold face. For brevity, the discussion for the components is less extensive than the discussion for DD.

Table 10.1   Summary of expectations and testable implications

$$\frac{X_{i,t}}{Y_{i,t}} = \alpha_i + \hat{\beta}\frac{RES_{i,t-1}}{Y_{i,t}} + \hat{\gamma}\frac{FLOWS_{i,t}}{Y_{i,t} + u_{i,t}} + u_{i,t}$$

Implications and expectations	Comments	Results
1. $\hat{\beta} > 0$ and $\hat{\gamma} \geq 0$	Implied by the conceptual framework (Section 2)	Table 10.2
2. $\hat{\beta}_{LA} > \hat{\beta}_{EA}$ and $\hat{\gamma}_{LA} > \hat{\gamma}_{EA}$	Implied by the conceptual framework, together with the recent economic history of the two regions (Section 3.2)	Table 10.2
3. East Asia's estimated $\hat{\beta}$ and $\hat{\gamma}$ should be higher when the high-reserve countries are excluded from the sample	Intra-region test of the chapter's testable implications. It is motivated by the very high reserves-to-GDP ratio of Singapore, Taiwan, and Malaysia (Section 3.2)	Discussed in the text
4. For LA, changes in bond flows may be a better measure of changes in the external debt ceiling; for East Asia, changes in syndicated loans	These *expectations* reflect the composition of the flows to the two regions. If they are true, bond flows should produce higher t-statistics for $\hat{\beta}$ and $\hat{\gamma}$, and higher R^2 for LA. The same applies to syndicated loans for Asia (Section 4.1)	Table 10.2

Domestic demand   In summary, LA's domestic demand was very sensitive to capital flows and foreign exchange reserves. In accordance with the chapter's model, this indicates that the region was close to facing a binding constraint prior to the return of private capital. In contrast, East Asia was seemingly enjoying an external debt ceiling so high that the flows did not affect perceptibly its demand. Comparing the two regions, LA's $\hat{\beta}$ and $\hat{\gamma}$ far exceed those of Asia, both in magnitude and significance. Thus, even though $\hat{\beta}$ and $\hat{\gamma}$ are biased estimates of the true coefficients, one could reasonably expect that LA's β and γ are higher than Asias, as suggested by

Table 10.2 *Regression results*

$$\frac{X_{i,t}}{Y_{i,t}} = \alpha_i + \hat{\beta}\frac{RES_{i,t-1}}{Y_{i,t}} + \hat{\gamma}\frac{FLOWS_{i,t}}{Y_{i,t}} + u_{i,t}$$

Variables		Latin America						East Asia					
$X_{i,t}$	$FLOWS_{i,t}$	$\hat{\beta}$	$\hat{\gamma}$	R^2	DW	DF	ρ	$\hat{\beta}$	$\hat{\gamma}$	R^2	DW	DF	ρ
Domestic demand	$\beta_{i,t} + L_{i,t}$	0.890 (5.13)***	1.113 (2.51)**	0.752	2.01	64		0.154 (1.15)	−0.363 (−0.95)	0.938	2.08	28	0.256 (2.06)**
	$\beta_{i,t}$	0.719 (5.02)***	2.499 (5.84)***	0.795	2.21	64		0.133 (0.85)	−0.304 (−0.47)	0.937	2.14	28	0.269 (1.93)*
	$L_{i,t}$	0.900 (6.55)***	−0.328 (−0.43)	0.726	1.80	64		0.116 (1.07)	−0.547 (−0.94)	0.938	2.05	28	0.237 (1.84)*
Private consumption	$B_{i,t} + L_{i,t}$	0.296 (2.12)**	0.230 (0.48)	0.960	1.55	45	0.244 (2.20)**	−0.010 (−0.15)	−0.174 (−0.60)	0.988	2.27	28	0.557 (4.28)***
	$B_{i,t}$	0.259 (1.99)**	1.275 (2.51)**	0.926	1.61	59		0.016 (0.27)	−0.345 (−1.22)	0.989	2.27	28	0.607 (4.61)***
	$L_{i,t}$	0.219 (2.13)**	−0.844 (−1.00)	0.962	1.51	45	0.227 (2.21)**	−0.033 (−0.63)	−0.107 (−0.22)	0.988	2.26	28	0.560 (4.50)***
Investment	$B_{i,t} + L_{i,t}$	0.430 (3.37)***	0.342 (1.94)*	0.860	2.22	49	0.567 (3.81)***	0.195 (4.64)***	0.349 (1.47)	0.943	1.61	37	
	$B_{i,t}$	0.381 (3.12)***	0.707 (3.38)***	0.865	2.24	49	0.589 (4.02)***	0.224 (4.31)***	0.225 (0.65)	0.941	1.62	37	
	$L_{i,t}$	0.411 (3.26)***	0.068 (0.19)	0.854	2.15	49	0.581 (4.08)***	0.213 (6.29)***	0.626 (1.90)*	0.944	1.66	37	

Government consumption $B_{i,t} + L_{i,t}$	0.104 (2.41)**	0.185 (1.64)	0.976	2.15	45	0.372 (3.79)***	0.033 (1.73)*	-0.019 (-0.29)	0.456	2.01	30	Estimated in Differences Time Dummies included
$B_{i,t}$	**0.082** (1.87)*	**0.306** (1.97)**	**0.976**	2.11	45	0.364 (3.66)***	**0.011** (0.58)	**0.242** (2.70)***	**0.489**	2.03	31	
$L_{i,t}$	0.106 (2.35)***	0.103 (0.50)	0.975	2.06	45	0.399 (4.11)***	0.033 (2.15)**	-0.109 (-1.68)*	0.482	1.93	30	

Notes

1. Sample: 1989 to 1994, annual data. Brazil, Mexico, Panama, Paraguay, China: missing data for 1994.
2. For Brazil, private consumption also includes change in stocks. For Argentina, it additionally includes government consumption.
3. Definitions:

- $Y_{i,t}$: gross domestic product of *i*th country, for *t*th, year.
- $RES_{i,t-1}$: foreign exchange reserves of *i*th country, for $t-1$ year, converted to local currency using the average exchange rate for the *t*th year.
- DF: degrees of freedom.
- ρ: first-order autocorrelation in the residuals. The error term is assumed to follow the process $u_{i,t} = \rho u_{i,t-1} + \epsilon_t$.

4. Estimation method: OLS. When $u_{i,t}$ exhibits autocorrelation, nonlinear least squares (NLLS).
5. The *t*-statistics have been calculated with a heteroscedasticity-consistent covariance matrix, using the ROBUSTERRORS option in RATS.
6. One, *, two, **, and three asterisks, ***, denote significance at the 10, 5 and 1 per cent levels, respectively.
7. **Bold face** denotes the best model which, presumably, corresponds to the best proxy of the debt ceiling.

Sources:

Macroeconomic variables: International Financial Statistics, plus *China Statistical Yearbook 1994* for China; *Industry of Free China* and DATA-STREAM database for Taiwan.

Bond flows, $B_{i,t}$, and syndicated loans, $L_{i,t}$: *International Capital Markets and Private Market Financing for Developing Countries*.

the model and the recent economic history of the two regions. Further, it appears that changes in bond flows are a better proxy for changes in LA's external debt ceiling, and changes in syndicated loans in Asia's.

In greater detail, using $B_{i,t} + L_{i,t}$ as a proxy for LA's debt ceiling produces $\hat{\beta} = 0.890$ and $\hat{\gamma} = 1.113$, which are significant at the 1 per cent and 5 per cent levels, respectively. The positive $\hat{\gamma}$ suggests that $B_{i,t} + L_{i,t}$ and $U_{i,t}$ are probably positively correlated. Thus, provided that λ is positive, $\hat{\beta}$ is likely to be a positively biased estimate of β. Taking into account equation (10.14) and that bonds and loans account for most of the flows to the region, the high $\hat{\gamma}$ implies that LA countries spent almost as much as they borrowed.

Using $B_{i,t}$ and $L_{i,t}$ separately reinforces the above conclusions. It additionally suggests that $B_{i,t}$ may be the best proxy for LA's $U_{i,t}$. With $B_{i,t}$, both $\hat{\beta}$ and $\hat{\gamma}$ are positive and significant at the 1 per cent level. R^2 also rises from 0.752 to 0.795, an indication that $B_{i,t}$ is a better proxy of the debt ceiling than $B_{i,t} + L_{i,t}$. Thus, according to equation (10.13), the decline in $\hat{\beta}$ from 0.890 to 0.719 is consistent with the conceptual framework, while $\hat{\beta} = 0.719$ is closer to the true β. Still, β in the neighbourhood of 0.7, which implies that 70 cents of each additional dollar of reserves were spent, is high. With $L_{i,t}$, $\hat{\beta}$ rises to 0.9 and is significant at the 1 per cent level, $\hat{\gamma}$ becomes negative but insignificant, while R^2 drops to 0.726.[7]

For Asia, both $\hat{\beta}$ and $\hat{\gamma}$ are insignificant for all three proxies. The first is positive though, as expected, but the second is negative. As equation (10.5) implies, an insignificant β is not fully consistent with the model. However, this may reflect the loss of efficiency resulting from the usage of a proxy for the debt ceiling. Using proxies effectively reduces the signal-to-noise ratio.

Overall, the conformity of the results with the model lends credibility to the latter's theoretical implications. That is, the return of private capital may have induced higher domestic demand and widening CA deficits through the perception of higher external debt ceiling, even in countries which were not facing a binding external financing constraint. In addition, LA's higher propensity to spend out of flows and reserves is consistent with the region's lower ceiling prior to the return. Consequently, for as long as the perception of a higher-than-before ceiling lasts, LA's decline in savings is unlikely to reverse.

Private consumption, investment and government consumption   The results for private consumption, investment and government consumption are qualitatively the same as those for domestic demand. Thus, in accordance with the model, it appears that the return of private capital affected LA more profoundly than Asia across the board.

In particular, for all three components of domestic demand, LA's $\hat{\beta}$ is positive and significant at the 5 per cent level or higher, the only exception being government consumption when $B_{i,t}$ is used. On the other hand, $\hat{\gamma}$ is always positive when significant. In fact, it is negative only for private consumption when $L_{i,t}$ is used. Further, R^2 attains its highest value (and $\hat{\gamma}$ its highest significance) when $B_{i,t}$ is used, another indication that $B_{i,t}$ may be the best proxy for LA's $U_{i,t}$. For Asia's investment, $\hat{\beta}$ is positive and significant at the 1 per cent level, while $\hat{\gamma}$ is significant at the 10 per cent level only when $L_{i,t}$ is used – an indication that $L_{i,t}$ may be the best proxy of Asia's $U_{i,t}$. The equation for Asia's government purchases has been estimated in differences, as the residual's autocorrelation coefficient ρ was very close to one. In it, $\hat{\gamma}$ is positive and significant at the 1 per cent level with $B_{i,t}$, but negative and significant at the 10 per cent level with $L_{i,t}$.

It is worth pointing out that several of these results do not fully conform with the perceived wisdom, although they are consistent with the chapter's hypotheses. First, it seems that investment and government consumption contributed to LA's widening CA deficits more than commonly thought; both $\hat{\beta}$ and $\hat{\gamma}$ are positive and significant (and higher than in Asia), with the exception of investment when $L_{i,t}$ is used. Further, contrary to the perception of fiscal consolidation in LA, capital flows contributed both directly and indirectly to government consumption; $\hat{\beta}$ is positive and significant at the 5 per cent, 10 per cent and 1 per cent levels for $B_{i,t}$ + $L_{i,t}$, $B_{i,t}$ and $L_{i,t}$, respectively, while $\hat{\gamma}$ is significant at the 5 per cent level for $B_{i,t}$. Finally, the flows contributed to Asia's CA deficits mostly indirectly, through the accumulation of reserves; $\hat{\beta}$ is significant for investment and the change in the G-to-CDP ratio, but $\hat{\gamma}$ usually is not.

The econometric analysis produced several other important results. Among them, the estimation of equation (10.12) with instrumental variables indicated that LA's significant results in Table 10.1 are not an artifact of the simultaneity bias. In particular, both $\hat{\beta}$ and $\hat{\gamma}$ remained positive and highly significant, and their point estimates were close to those reported in Table 10.2. Further, the estimation of equation (10.12) for Asia without the three high-reserve countries largely confirmed the chapter's predictions. That is, both $\hat{\beta}$ and $\hat{\gamma}$ rose in value and significance. For domestic demand, the two coefficients became positive and significant at the 1 per cent level. For investment, $\hat{\gamma}$ also became significant at the 1 per cent level. But for private and government consumption, the results were essentially the same as in Table 10.2.

5   Summary and conclusions

This chapter uses the model of a borrowing-constrained individual to analyse the economic impact of the forceful return of private capital to LDCs in the late 1980s. The empirical results are largely consistent with it, an indication that the model can provide credible answers to the questions posed in the introduction and useful lessons for similar episodes in the future. Reinforcing this optimism, it appears that the impact of the return was so strong that it could not be masked by differences among the recipient countries or by other forces operating at the same time. Such differences – across and within regions – pertain, but are not restricted, to stage of economic development, political and economic institutions, policy response to the surging capital flows, and stage of economic reforms (mainly in LA).

To summarize the answers, the return of private capital to LDCs in the early 1990s may have contributed to the widening CA deficits in two ways: by allowing higher demand in countries facing a binding external financing constraint, and by inducing higher demand through the perception of a higher external debt ceiling in the rest. Comparing the two regions, the higher sensitivity of LA's domestic demand (and components thereof) to foreign exchange reserves and capital flows can be explained by the region's lower external debt ceiling prior to the return. (LA's lower ceiling reflects the debt crisis of the 1980s and the region's poor economic performance relative to Asia.) The lower ceiling can also account for the fact that LA countries spent more of the flows and saved less in the form of reserves than their East Asian counterparts. Consequently, for as long as the perception of a higher ceiling lasts, it is unlikely that LA's savings ratio will recover.

What remains to be addressed is why LA's private consumption was more sensitive to capital flows than investment (their respective $\hat{\gamma}$'s are 1.275 and 0.707 when bond flows are used as a proxy for the external debt ceiling). A possible explanation is suggested by Kaminsky and Pereira (1994), who draw on the political economy literature to explain the collapse of growth in LA after the onset of the debt crisis in the eady 1980s. They argue that great income inequality made it almost impossible for LA countries to reduce spending and allocate more resources to investment, a policy that might have enabled them to cope with the reversal of capital flows in the 1980s as successfully as their Asian counterparts. Similarly, the income inequality may have made it impossible for LA governments to prevent a big share of the flows being diverted to finance consumption.

An alternative explanation, which is consistent with the chapter's forward-looking model, is suggested by the intertemporal trade-off between current and future consumption. Higher current consumption implies lower investment – due to limited resources – and, in turn, lower capital and income increases in the future. Since LA's investment was severely curtailed during the 1980s, the region probably entered the 1990s with a lower capital base than Asia. It is possible then that LA expected a higher marginal product of capital and, thus, higher future income increases with lower investment. By the same token, East Asian countries allocated more of the flows to investment. In short, the behaviour of both regions could be welfare maximizing. Supporting this explanation, the investment-to-GDP ratio has a negative coefficient when included as an additional explanatory variable for LA's consumption in equation (10.12). In contrast, the investment ratio is insignificant for Asia's consumption, an indication that the funds channelled to investment did not constrain consumption.

In addition to these answers, the chapter identifies several other developments in the recipient countries which, despite their economic and statistical significance, have not received sufficient attention in the literature. Among them, the flows contributed to the widening CA deficits both directly, as discussed above, and indirectly, through the accumulation of foreign exchange reserves. They also contributed significantly to LA's widening CA deficits via government consumption and investment, and affected investment in LA more than in Asia. Lastly, the low-reserve Asian countries responded to the return of private capital in a similar way as their LA counterparts.

Finally, the model, in conjunction with the empirical results, implies an important policy lesson. Namely, a consumption boom can occur even in countries which impose restrictions on capital inflows. This is so because higher demand is induced not by the lack of such restrictions, but by the perception of higher access to external financing. Thus, as long as economic agents believe that the government will allow sufficient inflows to cover a (widening) CA deficit, they may spend as if the restrictions did not exist. Such a policy is consistent with the government's goals of avoiding excessive money supply growth and a real appreciation in the country's currency, which may occur when the flows exceed the CA deficit. Yet, as this chapter argues, it may not prevent a surge in domestic demand and a deterioration of the CA deficit.

Notes

1. The model, however, is less restrictive than these explanations. Notably, it does not rely on Calvo's assumption of temporary, or *perceived* as such, reforms to explain the boom. In fact, it predicts that the boom will be bigger when the reforms and the associated increase in the external debt ceiling are perceived as permanent. Nor does the framework rely on McKinnon and Pill's assumption of over-optimistic expectations about higher future productivity, the increased ceiling by itself is sufficient to induce higher borrowing and spending and, thus, widening CA deficits.
   To save space, these alternatives are briefly discussed in Appendix 10A.2, while pertinent empirical results are available upon request.
2. Antzoulatos (1994) and Xu (1995) have shown the properties expressed respectively by inequalities (10.7) and (10.6). Combining them, one can prove the properties expressed by

(10.8) to (10.10), which, to the best of my knowledge, are analysed for the first time in this chapter. Finally, (10.5) has been explored by many authors.

3. In this case, $c_t^*[x_t, \bar{U}_t(x_t)] = c_t^*(x_t, U_t = \infty)$, where $U_t = \infty$ corresponds to the debt ceiling of the individual who faces only his/her lifetime budget constraint. This individual's PS2 is zero. In other words, $\bar{U}_t(x_t)$ is the minimum debt ceiling which will allow the individual to avoid a binding constraint in the worst-case scenario; that is, when the lowest possible income is realized in every period until the end of the planning horizon. See Xu (1995) for more details.

4. It should be noted though that the higher demand is entirely rational despite it leaving a recipient country more vulnerable to negative developments at home and abroad. Prominent examples of such developments are a global recession which may hurt the country's exports, and a reversal of the flows triggered by higher interest rates in the industrial world (the latter being particularly stressed by Calvo et al. 1992b and 1993). Moreover, since the life-time budget constraint (equation (10.4)) is satisfied, the higher demand does not rely on a Ponzi scheme where the debt incurred today will be serviced by future borrowing. Simply, the higher ceiling provides a bigger buffer to smooth the impact of a negative shock, thus weakening the precautionary saving motive – the PS2 component.

5. As noted above, $U_{l,t}$ represents the maximum amount a country could borrow after 1989 in addition to its preexisting debt. Thus, for the short sample period, 1989 to 1994, one can reasonably expect that new borrowing – a flow variable – is correlated with $U_{l,t}$ – a stock variable.

   Related to this, some countries restricted foreign borrowing by private entities in an effort to avoid the undesirable side-effects of excessive inflows. Such policies, however, do not affect the analysis, for the reason that private agents base their spending decisions on the available credit. The latter is correlated with actual flows. See, also, the related discussion on consumption in Section 3.1.

6. The sign of λ is not known *a priori*. It is likely, though, to be positive. On the one hand, high reserves may reflect high precautionary savings because of a low debt ceiling. Provided the low ceiling is manifested in low borrowing, λ would be negative. On the other hand, high reserves may reassure potential lenders about a country's ability to meet its payments obligations on schedule, thus inducing them to lend more to this country or buy its bonds. In this case, λ would be positive. Some evidence in support of this case is provided by Edwards (1984). In his empirical study of the determinants of the spreads over LIBOR, LDCs paid for their Euroloans during the period 1976 to 1980, he finds that the reserves-to-GNP ratio has a negative coefficient; that is, high reserves were associated with low spreads, and vice-versa. Edwards interprets this as evidence that high reserves were associated with lower (perceived) probability of default.

   Nor is the sign of μ known *a priori*. High $B_{l,t}$ may reflect a high $U_{l,t}$, in which case μ would be positive. Yet, an increase in $B_{l,t}$ might reflect a decline in the expected future ceiling, indicating that μ could be negative. Also, μ is likely to be greater than one, as $U_{l,t}$ exceeds $B_{l,t}$.

7. The negative sign of $\hat{\gamma}$ is consistent with the hypothesis that $B_{l,t}$ is a better proxy for $U_{l,t}$ and the fact that bond and loan financing are complementary. Thus a decrease in $U_{l,t}$, manifested on lower $B_{l,t}$, may have induced LA countries to (i) reduce demand and (ii) turn to bank loans for their external financing needs. This is supported by the observation that, when the international bond market collapsed in the second quarter of 1994, following the Federal Reserve's tightening of monetary policy in February 1994, LA countries borrowed more in the syndicated loan market. But when the bond market recovered in the third quarter, they again borrowed more in the bond market. More precisely, the value of new international bonds by all issuers worldwide declined by approximately 45 per cent between the first and second quarter of 1994, and recovered by almost 20 per cent in the third. Following this trend closely, the volume of new international bonds issued by LA countries declined by approximately 60 per cent in the second quarter and recovered by 25 per cent in the third.

References

Antzoulatos, Angelos A. (1994), 'Credit Rationing and Rational Behavior'. *Journal of Money, Credit, and Banking*, **26** (2), May, pp. 182–202.

Bartolini, Leonardo and Allan Drazen (1995). 'Financial Openness as News: Can More be Less?', Mimeo, Federal Reserve Bank of New York, November.

Calvo, Guillermo A. (1986), 'Temporary Stabilization: Predetermined Exchange Rates', *Journal of Political Economy*, **94** (6), 1319–29.

Calvo, Guillermo A. (1988), 'Costly Trade Liberalizations: Durable Goods and Capital Mobility', *IMF Staff Papers*, No. 35, 461–73.

Calvo, Guillermo A., Leonardo Leiderman and Carmen M. Reinhart (1992a), 'Capital Inflows and Real Exchange Rate Appreciation in Latin America: The Role of External Factors', IMF Working Paper, WP/92/62, August.

Calvo, Guillermo A., Leonardo Leiderman and Carmen M. Reinhart (1992b), 'Capital Inflows to Latin America: The 1970s and the 1990s', IMF Working Paper, WP/92/85, October.

Calvo, Guillermo A., Leonardo Leiderman and Carmen M. Reinhart (1993), 'The Capital Inflows Problem: Concepts and Issues', IMF Paper on Policy Analysis and Assessment, PPAA/93/10, July.

Calvo, Guillermo A., Ratna Sahay and Carlos A. Végh (1995), 'Capital Inflows in Central and Eastern Europe: Evidence and Policy Options', IMF Working Paper, WP/95/57, May.

Calvo, Sara and Carmen M. Reinhart (1995), 'Capital Flows to Latin America: Is There Evidence of Contagion Effects?', Mimeo, World Bank and IMF, April.

Carneiro, Dionísio Dias and Márcio G.P. Garcia (1995), 'Private International Capital Flows to Brazil', Mimeo, Department of Economics, Pontifical Catholic University of Rio de Janeiro.

Chuhan, Punam, Stijn Claessens and Nlandu Mamingi (1993), 'Equity and Bond Flows to Asia and Latin America: The Role of Global and Country Factors', Working Paper, WPS 1160, World Bank, July.

Copelman, Martina (1994), 'The Role of Credit in Post-stabilization Consumption Booms', Mimeo, MIT, Department of Economics, January.

Culpeper, Roy (1994), 'Resurgence of Private Flows to Latin America: The Role of American Investors', Mimeo, North–South Institute, February.

Deaton, Angus (1991), 'Saving and Liquidity Constraints', *Econometrica*, **59** (5), September, 1221–48.

Dooley, Michael R (1994), 'Are Recent Capital Inflows to Developing Countries A Vote For or Against Economic Policy Reforms?', Working Paper, No. 295, University of California at Santa Cruz, May.

Dooley, Michael P, Eduardo Fernandez-Arias and Kenneth M. Kletzer (1994), 'Recent Private Capital Inflows to Developing Countries: Is the Debt Crisis Over?', NBER Working Paper, No. 4792, July.

Edwards, Sebastian (1984), 'LDC Foreign Borrowing and Default Risk: An Empirical Investigation, 1976–80', *American Economic Review*, **74** (4), September, 726–34.

Eichengreen, Barry (1996), 'International Lending in the Long Run: Motives and Management, Paper presented at the conference on The Future of Emerging Market Capital Flows at the STERN School of Business, New York University, May.

Fernandez-Ansola, Juan Jose and Thomas Laursen (1995), 'Historical Experience with Bond Financing to Developing Countries', IMF Working Paper, WP/95/27, March.

Glick, Reuven and Ramon Moreno (1994), 'Capital Flows and Monetary Policy in East Asia', Working Paper, No. PB94-08, Federal Reserve Bank of San Francisco, November.

Gooptu, Sudarshan (1993), 'Portfolio Investment Flows to Emerging Markets', Paper presented in the World Bank Symposium Portfolio Investment in Developing Countries, 9–10 September.

International Monetary Fund, *Exchange Restrictions and Exchange Arrangements*, various issues.

International Monetary Fund, *International Capital Markets*, various issues.

International Monetary Fund, *Private Market Financing for Developing Countries*, various issues.

International Monetary Fund, *World Economic Outlook*, various issues.

Johnston, J. (1984). *Econometric Methods*, New York: McGraw-Hill.

Kaminsky, Graciela L. and Alfredo Pereira (1994), 'The Debt Crisis: Lessons of the 1980's for the 1990's', International Finance Discussion Paper, No. 481, Board of the Governors of the Federal Reserve System, September.

Mas, Ignacio (1995), 'Things Governments Do to Money: A Recent History of Currency Reform Schemes and Scams'. *Kyklos*, **48**, 483–512.

McKinnon, Ronald I. and Huw Pill (1994), 'Credible Liberalizations and International Capital Flows: The Over-borrowing Syndrome', Working Paper, Department of Economics, Stanford University, May.

Reinhart, Carmen M. and Carlos A. Végh (1994), 'Intertemporal Consumption Substitution and Inflation Stabilization: An Empirical Investigation', Mimeo, International Monetary Fund, June.

Rojas-Suarez, Liliana and Steven Weisbrod (1995), 'Achieving Stability in Latin American Financial Markets in the Presence of Volatile Capital Flows', Working Paper Series, No. 304, Inter-American Development Bank.

Rosende, Francisco (1995), 'Handling Capital Inflows: Some Comments on the Chilean Experience', Mimeo, Catholic University of Chile, June.

Rossi, Nicola (1988), 'Government Spending, the Real Interest Rate, and the Behavior of Liquidity-Constrained Consumers in Developing Countries', *IMF Staff Papers*, No. 85, 104–140.

Sachs, Jeffrey, Aaron Tornell and Andrés Velasco (1995), 'The Collapse of the Mexican Peso: What Have We Learned?', NBER Working Paper, No. 5142, June.

Spiegel, Mark M. (1995), 'Sterilization of Capital Inflows Through the Banking Sector: Evidence from Asia', Working Paper, No. 95–06, Economic Research Department, Federal Reserve Bank of San Francisco, June.

World Bank (1988), *External Debt: Definition, Statistical Coverage and Methodology*, Paris: World Bank.

Wijnbergen, Sweder van (1990), 'Cash/Debt Buy-backs and the Insurance Value of Reserves', *Journal of international Economics*, **29**, 123–31.

Xu, Xiaonian (1995), 'Precautionary Savings Under Liquidity Constraints: A Decomposition', *International Economic Review*, **36** (3), August, 675–90.

Zeldes, Stephen P. (1989), 'Optimal Consumption with Stochastic Income: Deviations from Certainty Equivalence', *Quarterly Journal of Economics*, **104**, 275–99.

Appendix 10A.1   Data description

Aggregate data come mostly from the International Financial Statistics database (IFS). Consumption corresponds to private consumption (line 96f in IFS), while income corresponds to GDP (line 99b). Government consumption (line 91f) and gross fixed capital formation, that is, investment, (line 93i) are also used. For Brazil, private consumption includes the change in stocks (line 93e), while for Argentina it further includes government consumption. The composition of GDP for the People's Republic of China (China), for which there is no information in IFS, is taken from the *China Statistical Yearbook 1994*, a publication of the country's State Statistical Bureau. In it, the main components are personal consumption, government consumption, and 'accumulation', the latter closely corresponding to IFS's gross fixed capital formation. For Taiwan, which is not included in IFS, all data come from the *Industry of Free China* and the DATASTREAM database.

Total foreign exchange reserves minus gold (line 1/d in IFS) at the end of the $t-1$ year are converted to local currency using the average exchange rate for the t year (line rf). For China, prior to July 1992, line 1/d comprises the foreign exchange holdings of the People's Bank of China and the Bank of China. Beginning July 1992, foreign exchange holdings at the Bank of China are not included any more. Thus, the post-1991 IFS figures have been adjusted with the Federal Reserve Bank of New York (FRBNY) staff estimate of the reserves held at the Bank of China. Noteworthy, currency fluctuations should not affect the interpretation of the results, despite them affecting the reserves-to-GDP ratio, $(S_{i,t-1})/(Y_{i,t})$. Consider the two cases below. First, let real GDP be the same at $t-1$ and t. Let also dollar reserves, $S^{\$}_{i,t-1}$, remain the same between $t-2$ and $t-1$. Further assuming that purchasing power parity holds and US inflation is zero, it follows that the nominal exchange rate e(National Currency/\$) depreciates by the same rate as inflation $\pi_{i,t}$, the latter measured by the GDP price deflator. In this case, the reserve-to-GDP ratio does not change between $t-1$ and t:

$$\frac{S_{i,t-1}}{Y_{i,t}} = \frac{S^{\$}_{i,t-1}e_{i,t}}{Y_{i,t}} = \frac{S^{\$}_{i,t-2}e_{i,t}}{Y_{i,t}} = \frac{S^{\$}_{i,t-2}e_{i,t-1}(1+\pi_{i,t})}{Y_{i,t-1}(1+\pi_{i,t})}$$

$$= \frac{S^{\$}_{i,t-2}e_{i,t-1}}{Y_{i,t-1}} = \frac{S_{i,t-2}}{Y_{i,t-1}}.$$

Next, consider the case where the nominal exchange rate depreciates by less than the inflation rate. The same calculations as above show that the reserves' purchasing power increases, even though the dollar reserves have not changed. Yet, this exchange rate driven increase can lead to higher consumption.

$$\frac{S_{i,t-1}}{Y_{i,t}} > \frac{S_{i,t-2}}{Y_{i,t-1}}.$$

Finally, the data on bond flows, $B_{i,t}$, and syndicated loans, $L_{i,t}$, are collected from several issues of the *International Capital Markets* and *Private Market Financing for Developing Countries*. $B_{i,t}$ and $L_{i,t}$ are converted to local currency using the average exchange rate for the year t.

Appendix 10A.2   Alternative explanations for demand surges and post-stabilization consumption booms

Alternative	Comments
Capital flows and credit expansion to private sector (Copelman 1994)	The chapter's model is consistent with Copelman's evidence that capital flows supported a credit expansion to the private sector and, through it, the consumption boom that followed Mexico's stabilization programme in the late 1980s. Implicit in her analysis, however, is the assumption that Mexican households were facing a binding constraint. In contrast, the chapter's model suggests that the increased availability of credit could have the same effect even when people were not facing a binding constraint. In addition, the chapter argues that foreign exchange reserves carried over from the previous period may have supported the credit expansion and the associated consumption boom.
Role of temporary, or perceived as such, reforms (Calvo 1986)	Using a cash-in-advance model, Calvo suggests that a temporary, or *perceived* as such in the case of non-credible reforms, exchange rate-based stabilization programme may cause a consumption boom. Briefly, under perfect capital mobility, a temporary reduction in the rate of currency depreciation leads to a temporary reduction in the nominal interest rate. The latter, reduces the opportunity cost of holding money and, through it, the cost of current consumption relative to future consumption. In response, forward-looking individuals substitute current for future consumption. Unlike Calvo's model, however, the present one predicts that the consumption boom will be stronger and longer lasting when the capital flows are perceived as a permanent increase in the debt ceiling. Combining the two models, to the extent that credible reforms increase a country's access to external financing, they can cause a consumption boom even when the cost of current and future consumption is the same.

Expansionary
effect of lower real
interest rates

The argument goes as follows: the stabilization programme leads to lower nominal interest rates. But as inflationary expectations recede slowly, real rates decline thus leading to higher consumption. This effect is consistent with the chapter's model, as a lower real rate is likely to induce more borrowing and higher demand even in an explicit intertemporal optimizing framework, in which both the income and substitution effects operate. However, in support of the chapter's explanation, a consumption boom has occurred even in countries in which the real interest rate rose (Reinhart and Végh 1994).

'Over-borrowing
syndrome'
(McKinnon and
Pill 1994)

This syndrome was experienced by several countries – developing and developed alike – in the aftermath of policy reforms. McKinnon and Pill's analysis, however, relies on the banking sector's superior information relative to the information of other economic actors, and on the moral hazard created by the expectation that governments will not allow banks to collapse under the burden of bad loans. Briefly, over-optimistic agents want to consume and invest more in anticipation of higher future income, while the banking sector is willing to satisfy their demand for credit even if it does not share their optimism. Banks act so in the knowledge that they will be bailed out if the overoptimistic expectations do not materialize and their borrowers default. In contrast, this chapter does not rely on informational asymmetries or over-optimistic expectations to justify higher borrowing and spending in the event of a surge in capital flows; the perception of a higher external debt ceiling is sufficient.

PART III

LESSONS FROM THE NORDIC ENLARGEMENT AND THE EXPERIENCE OF THE SOUTHERN PERIPHERY

11 Swedish integration with the European Union: effects on growth and the structure of trade

P. Nandakumar and Bala Batavia

1 Introduction

As is well known from the theory of customs unions, when trade is liberalized between a group of countries, there is trade creation between the countries forming the union, while there is trade diversion away from countries outside. The growth in exports will be marked in sectors of relative comparative advantage, an impetus for *inter-sectoral* trade. But according to the theories of trade emphasizing imperfect competition, there will be growth in *intra-industry* trade as well, assuming more importance when the relative factor endowments in the countries become more similar. As integration proceeds there may be also changes in relative comparative advantage positions as 'false' comparative advantages (in Lancaster's (1980) terminology) are eliminated under the new-found economies of scale, and this can also fuel intra-industry trade.

The gradual lowering of tariff barriers between the European Free Trade Association (EFTA) and the European Union (EU) during the 1970s and the early 1980s has meant that Sweden has already benefited from the general ongoing liberalization process in Europe. But the benefits of the creation of the internal market under the 1992 programme would be realized only now, with Sweden taking the final decisive step of full EU membership. The barriers that are falling now and the possibilities that are opening up are of a different kind compared to the EFTA–EU liberalization processes. This chapter tries to evaluate the effects of the Swedish EU integration process reaching back to the1980s, paying attention to the structural effects (that have implications beyond the static) that would vary between periods.

Section 2 presents the background *for* the analysis, touching upon previous studies of the liberalization process between Sweden and the European Union. This is followed by the main empirical section, rounded off by the concluding part of the chapter.

2 Background and earlier work

A study by a Swedish Parliamentary Committee (SOU 1994) of the probable effects (benefits) of Swedish membership of the EU singles out an increase in the investment–GDP ratio and the resulting rise in the GDP growth rate as the key benefit. This result seems to hinge upon certain assumptions or propositions (not formally derived), one being that full-fledged EU membership will attract increased foreign direct investment, particularly into high-tech, skill-intensive sectors.

But, as Kokko (1994) remarks, such a presumption *may* be misplaced; EU membership may not be the sole criteria on which multinational companies base their foreign direct investment decisions. Indeed, in the mid-1980s, Swedish multinationals (MNCs) have stepped up *their* foreign investment, resulting in negative net foreign domestic investment (FDI) flows to Sweden. Not only that, these MNCs have been shifting out the skill-intensive part of their vertically integrated activities to locations outside Sweden.

A key role for skill-intensive industries also has certain implications for the pattern of relative comparative advantage and structural change. Sweden's traditional relative comparative advantage has been in natural resource and energy-intensive industries. In terms of skill intensity, Swedish industry does not fare well in international comparisons, even though in terms of the percentage of skilled labour in the total labour force, Sweden nears the top of the table. The reason for this seemingly contradictory state of affairs is that much of the skilled labour in Sweden is in the government sector. In recent years, the Swedish competitive position might have improved, according to OECD (1986).

Of course, the growth (in exports) of a particular sector need not be due to trade policy alone; there could be shifts in relative comparative advantage over time. Or it may be due to the elimination of 'false' comparative advantages (Lancaster 1980) as new vistas offering greater economies of scale open up in the wake of economic integration. Often, skill-intensive industries are new-product industries that depend on a large *home* market before integration, which is no longer a constraint with the economies of scale offered by a programme such as the internal market for Europe. Typically, the growth in exports of these sectors constitute intra-industry trade, in the presence of product differentiation and demand for variety. The programme for the internal market in Europe, with the removal of several constraining factors such as technical barriers, discriminatory government procurement, protected investment areas and so on, should give a much larger impetus to the growth in such trade than a pure reduction in tariffs.

Lundberg (1992) has studied the impact on Swedish trade of the liberalization process in Europe, for the period 1970–84. He finds that while exports have grown for sectors in which Sweden has traditionally possessed relative comparative advantage, the dominant increase has been in intra-industry trade which is seen to be positively influenced by growth orientation (typically in new-product industries), technology and skill intensities. Lundberg's results are for time periods prior to full-fledged Swedish participation in Europe's internal market. Such a participation may be expected to magnify these effects, and viewed in such a fashion, the Parliamentary Committee's predictions (which are based on a key role for the high-tech, skill-intensive sectors) fall in line with these results.

The next section analyses the effects of trade liberalization and economic integration in Europe on Swedish inter-industry and intra-industry trade with the EU members, for the period 1983–94. The industry classification according to factor intensities is as in Ohlsson and Vinell (1987). This section, based on assumptions about expectations formation and their influence, also uses FDI data to sketch scenarios for investment flows into key sectors.

3   Empirical analysis

Table 11.1 provides the net export figures (as ratios to total trade) for industries classified according to factor intensities as in Ohlsson and Vinell (1987). The figures are for Swedish–EU trade. The figures for each year represent in effect relative comparative advantage positions. The shifts in these ratios cannot be attributed to trade policies alone; there could be exogenous shifts in comparative advantage over time. Still, trade policies may be considered to exert an important influence. The table shows that towards the end of the 1980s and the early 1990s the R&D-intensive and the skill-intensive sectors are being benefited at a rate even greater than that for the capital- and energy-intensive sectors (the traditional comparative advantage sectors).

The easing of tariff barriers on manufactured goods between the EU and EFTA during the 1970s and the early 1980s ought to have benefited Sweden's industrial sectors, embedding traditional comparative advantage

Table 11.1   Net export ratios

Year	Labour-intensive industry	Capital-intensive industry	Skill-intensive industry	R&D-intensive industry
1983	−0.31	+0.18	−0.04	−0.12
1989	−0.42	+0.31	−0.06	−0.05
1994	−0.34	+0.346	+0.02	+0.03

such as forest-based and energy-intensive ones. There is a data-based problem here in that there is extensive overlap between the capital-intensive industries and the ones that fall into the definition of energy-intensive and resource-intensive industries. Because of this, an enhancement of the net export position of capital-intensive industries will be construed as an improvement in the position of Sweden's industries of traditional comparative advantage.

Preliminary work indicates that the period of trade liberalization between the EU and the EFTA (up to the mid-1980s or so) has benefited these traditional industries, which amounts to an increase in inter-sectoral trade. But this period has also seen an improvement in the position of skill- and R&D-intensive industries (manifested in the table as a reduction in the negative net export ratios). The later period, up to 1994, seems to have benefited these latter type of industries strongly, so that trade flows have become increasingly of the intra-industry type. This seems to stand to reason, since the change in factor endowments during this period, if any at all, must have only made Sweden more similar to the EU countries. Also, during the tail end of this latter period, expectations about EU membership could have benefited exports of high-tech, skill-intensive industries, as we argue later. The increase in exports of the skill-intensive goods as well as that of the goods of traditional comparative advantage during the period under study, is consistent with the relevant models of international trade.[1]

Lundberg (1992) has used a cross-section analysis of Swedish industries to illustrate, among other things, the importance of factors such as skill intensity and growth orientation in explaining the growth in intra-industry trade. New-product industries are often fast growing, and the rationale for the presumption that they benefit from trade liberalization and economic integration is as follows: these new-product industries need a large market in their initial, experimental, take-off stages, and this requirement can be met only by a *large* home market in the presence of trade barriers. But the large home market provides a low-cost comparative advantage only under protection, since with the freeing of trade and the removal of investment barriers, economies of scale become available even to a small country; so, with liberalization and integration, exports of new-product, growth-orientated industries from the small country can get a fillip.

Here we extend Lundberg's analysis to a later time period, where economic integration has proceeded further, and the results ought to be more pronounced.

The following equation was estimated for conventionally defined intra-industry trade for a cross-section of manufacturing industries:

$$y = a_0 + a_1 m + a_2 f \qquad (11.1)$$

where y is the intra-industry trade variable and is defined as [(exports + imports) − absolute value of (exports−imports)]/total output in the industry, m is market growth (of the total output) in the industry, and f is expenditure on research and development in the industry as a proportion of total output. Other variables used in place of f are t the share of technicians in the labour force in the industry, and also u the share of university graduates in the labour force in the industry.[2] Lundberg (1992) had also used a variable representing product substitutability, which we omit since some further development in the suitability of this variable may be desirable.

The results of the estimation for the years 1983–91 and for the individual years 1985, 1987, 1989 and 1991 are shown below. The t-values are given in brackets under the values of the estimated coefficients (significance levels are given by *** for 1 per cent, ** for 5 per cent, and * for 10 per cent levels).

- *Aggregate model for years 1983–91*

$$y = 0.56 \quad + \quad 0.073\,m \quad + \quad 2.96\,f \qquad R = 0.24$$
$$\quad (8.48)^{***} \qquad (0.30) \qquad (4.54)^{***} \quad F(2,65) = 10.48$$

- *Models for the individual years*

Year 1985

$$y = 0.39 \quad + \quad 3.18\,m \quad + \quad 2.65\,f \qquad R = 0.57$$
$$\quad (2.58)^{**} \qquad (2.90)^{**} \qquad (2.07)^{***} \quad F(2,12) = 8.05$$

Year 1987

$$y \quad 0.86 \quad - \quad 4.19\,m \quad + \quad 4.24\,f \qquad R = 0.53$$
$$\quad (4.88)^{**} \qquad (-2.21)^{**} \qquad (3.31)^{***} \quad F(2,12) = 6.77$$

Year 1989

$$y \quad 0.43 \quad + \quad 0.36\,m \quad + \quad 2.08\,f \qquad R = 0.27$$
$$\quad (2.79)^{**} \qquad (1.15) \qquad (1.85)^{*} \quad F(2,12) = 2.21$$

Year 1991

$$y \quad 0.04 \quad - \quad 5.04\,m \quad + \quad 6.91\,f \qquad R = 0.57$$
$$\quad (0.20) \qquad (-3.46)^{***} \qquad (3.93)^{***} \quad F(2,12) = 7.80$$

When the variables t and u were substituted for the variable f, similar results were obtained. The results above compare well with the figures in Table 11.1, where the skill- and R&D-intensive sectors are seen to boost their exports in these years. The variable f is positive and statistically significant at least the 0.05 level for the aggregate model for the years 1983–

91 and for all the individual years (except for 1989 where it is significant at the 0.1 level). The estimation also shows that the rate of growth of the sector variable m was not statistically significant for the aggregate model 1983–91 years. For the individual years 1991 and 1987 the sign for this variable was negative, and for the years 1985 and 1989 it was positive. The hypothesis that intra-trade grows faster in the new products industries in their initial high-growth periods is measured by the rate of growth of output and a high rate of technological change measured by the R&D intensity. Given the significance of the f variable and the mixed results for the m variable, there is some marginal support for the above hypothesis. Similar results were also obtained by Lundberg (1992) for the data period 1970–84. The explanatory values of the regressions while low are considerably higher than those obtained by Lundberg for the earlier years. Since the data for the individual years is limited (each year has a cross-section of only 15 industries), the results for the individual years should be viewed with caution.

These results, however, need not derive from the effects of trade (and market integration) policy alone; exogenous shifts in comparative advantage may have occurred. If it is a case of 'false' comparative advantages being eliminated by market integration, and if integration does have such a dominant role, it should be reflected somehow in the FDI patterns. The Parliamentary Committee report (SOU 1994), indeed, stresses these aspects.

Table 11.2 gives the aggregate foreign direct investment figures, exact figures disaggregated by sectors not being available.

Kokko (1994) points out that in recent years (in the mid-1980s) heavy investment by Swedish MNCs abroad has meant a smaller, sometimes negative, inflow of domestic investment to Sweden, so that the Parliamentary Committee's emphasis on more, strategically important, FDI of trade liberalization and economic integration in Europe may be belied. But, now, if the increased outflow of FDI was due to the strategic interest in being a part of (and being able to influence) the integration process in Europe, the reverse must also be true: with expectations of Sweden playing a full part in the internal market, FDI (as well as domestic investment), particularly in key high-tech, skill-intensive, sectors should have increased.

By this reasoning, since the 1992 programme for the European internal market was known by 1986/87, net FDI inflow to Sweden should have started decreasing around that period. Similarly, since expectations about full Swedish EU membership also started getting a boost from perhaps around 1993, the tail end of the FDI data should reflect that positive impact. But no such clear pattern seems to emerge. Figures for FDI in the 1990s in Table 11.2 seem to suggest that the FDI may be increasing with *expectations* about Sweden's entry into the EU.

Table 11.2 Aggregate net FDI to Sweden (million kronors)

Year	Net FDI Inflow
1983	−997
1984	−882
1985	−1 028
1986	−2 249
1987	−3 911
1988	−5 719
1989	−8 484
1990	−12 287
1991	−911
1992	−325
1993	+2 209
1994	−387

4 Conclusion

In this chapter, the growth and the change in the structure of Swedish trade with the European Union during the period 1980–94 (encompassing the gradual process of Swedish integration with the Union) were studied. It was noted that the industries embedding traditional Swedish comparative advantage, the natural resource and energy-intensive ones, did benefit, increasing their export surplus, particularly in the period up to the mid-1980s. However, skill- and R&D-intensive industries also improved their net trade positions. A cross-sectional analysis of industries revealed that these characteristics of skill and R&D intensities, as well as to a smaller extent that of growth orientation typical of new-product industries, were important in explaining the growth in intra-industry trade, particularly so in the later part of the period when the integration process intensified. These results with the extended period embracing the 1990s, compare well with earlier work.

The improved performance of the skill-intensive sectors need not be traced to the liberalization policies alone. It could also be due to exogenous shifts in comparative advantage, with the Swedish traditional disadvantage (relative to EU members) in skill endowments in industry being eliminated over time. But it could equally well be a case of 'false' comparative advantages being eliminated because of the economies of scale offered by the process of market integration.

In fact, in terms of skill levels for the labour force *as a whole*, inclusive of the public sector, Sweden compares favourably with other EU members, and if this (rather than skill levels in industry alone) is taken as the measure of comparative advantage, then Sweden's traditional disadvantage in this genre disappears. But the large internal market in the EU might have offered a comparative advantage because of economies of scale (rather than relative factor endowments), particularly for the skill-intensive, growth-orientated industries. Such a 'false' comparative advantage might have been gradually vanquished as Sweden became integrated into the community, the process being more intensified in recent years.

These developments on the trade front ought to have been reflected, at least to some extent, in the structure of foreign direct investment flows as well. As the 1992 programme for Europe's internal market was known by the latter half of the 1980s, it is reasonable to expect that the Swedish MNCs would have opted to direct investment flows increasingly to the Union (thus reducing net FDI flows to Sweden) to take part and to become influential in the process of integration being played out there. By the same token, with full EU membership becoming closer, net FDI inflows should have been enhanced towards the middle of the current decade. But the data do not bear out this kind of reasoning fully. Hence the optimism expressed by a Parliamentary Committee (set up to study the benefits of EU membership) regarding increased strategic FDI inflows to Sweden may not be immediately apparent.

Notes

1. Assume that the skill-intensive good could be of different qualities. It requires two inputs, one composite factor consisting of labour and capital (also representing energy, here), the other factor being 'skill'. The unit cost of the composite factor is represented by W and that of the skill input (embedded in high-skilled workers) by R. In skill-abundant Sweden, R is higher than in the EC, so that $R_{EC} < R_{SW}$, while $W_{EC} > W_{SW}$.

    Representing the cost of production in a simple fashion by $C = W + a.R$, assuming inputs per unit of output of one unit of the composite factor and 'a' units of skill, the costs are *equal* in the EC and Sweden if

    $$W_{EC} + a.R_{EC} = W_{SW} + a.R_{SW}$$

    that is, if

    $$a = \frac{W_{EC} - W_{SW}}{R_{SW} - R_{EC}}.$$

    For skill-intensities *below* this level, Sweden has a comparative advantage and, with the freeing of barriers, pushes up exports of (those qualities of) the skill-intensive good, *as well as* that of the traditional goods. The elimination of 'false' comparative advantages provided by a large home market before integration can also give rise to this pattern.

2. Data for the variables was obtained from OECD, *Industrial Structure Statistics*, 1990 and 1992, and also OECD *Science and Technology Indicators*, 1991, 1993 and 1995. The 15 industries selected were Food, Beverages and Tobacco; Textiles, Apparel and Leather; Wood Products and Furniture; Paper, Paper Products and Printing; Chemical Products; Drugs and Medicines; Rubber and Plastic Products; Non-metallic Mineral Products;

Basic Metal Industries; Metal Products; Office and Computing Machinery; Electrical Industrial Machinery; Machinery and Equipment; Motor Vehicles; Metal Products; and Electronic Equipment.

References

Buiques, P. and A. Jacquemin (1989), 'Strategies of Firms and Structural Environment in the Large Internal Market', *Journal of Common Market Studies*, **28**, 53–67.

Caves, R. (1981), 'Intra-industry Trade and Market Structure in the Industrial Countries', *Oxford Economic Papers*, **38**, 203–23.

Hansson, P. (1989), 'Intra-industry Trade: Measurement, Determinants and Growth', *Umeå Economic Studies*, No. 205, University of Umeå.

Hansson, P. (1991), 'Determinants of Intra-industry Specialization in Swedish Foreign Trade', *Scandinavian Journal of Economics*, **93**, 391–406.

Helpman, E. and P. Krugman (1985), *Market Structure and Foreign Trade*, Cambridge, MA: MIT Press.

Kokko, A. (1994), 'Sweden: Effects of EU Membership on Investment and Growth', *World Economy*, **17** (5), 667–77.

Lancaster, K. (1980), 'Intra-industry Trade Under Perfect Monopolistic Competition', *Journal of International Economics*, **10**, 151–76.

Lundberg, L. (1992), 'Economic Integration, Inter- and Intra-industry Trade: The Case of Sweden and the EC', *Scandinavian Journal of Economics*, **94** (3), 393–408.

Ohlsson, L. and L. Vinell (1987), 'Driving Forces of Growth. A Study of Industries' Future Possibilities', *Industriforbundets Forlag*, Stockholm.

OECD (1990, 1992), *Industrial Structure Statistics*, Paris: OECD.

OECD (1986, 1991, 1993, 1995), *Science and Technology Indicators No. 2. R & D. Invention and Competitiveness*, Paris: OECD.

Smith, A. and A.J. Venables (1988), 'Completing the Internal Market in the European Community: Some Industry Simulation', *European Economic Review*, **32**, 1501–25.

Swedish Parliamentary Committee (1994), 6, 'Sweden and Europe: An analysis of the Socioeconomic Impacts', *Nordstedts*, Stockholm.

12 Did the ERM stabilize real exchange rates? The experience of the southern members of the EU

Bernd Kempa

1 Introduction

This chapter studies the bilateral real exchange rates of the four southern EU members – Greece, Italy, Portugal and Spain – a group of countries which have experienced the highest rates of real exchange rate variability within the union. The analysis attempts to ascertain whether participation in the exchange rate mechanism (ERM) of the European monetary system (EMS) has been a significant factor in bringing about a reduction in real exchange rate variability. The sample countries had very different degrees of exposure to the ERM. While Italy participated in the system since the inception of the EMS in 1979, Portugal and Spain joined in 1989 and 1992, respectively, while Greece was never a member. The four countries are thus ideal for analysing whether the ERM helped to stabilize real exchange rates.

The level of real exchange rate variability has been the subject of much of the recent empirical research on exchange rate systems. An important strand of the literature has focused on the question whether nominal exchange rate regimes affect the behaviour of real exchange rates. The overwhelming evidence suggests real exchange rates to be much more volatile under floating rate regimes compared to systems of pegged nominal exchange rates.[1] Since real exchange rates reflect the relative prices of the outputs of different countries, the former should be affected mainly by real factors such as technology or demand. However, in an environment of price sluggishness, (nominal) shocks in the money market may also impinge on the real exchange rate by inducing the latter to overshoot its equilibrium level, giving rise to 'excess volatility' in foreign exchange markets.[2] Nominal exchange rate regimes can reasonably be expected to lower the incidence of nominal shocks due to the closer monetary cooperation among the member countries. The closer monetary cooperation in turn reduces the degree of 'excess volatility' of real exchange rates.

Monetary and real shocks are generally unobservable but can potentially be identified from the joint behaviour of the time series on real exchange rates and relative price levels. To this end, monthly data on the bilateral real exchange rates and relative price levels of the four sample countries *vis-à-vis* Germany are decomposed into their underlying nominal and real sources by employing the structural bivariate vector autoregression (SVAR) analysis pioneered by Blanchard and Quah (1989), as extended by Lastrapes (1992). The decomposition is obtained by imposing the identifying restriction that monetary shocks have no long-run effect on the level of the real exchange rate. The SVAR decomposition can be used to determine whether monetary shocks are significant and how these shocks influence the time paths of the bilateral real exchange rates.

The remainder of the chapter is organized as follows. Section 2 defines the real exchange rate and presents data on the level of real exchange rate variability in the sample countries. Section 3 discusses how a bivariate SVAR applied to the rates of change of real exchange rates and relative price levels can be used to identify the underlying monetary and real shocks. Section 4 applies the SVAR on the exchange rate data of Greece, Italy, Portugal and Spain. After testing for the significance of monetary shocks in the four countries, the incidence of these shocks is related to the different stages of monetary coordination in Europe. The results are summarized in Section 5.

2   Some evidence on real exchange rate variability

Monthly data have been taken from the IMT International Financial Statistics database for the time period 1972:1 to 1994:12. Real exchange rates are constructed using national consumer price indices and own-currency to dollar exchange rates. The real exchange rates are bilateral rates of Greece, Italy, Portugal and Spain, all expressed *vis-à-vis* Germany. These bilateral rates are computed using the following formula:

$$q_i = \frac{P_i \cdot \pi_{ger}}{P_{ger} \cdot \pi_i} \tag{12.1}$$

where q_i is the bilateral real exchange rate of country i, P denotes the consumer price index, π is the nominal exchange rate and *ger* is shorthand for Germany.

Table 12.1 reports on the mean rates of change of the real exchange rates in the four sample countries. Numbers are presented for four different subperiods of the sample. The first ranges from 1972:2 to 1979:2 and is the period preceding the EMS when all four countries in the sample had floating exchange rates *vis-à-vis* Germany. The second period extends from 1979:3 to 1986:12 and represents the phase immediately following the inception of the EMS, which was characterized by frequent realignments of the ERM parity grid. The third period covers the time span from 1987:1 to 1992:8, a period during which no more realignments occurred within the

Table 12.1   Mean rates of change of the real exchange rate (in %)

	1972:2– 1979:2	1979:3– 1986:12	1987:1– 1992:8	1992:9– 1994:12
Greece	2.21	1.82	1.21	1.06
Italy	1.72	0.77	0.49	2.08
Portugal	1.77	1.50	0.88	1.19
Spain	1.93	1.15	0.96	1.29

ERM. Finally, the period 1992:9 to 1994:12 witnessed the loosening of the ERM in response to the European currency crises of 1992 and 1993 when the Italian lira was forced to float and the Portuguese escudo and the Spanish peseta experienced successive devaluations of their central parities. The first three periods are thus characterized by increasingly tighter monetary coordination within the ERM while the last period reflects the recurrence of instability in European currency markets. Table 12.1 implies that the level of real exchange rate variability declined steadily as more countries joined the ERM and the EMS became increasingly more credible. However, real exchange rate variability picked up again in the wake of the European currency crises of 1992 and 1993. The evidence of Table 12.1 immediately raises the questions whether the operation of the ERM has been instrumental in bringing about the stabilization of the real exchange rates in the 1980s and whether the exchange rate system has been responsible for the recurrence of real exchange rate instability in the 1990s. The subsequent analysis turns to these issues.

3   The empirical model
This section discusses an empirical model which allows for a decomposition of the time series on real exchange rates into their underlying monetary and real sources. In the Dornbusch (1976) scenario, the assumption of sluggish adjustments of commodity prices implies that monetary shocks displace the real exchange rate on impact. In the long run, however, relative price levels adjust and the real exchange rate returns to its pre-shock level. The Dornbusch framework therefore suggests that monetary shocks should be identified as the component of mean-reversion in the time series on real exchange rates. In contrast, the equilibrium approach to exchange rates implies that real shocks with large permanent components will persistently alter the equilibrium position of the real exchange rate (see, for example, Stockman 1987). According to the equilibrium approach,

then, permanent displacements of real exchange rates can be attributed to the incidence of real shocks.

Based on the above distinction, a bivariate structural vector autoregression (SVAR) in the tradition of Blanchard and Quah (1989) is used to recover monetary and real shocks from the first differences of the data on real exchange rates and relative price levels.[3] The following unrestricted bivariate SVAR is estimated:

$$X_t = B_1 X_{t-1} + B_2 X_{t-2} + \ldots + B_p X_{t-p} + e_t \qquad (12.2)$$

where $X_t \equiv [d\ln(q_t), d\ln(P_t/P_t^*)]'$ and e_t, is a 2×1 vector of multivariate normal residuals. The reduced form of (12.2) just identifies the unobservable structural disturbances by imposing the restriction of long-run neutrality of monetary shocks on the real exchange rate. The SVAR procedure can be used to estimate the speed of adjustment of the real exchange rate to a standardized monetary shock (innovation accounting) as well as the relative importance of monetary and real shocks in the data (variance decomposition).

The insights obtained by the approach chosen in this chapter come at the cost of accepting two kinds of restrictions on the generality of the results. First, any bivariate SVAR is restricted to the identification of only two kinds of shocks by construction. If exchange rates are driven by more than two shocks, the reduction to a two-dimensional system may render the decomposition meaningless. Blanchard and Quah (1989, pp. 659 and 669–72) derive conditions under which the bivariate SVAR continues to yield a meaningful decomposition in the presence of multiple shocks, and the results reported below are based on the assumption that these conditions hold.[4] Second, our results may be biased if nominal shocks have a permanent effect on the real exchange rate. However, our identification scheme will still be approximately correct as long as these effects are small relative to the size of real shocks (Blanchard and Quah 1989, pp. 659 and 668–9). The results presented below should therefore be interpreted with these qualifications in mind.

4 Results

The SVAR of equation (12.2) exists if the vector process X_t, is stationary and if there is no cointegration between q_t, and (P_t/P_t^*). Augmented Dickey–Fuller tests for unit roots in q_t, and (P_t/P_t^*) and in the residuals from restricted cointegrating regressions imply that all series have a unit root in levels but not in first differences.[5] In order to preserve symmetry, equation (12.2) was estimated with the lag length for all countries set equal to $p = 12$.

Table 12.2 Shares of monetary shocks in a variance decomposition of structural vector autoregressions*

Greece	25.27	(13.92, 59.96)
Italy	70.90	(36.56, 88.69)
Portugal	4.96	(−3.08, 19.46)
Spain	37.95	(4.27, 59.32)

Note: *Shares of monetary shocks as percentage of the total forecast error variance, 12-month averages; numbers in parentheses are (asymmetric) one-standard-error empirical confidence bounds obtained from a bootstrap simulation with 1000 replications.

Table 12.2 reports the results of forecast error variance decompositions of the vector autoregressions which can be used to check for the significance of the incidence of monetary shocks in the sample countries. The variance decompositions of Table 12.2 are the shares of overall variability due to monetary shocks.[6] By construction, the influence of monetary shocks disappears in the long run and the table presents numbers for the average impact of monetary disturbances at a 12-month forecast horizon. Monetary shocks are significant for all countries except Portugal, the only country for which the confidence interval of the variance decomposition includes a zero. For the remaining three countries, the shares of monetary shocks account for more than a quarter of each country's real exchange rate variability and range from 25.27 per cent for Greece to 70.9 per cent for Italy.

In order to investigate whether the responses of the real exchange rates to a monetary shock are in line with the predictions of the Dornbusch model, the estimated SVAR system can be used to trace experimentally the impact of a one-standard-deviation money demand shock on the real exchange rate. Figure 12.1 plots the impulse response functions of the real exchange rates for the four countries of the sample.[7] With the exception of Portugal, the real exchange rate effect of a monetary disturbance accords with the Dornbusch scenario. The real exchange rate depreciates on impact and overshoots its equilibrium level. Moreover, the depreciation peaks within the first 12 months after the shock hits the system, reverts thereafter and gradually converges to zero as time progresses. The broken lines in the panels are one-standard-deviation confidence bounds obtained from a bootstrap simulation with 1000 replications.[8] On impact, the impulse response functions are significant for Greece and Italy, marginally significant for Spain and not significant for Portugal. All responses become insignificant after about 12 to 24 months.

The evidence contained in Table 12.2 and Figure 12.1 implies that monetary shocks significantly influence the time paths of the real exchange rates in all countries except Portugal. Consequently, the remainder of the paper restricts the attention to Greece, Italy and Spain and turns to an assessment of the impact of the ERM on the incidence of monetary shocks relative to real shocks in these three countries.

Table 12.3 displays the standard deviations of monetary and real shocks for the four different subperiods discussed in Section 2. In the table, standard deviations above (below) unity indicate subperiods of above-average (below-average) variability of shocks relative to the incidence of shocks across the full sample period.[9] Table 12.3a implies that the incidence of real shocks declined steadily throughout the sample period with the exception of Italy where the variability of real shocks increased in the last subperiod. The observation that real shocks declined for all three countries regardless of their exchange rate system in place suggests that the operation of the EMS did not affect the incidence of real shocks in its member countries.

Turning to the evidence regarding monetary shocks contained in Table 12.3b, a comparison of the first and second subperiods reveals that Greece witnessed an increase in the level of monetary variability while both Italy and Spain experienced a substantial decline of monetary shocks after 1979. This may be surprising in so far as Spain was not among the founding members of the EMS. However, the numbers may reflect a policy of monetary stabilization as Spain became a member of the European Community towards the end of that time period and could reasonably expect to be admitted into the ERM in due course. Italy witnessed the most significant reduction of monetary variability in that subperiod, possibly reflecting a stabilizing 'ERM effect'.

The third column of Table 12.3 covers the period of the stable EMS during which Spain joined the ERM. All three countries gained real and monetary stability during that period. Greece, although not a member of the ERM, experienced a dramatic reduction of monetary shocks *vis-à-vis* Germany, likely to be due to a policy of 'shadowing the mark'. The last subperiod covers the time of the turmoil in European currency markets when the Italian lira was forced to float and the Spanish peseta was devalued repeatedly within the ERM parity grid. These events are reflected in the figures for monetary variability. Spain saw her level of monetary variability increase considerably and Italy's jumped dramatically. Interestingly, Greece is the only country to experience a substantial reduction in monetary variability during that time period.

Evaluating the evidence presented in this section, it appears that the ERM was not instrumental in bringing about the stabilization of real

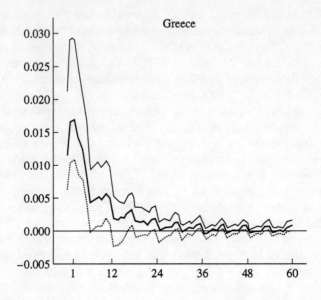

Greece

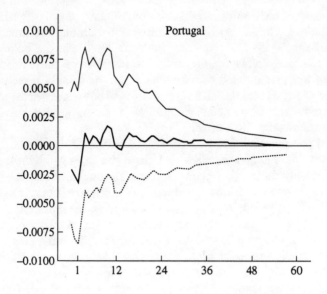

Portugal

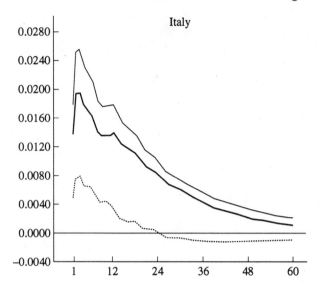

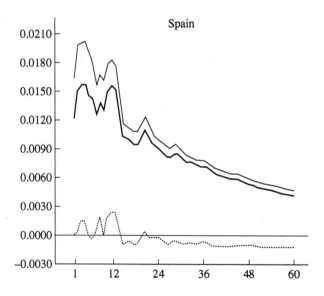

Note: *Dynamic response of the real exchange rate to a one-standard-deviation impulse in the nominal shock over forecast horizons from 1 to 60 months. Broken lines are empirical one-standard-error confidence intervals obtained from a bootstrap simulation with 1000 replications.

*Figure 12.1 Impulse response functions of the real exchange rate**

Table 12.3   Standard deviations of monetary and real shocks*

	1972:2– 1979:2	1979:3– 1986:12	1987:1– 1992:8	1992:9– 1994:12
a) Real shocks				
Greece	1.334	0.974	0.716	0.509
Italy	1.291	1.033	0.591	0.811
Spain	1.285	0.915	0.805	0.764
b) Monetary shocks				
Greece	1.039	1.247	0.652	0.443
Italy	1.351	0.657	0.424	1.563
Spain	1.457	0.903	0.489	0.717

Note: *The standard deviations of monetary and real shocks are normalized to unity for the sample period as a whole.

exchange rates in the 1980s as reported in Table 12.1. The incidence of real shocks has declined in all countries and has been independent of the association with the ERM. Moreover, membership of the ERM does not appear to have been a prerequisite for monetary stabilization. At different times, both Greece and Spain have achieved monetary stabilization while not being a member of the ERM. This stabilization may have been due to a central bank policy of accommodating money demand shocks.

The operation of the ERM seems to have been responsible for the renewed surge of monetary and real exchange rate instability in the wake of the European currency crises of the early 1990s. Persistent inflation differentials coupled with nominal exchange rate rigidities among the member countries of the ERM led to cumulative misalignments of real exchange rates and put a strain on the system's nominal parity grid.[10] By staying outside of the ERM, Greece was able to prevent any major real exchange rate misalignment from occurring. This view is corroborated by the observation that Greece has been the only country in the sample whose monetary and real exchange rate stability did not fall prey to the turmoil in European currency markets.

5   Summary
It is widely believed that pegging nominal exchange rates entails a stabilization of real exchange rates. The stabilization can be associated with a reduction of 'excess volatility' in foreign exchange markets due to the closer monetary cooperation of the member countries of the nominal

exchange rate regime. The present chapter has investigated whether participation in the exchange rate mechanism (ERM) of the EMS has been instrumental in decreasing member currencies' levels of 'excess volatility' and real exchange rate variability. To this end the bilateral real exchange rates, *vis-à-vis* Germany, of the four southern EU members, Greece, Italy, Portugal and Spain have been analysed. Not only did these countries experience high levels of real exchange rate variability throughout the sample period but they also had a diverse history of association with the ERM. While Italy is a founding member, Portugal and Spain joined the mechanism more recently and Greece does not yet participate.

The results cannot consistently identify a stabilizing 'ERM effect'. The incidence of real shocks has declined in all countries and has been independent of the association with the ERM. Monetary shocks were found to make up a sizeable portion of overall variability and exert a significant short-run impact on real exchange rates in all countries except Portugal. At different times both Spain and Greece have achieved monetary stabilization while not being a member of the ERM. These results imply that the ERM was not instrumental in bringing about the stabilization of real exchange rates in the 1980s. In contrast, the operation of the ERM seems to have been responsible for the renewed surge of monetary and real exchange rate instability in the wake of the European currency crises of the early 1990s by inducing cumulative misalignments of real exchange rates which put a strain on the system's nominal parity grid.

Notes

1. Mussa (1986) presents extensive evidence in support of the case for exchange rate regime non-neutrality. For a recent overview of the literature with further references therein, see Taylor (1995).
2. This argument was first expounded by Dornbusch (1976).
3. Bayoumi and Eichengreen (1993) use a bivariate SVAR to identify supply and demand shocks in order to gauge the desirability of European monetary unification.
4. Clarida and Gali (1994) estimate a trivariate SVAR to identify two real shocks (to supply and demand) as well as a monetary shock.
5. These tests are standard and are not reported to save space.
6. With only two shocks in the model, the shares of monetary and real shocks always add up to unity.
7. The impulse response functions for the relative price levels are not reported since the latter displayed little or no impact reaction while converging to a permanently lower level after being shocked by an expansionary money demand shock.
8. The simulation is based on drawings from a bivariate normal distribution of the empirical covariance matrix. The resulting process can be transformed into a new (artificial) data set by using the estimated SVAR equation as a filter with the first 12 observations of the original data set functioning as startup values.
9. The structural vector autoregression achieves exact identification of monetary and real shocks by standardizing the latter to have unitary variances. While this standardization makes it impossible to estimate the relative magnitudes of monetary and real shocks across countries, it allows for comparisons of the *relative* importance of these shocks for each individual country across different subperiods.

10. Svensson (1994) compares the nominal and real exchange rates of a number of ERM and non-ERM countries and finds that Italy, Portugal and Spain were the three countries within the ERM experiencing the most significant real exchange rate appreciations relative to the German mark. Svensson identifies these real exchange rate appreciations as a major force in triggering the European currency crises.

References

Bayoumi, Tamim and Barry Eichengreen (1993), 'Shocking Aspects of Monetary Unification', in Francisco Torres and Francesco Giavazzi (eds), *Adjustment and Growth in the European Monetary System*, Cambridge: Cambridge University Press, pp. 193–229.

Blanchard, Olivier, and Danny Quah (1989), 'The Dynamic Effects of Aggregate Demand and Supply Disturbances', *American Economic Review*, **79**, 655–73.

Clarida, Richard, and Jordi Gali (1994), 'Sources of Real Exchange Rate Fluctuations: How Important are Nominal Shocks?', *Carnegie–Rochester Conference Series on Public Policy* Discussion Paper No. 951, **41**, 7–56.

Dornbusch, Rudiger (1976), 'Expectations and Exchange Rate Dynamics', *Journal of Political Economy*, **84**, 1161–76.

Lastrapes, William D. (1992), 'Sources of Fluctuations in Real and Nominal Exchange Rates', *Review of Economics and Statistics*, **74**, 530–39.

Mussa, Michael (1986), 'Nominal Exchange Rate Regimes and the Behavior of Real Exchange Rates: Evidence and Implications', *Carnegie–Rochester Conference Series on Public Policy*, **25**, 117–214.

Stockman, Alan C. (1987), 'The Equilibrium Approach to Exchange Rates', *Economic Review*, Federal Reserve Bank of Richmond, 12–30.

Svensson, Lars E.O. (1994), 'Fixed Exchange Rates as a Means to Price Stability: What Have We Learned?', *European Economic Review*, **38**, 447–68.

Taylor, Mark P. (1995), 'The Economics of Exchange Rates', *Journal of Economic Literature*, **33**, 13–47.

Index

Aggregate Method of Support (AMS)
117 n.8
Agricultural Bank of Greece 111
agriculture *see* Common Agricultural
Policy (CAP); Greece
Akaike, H. 34, 37
Alesina, A. 22, 24
Amin, A. 125, 128
Antzoulatos, Angelos A. 2–3, 148, 150–
51
Arestis, P. 122
Argentina 169
Artis, M.J. 32, 72
Artus, P. 32, 44
Asia, East
capital inflows 3, 147–9, 156–65, 169
Asian Tigers 124
Austria 23, 95

Backus, D. 57
balance of payments 57, 71
balance of trade 60, 62–7, 70, 112–13,
114, 126–7
Baldwin, R.E. 121
Baltas, Nicholas C. 2, 110, 112, 114, 116
n.7
Banerjee, A. 35
Barry, F. 127
Bartolini, L. 55
basic products 105, 111
Basle-Nybord Agreement (1987) 57,
61–7
Batavia, Bala 3
Baumol, W. 121
Bayoumi, Tamin 23, 193 n.3
Belgium 21, 23
capital stock per capita variation 142
exchange rates 142
FDI in 126
GDP per capita variation 142
interest rates 36, 38–40, 44–9
VAT rates 95
benefits of monetary union 71–2, 77,
137

benefits curve 74–5, 76, 80
in cooperative games 76–84
marginal 72–6
net benefits function 74, 75, 76,
80–85
Berglas 94
Bertola, G. 55
Biltoft, K. 32
bivariate structural vector
autoregression (SVAR) *see*
SVAR (structural vector
autoregression)
Blanchard, Oliver 185, 187
Blaupunkt 128
Boersch, C. 32
Bondar, A. 55
bond flows 158, 159, 162, 164,
170
Borkakoti, Jiten 2
Brazil 161, 169
Bretton Woods system 7, 8, 13, 14
Brusco, S. 129
budget deficits 9, 11, 13, 20, 25, 58, 106,
134
Buiter, W. 18
Bundesbank 11, 21, 24–5, 32, 47

California 143–4
Calvert, R. 26
Calvo, Guillermo A. 147, 148, 149, 155,
156, 158, 166 n.4, 171
Carneiro, Dionisio Dias 147
Canada 21, 143
capital
capital flows, foreign exchange
reserves and aggregate demand
3, Ch.10
composition of capital inflows 158,
159, 162
data description 169–70
differing responses of LDCs *see*
Asia, East; Latin America
econometric considerations in
empirical analysis 157–8

post-Fordism 129
primary convergence
  in Canada 143
  definition of 135, 144
  of EU 137–44
  in OECD countries 143
  in United States 142–4
Prodromidis, Kyprianos 2
production-possibility curves 136, 137
product substitutability 179

Quah, Danny 185, 187
quotas 104, 116 n.4, n.5, n.7, 131

rationality, individual and group 79
real exchange rate variability 85–6
  n.3, n.4
regional market efficiency 137
regional policies 130–31
Reinhart, Carmen M. 147, 172
relative price levels, time series on 184–
  5, 186–7
research and development 120–21, 124,
  125, 128, 130–31, 136, 177, 178–
  80, 181
revenue transfers, inter-country 92, 96–
  9, 100
Rojas-Suarez, Liliana 147
Rome, Treaty of (1957) 7
Romer, P. 120, 121
Rose, A.K. 2, 56, 68 n.1
Rosende, Francisco 147
Rowley, Robin 2, 18

Sabel, C. 129
Sachs, Jeffrey 122, 147
Sala-i-Martin, X. 138, 142–3
Sandholtz, W. 16, 18
Sarris, A. 116 n.1
savings, precautionary 148, 151–3
  foreign exchange reserves as 148,
  153–4
Sbragia, A. 18–19
Schengen agreement 17
Schneider, G. 19
Schumpeter, J.A. 131
Schwarz, G. 34, 37, 38, 43
secondary convergence 135
Shapley, L.S. 86 n.8
Shibata, M. 94

Shubik, M. 86 n.8
Silicon Valley 143
Singapore 156, 159
Single European Act (1986) 8, 16, 17, 58
Single European Market (SEM) 91, 97,
  101, 119, 120, 124, 125
  potential gains from 121–2
  Swedish participation in Ch.11
small and medium enterprises (SMEs)
  129–30
Smeets, H.D. 32
Smithsonian Accord 8
snake 8
social policy, common 19, 27
Solow, R. 120
Spain
  accession into EU (1986) 138, 139,
    191–2
  capital controls 11
  capital stock per capita variation 142
  convergence experienced by 2, 131
  exchange rates 11, 142
    ERM and stability of 3, 184–6,
      188, 190–93
  exports 129
  FDI in 126, 128
  GDP growth 122–4
  GDP per capita variation 142
  labour cost 126
  R & D expenditure 131
  Structural and Cohesion Funds 130
  VAT rates 95, 96–7
  VAT revenue losses 96–7
speculative attacks 10–11, 58–9, 67
Spiegel, Mark M. 147
stability of a monetary union *see*
    optimum currency areas
    (OCAs), determination of
Stockman, Alan C. 186
Structural and Cohesion Funds 119,
  130, 131, 132
subsidiarity 17, 25–6, 27
subsidies
  agricultural 104–8, 110, 111, 113,
    114–15, 117 n.8, 118 n.9
  and growth 120–21
  Structural and Cohesion Funds 119,
    130, 131, 132
superadditivity 77
Suppel, R. 26